Adventures In The Big Bend

Adventures In The

BIG

BEND

A TRAVEL GUIDE

Fourth Edition

by Jim Glendinning

IRON MOUNTAIN PRESS
Houston, Texas
2010

Fourth Edition

May 2010

ISBN-10: 0-9745048-9-0
ISBN-13: 978-0-9745048-9-6

Printed and Bound in
United States of America

Cover Photos by Blair Pittman, Terlingua, Texas:
Front: *Boquillas Canyon, Agave, Eagle Claw Cactus*
Back: *Roundtail horned toad, Aplomado falcon, Yellow columbine*

Maps: Bob Bell, Alpine, Texas

Cover Design: Leisha Israel, Digital Tractor
Austin, Texas

Iron Mountain Press
Houston, Texas

www.ironmtnpress.com

To Pilar Pedersen

Horse lover, Mexicophile, aspiring writer and good neighbor.

ALSO BY JIM GLENDINNING

From Big Bend to Carlsbad, A Traveler's Guide
Published by Texas A&M University Press

Mexico — Unofficial Border Crossings & Copper Canyon
Published by The Alpine Company Press, Alpine, TX

Acknowledgements

For help with factual recommendations and for checking text: the staff at the Chambers of Commerce in Alpine, Fort Davis, Fort Stockton, Marathon, Monahans, Presidio and Van Horn.

For compiling the Book List, thanks to the staff at Front Street Books in Alpine and Marathon; and to Sarah Bourbon for revising the reading list suggested by the Big Bend Natural History Association.

For contributing the Birds Galore section, Carolyn Ohl and to Marsha J. Seyfferts for the accompanying photograph (Lucifer Hummingbird). Cathryn Hoyt brought me up to date on the Chihuahuan Desert Visitor Center, and Mary C. Williams made corrections and additions to the Fort Davis National Historic Site section.

For permission to use extracts from existing published works: Lovika de Koninck for the introduction to Terlingua (from *The Terlingua Area* by Dimitri Gerasimou. DeGe Verlag, 1994); Kirby Warnock's *Big Bend Quarterly* for the articles "Chili Cookoff" and "Taking a walk with the Creator"; the late David Alloway, author of *Desert Survival Skills* (UT Press, 2000) for the chapter "Desert Survival Basics"; Cecilia Thompson, author of *The History of Marfa and Presidio County* (Nortex Press, 1985) for the extract "Retrospect." Thanks to the Big Bend Natural History Association for statistics and articles on Big Bend National Park, and to the Texas State Historical Commission for permission to reprint from the *Handbook of Texas Online*.

Table of Contents

Maps & Photos

Introduction

I have tried in this guidebook to combine facts with anecdotes to make places more interesting. In between the major parts of the book, I have inserted articles describing prominent persons (such as Barton Warnock) and historical events (a cattle drive) to add flavor to the mixture.

Adventures In The Big Bend is divided into six parts. We start with a look at Big Bend's best known attraction, the Big Bend National Park, and then move next door to newer, lesser known Big Bend Ranch State Park. Part II covers a variety of other sites, natural and man-made, which are scattered across the region.

To some people, an adventure may involve action, sweat, and fear. To others, it may be a more placid experience like a new bird sighting. Part III lists seven different adventures, fairly energetic on the whole, which you can experience by buying a prebooked package (rafting, hiking, riding into Mexico). In most cases you can also do these adventures independently. The do-it-yourself option is listed at the end of each specific adventure.

Scenic Routes, Part IV, describes the two main driving circuits around Big Bend as well as three shorter routes, some on dirt or gravel roads. In the first two instances, you may need to use the Big Bend Area Map (following the introduction) or a Texas road map. In the case of the three other routes, each has its own detailed map. Take plenty of water and keep your gas tank full whenever or wherever you drive in the Big Bend.

Part V covers towns and communities and follows the same layout for each place. Lodging precedes restaurants, followed by shopping, then what to do/where to go, with events coming at the end. Please note that all local phone numbers are within the 432 area code, unless stated otherwise.

A lot of changes have taken place recently across the region and continue to do so. Businesses close, prices change, and new services start up. Please write, phone, or email us with information on any changes you come across when you visit Big Bend (see page 305 for contact information).

Have a Great Adventure!

J.G.

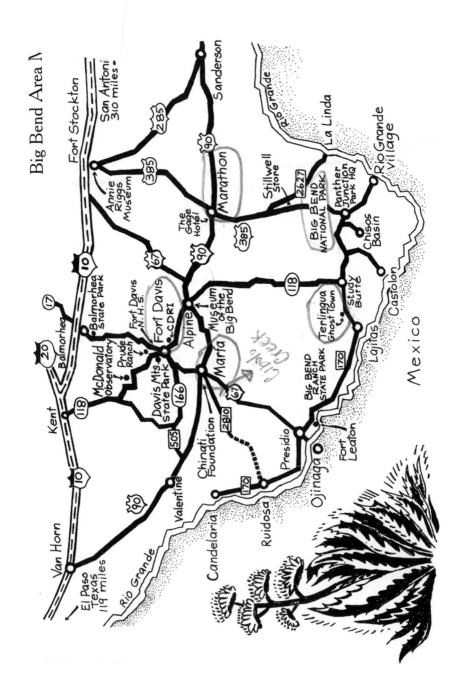

Big Bend Area Map

Part I
The Big Bend

Big Bend National Park

Almost 225 miles from the nearest commercial airport, awkwardly located on the way to nowhere, experiencing seriously hot temperatures at the lower elevations during five months of the year, the Big Bend National Park (BBNP) nevertheless attracts up to 400,000 visitors annually. It lends its name to the whole region and is the number one visitor attraction in West Texas.

The unique appeal of the park comes from a mix of river, desert, and mountain scenery. The river is the Rio Grande or, to the Mexicans who share its southern bank, the Rio Bravo del Norte (Wild River of the North). The desert is the northern part of the Chihuahuan Desert, the largest in North America, of which four-fifths lies in Mexico. The mountains in the center of the park are the Chisos Mountains and reach to 7,835 feet. The whole package extends to 1,251 square miles, the fifth largest national park in the lower 48 states.

The name "Big Bend" was coined in 1849 by Lt. William H. C. Whiting, who headed one of a number of military expeditions exploring and mapping the area. He found that the Rio Grande, which followed a southeasterly course towards the Gulf of Mexico, turned abruptly northeast when it encountered the extreme southern tip of the Rocky Mountains. He named this feature "The Big Bend," and the title stuck. The BBNP is wedged tightly into this bend in the river. Today's rafters traversing Mariscal Canyon, second of the three canyons in the BBNP, follow the same turn in the river at the evocatively named "Tight Squeeze."

What makes this remote park different is its geologic history. "A heap of stones thrown down by the Great Spirits after they had finished creating the Earth" was the explanation of the Apache Indians for the origins of the Chisos Mountains. Certainly today's visitor can't ignore the profusion of scattered and jumbled rocks spread across the landscape, all the more visible because of the sparse vegetation. This is a geologist's dream.

The Chisos Mountains, the centerpiece of the national park, were thrown up by volcanic activity 30 million years ago. They are part of a wider geologic picture that includes the southeastern extremity of the Rocky Mountains, and vestiges of a much older range called the Ouachitas, which are linked to the distant Appalachians. A third feature, the Sierra Madre, extends south and east into Mexico. However, the Chisos essentially stand on their own, a biological island in a desert sea. It is this feature that makes the BBNP unique and produces an exceptional diversity in plant and animal habitats.

Birders have as much to excite them as geologists, since over 450 species inhabit BBNP, more than in any other national park. For other naturalists there are over 1,200 plant types and 75 species of mammals. Mountain lions and black bear make the Chisos their home, and there are regular sightings of the latter throughout the Chisos Mountains.

At the lower elevations (1,800 feet) along the riverbank, a narrow band of lush green vegetation predominates. Up to 3,500 feet the terrain is desert scrubland, giving way to grassland up to 5,500 feet. As the visitor drives up through "Green Gulch" en route to the Chisos Basin, a bowl in the middle of the mountains, he reaches a woodland zone where piñon, juniper, and oak trees thrive. If he gets out of his car and takes a hike up Lost Mine Trail he will encounter Rocky Mountain-type vegetation as the trail tops out at 6,800 feet.

In and around the park visitors will find relics of earlier inhabitants: Native Americans, homesteaders, and miners. They will also find at roadside exhibits vestiges of the life of primitive hunters from tens of thousands of years ago, or of much earlier animal life, such as dinosaurs and pterosaurs. This is the Big Bend National Park, vast in size, varied in topography, and remote.

When To Visit

Most visitors (60%) come during the winter and spring months when the temperatures, particularly at the lower elevations along the Rio Grande, are more comfortable. Spring, starting in late February, is a popular time to visit as wildflowers bring color to the desert. It is also the busiest time. Spring break is the peak time — even the primitive campsites fill up. In this case you may have to resort to "zone camping" (out of sight of the highway, in desert area only, with no facilities) providing you have the right camping equipment. Thanksgiving and Christmas/New Year are also heavily visited times when there is maximum demand for motel accommodation in and near the park.

May, June, and July are the hottest months. The average maximum temperature on the desert floor can be over 100°F and can reach 115°F in the deep river canyons. During the winter, the average minimum temperature in the higher campsites can easily fall below freezing. Average daily temperatures range from a minimum of 35°F in January to 68°F in July with maximum temperatures ranging from 61°F in January to 94°F in June. Add five to ten degrees along the Rio Grande, and take off the same amount for the higher mountain elevations.

Chisos Mountains From Old Ore Road

Annual rainfall averages 15-16 inches with August being traditionally the rainiest month. Again, the specific rainfall amount varies from point to point within the park. Along the Rio Grande at Castolon annual rainfall can be as low as 4 inches, while in the high Chisos it may rain as much as 25 inches in a year. For month-by-month temperatures ask for the National Park Service's free pamphlet, *Big Bend General Information*. Once you are in the park, the park staff posts a daily notice of rainfall, hours of sunshine, river level, and visibility at the park's five-visitor centers: Panther Junction headquarters, Persimmon Gap at the north entrance, Chisos Basin, Castolon (seasonal) and Rio Grande Village (seasonal).

Park History

When the State of Texas deeded 707,894 acres to the U.S. National Park Service in 1944, it marked the end of many years of planning and action by scores of people. Principal among these planners was Everett Ewing Townsend, the "father" of Big Bend National Park. Townsend, a cowboy and later a Texas ranger, sheriff of Brewster County, and subsequently a member of the Texas legislature, was probably the first to think of the region as a park.

Another vital figure was Amon Carter, publisher of the *Fort Worth Star-Telegram* and an early influential advocate of the national park idea. He became the chairman of the Texas Big Bend Park Association, an organization of prominent citizens across the state whose goal was to raise money to buy land for the park.

Ross Maxwell, however, was the man on the spot at the time of acquisition. By training a geologist, Maxwell saw the immense potential of the terrain as a location for a park. He was also a diplomat. Previously, over three thousand people owned land in the Big Bend, although only fifty-five actually lived there. It was Maxwell, living in the region and knowing the local ranchers, who was critical in seeing the project become a reality.

During a difficult time of drought, he convinced the ranchers to move their stock off the park land — no easy task. His name is rightly remembered for the work he did during the transition period from private to public land. Even today pockets of private land still remain within the park boundary towards the northern limit. Maxwell was appointed first superintendent of the park, and his name is commemorated in Ross Maxwell Scenic Drive.

History Of The Area

While people have lived in the Big Bend area for ten to twelve thousand years, evidence of early human activity is scarce. The Spanish called the area "El Despoblado," (the unpopulated place) a reference to the scarcity of people.

The Spanish explorer, Cabeza de Vaca, was the first European to visit the area when he skirted the Big Bend region on his epic journey across Texas in 1535. He was amazed to find Indian settlements with houses and land cultivation at the junction of the Rio Grande and Rio Conchos, 50 miles west of today's national park, near Presidio/Ojinaga. These were the Jumanos, a farming people. They were neighbors to the Chisos, a tribe from North Mexico, which moved into the mountains of Big Bend during the summer months. The Chisos were soon to be driven out by the Mescalero Apaches.

When the Spanish extended their northern frontier, it was the aggressive Apaches whom they encountered. Trying to control the Apaches, they built a series of forts along the Rio Grande, starting in 1720, but just as quickly abandoned them. The subsequent chaotic period up to the latter part of the nineteenth century ended with the establishment of U.S. Army forts across the area and the death of the Indian chief Victorio in 1880.

With Indian resistance subdued, the way was open for Anglo ranchers and mining concerns to exploit the rich pasture and even richer underground wealth of the area. The waving sea of waist-high grasses, which J. O. Langford described in *A Homesteader's Story* in 1905, had largely disappeared 50 years later due to over-grazing. Unaware of the sensitivity of the desert terrain, and buoyed by high prices for beef during the First World War, the early ranchers piled more and more cattle, as well as sheep and goats, onto a land that could not sustain them.

Similarly, the first part of the twentieth century saw considerable mining activity on both sides of the Rio Grande. The mining companies dug for lead, zinc, silver, and, in particular, cinnabar (mercury). Within today's national park boundary near Rio Grande Village remains of an overhead tramway can still be seen. It was used to transport the ore across the river from the Mexican mine. The ore was then unloaded onto freight cars pulled by traction engines traveling along the Old Ore Road to the railhead in Marathon, 80 miles away.

By the 1980s, mining had all but ceased, and ranching was on the ropes. But a new business offering employment to locals and enjoyment for visitors was underway: tourism. The environment is particularly suited to nature tourism and offers opportunities such as hiking, camping, rafting, and especially birding. Other visitors who seldom get out of their cars nevertheless seem to like what they see. Despite heat and distance the visitors keep coming, and this is a promising sign for the economy of the region.

Statistics

The most recent survey by the National Park Service (1992) showed that almost two thirds of visitors were families, and just under half were in the 50–70-year-old age group. Three quarters of them spent more than one day in the park, and eighty percent visited the Chisos Basin. Only fifty-three percent hiked trails, while forty percent camped without hookups.

The National Park Service encourages visitors to stay longer so that they can learn more about the park and to get out of their cars so they can savor the aroma of the desert and listen to their surroundings. Many people dismiss the desert as an empty or dangerous wasteland. However, a guided walk with a park ranger or an evening slide show, one of the many year-round interpretive programs at various points in the park, will show how full of life the desert is.

Planning

By getting some basic materials from the NPS in advance, you can read them during the long drive to the park and then make the best use of your time upon arrival.

The National Park Service	
Big Bend National Park P. O. Box 129 Big Bend National Park, TX 79834	Phone: 432-477-2251 Web: www.nps.gov/bibe

The NPS publishes two free general information pamphlets. The first, *Big Bend*, is a comprehensive color foldout with a map of the park on one side and a wealth of detailed information about animal and plant life on the other. The second pamphlet is a black and white folder, *General Information*, which gives all the necessary practical information such as temperatures, camping fees, do's and don'ts, pets (not allowed on trails) and so forth.

There are also 20 free pamphlets covering specific topics: *Archeology; Glenn Springs; Hiking & Backpacking; Biodiversity; History; Air Quality; Black Bears; Mariscal Mine; Window Trail; Border Towns; Survive the Sun; Biosphere Reserves; C.C.C.; Mountain Lions; Comanche Trail; Dinosaurs; Rio Grande; Floating the Rio; Geology; Fire at Big Bend.*

Trail Guides available from dispensers at trail heads (50-75¢): *Dagger Flat Auto Trail; Lost Mine Trail; Panther Path; Window View Trail; Hot Springs; Rio Grande Village Nature Trail.*

Recommended Reading

The following books and a collection of more than six hundred other publications, plus maps, videos, posters, and cassettes, can be purchased in the bookstore at Panther Junction. You can also buy these outside of the area at any good bookshop. Available from the Big Bend Natural History Association by phone or at their web site.

Big Bend Natural History Association	
Big Bend Natural History Association P. O. Box 196 Big Bend National Park, TX 79834	Phone: 432-477-2236 Web: www.bigbendbookstore.org

Among a large collection of books on the Big Bend, the following stand out: *Naturalist's Big Bend* by Roland Wauer ($15.95)— the bible for this sort of thing. *Chronicles of the Big Bend* by W. D. Smithers ($29.95)—gripping tales collected from locals. *Big Bend* by Ron C. Tyler ($15.95)—thorough, extensive and well-written history of the region. *Big Bend: A Homesteader's Story* by J. O. Langford ($17.95) — evocative history of the early days at Hot Springs. *Big Bend Country: Land of the Unexpected* by Kenneth Ragsdale ($24.95) 1900–1955—

tales of extraordinary women, violent incidents, and unusual events. *Big Bend Vistas* by William MacLeod ($27.95)—geological exploration of the Big Bend, new and readable. *Hiking Big Bend* by Laurence Parent ($14.95)—talented writer/photographer's detailed trail descriptions.

The most practical and popular small guidebooks bought upon arrival are the Natural History Association's publications: *Hiker's Guide to Trails of Big Bend National Park* ($1.95)—describes 39 trails: self-guiding, developed, and primitive trails. *Road Guide to Paved and Improved Dirt Roads* ($1.95)—44 pages, details of the landmarks. *Road Guide to Backcountry Dirt Roads* ($1.95)—Old Ore Road, 26 miles; Glenn Springs Road, 14 miles; River Road, 50 miles; Paint Gap Road, four miles.

For a full listing of the 600-volume inventory in the Panther Junction store, visit the Big Bend Natural History Association website at www.bigbendbookstore.org, where you can also order by mail. Profits go back to the park.

The Chisos Mountains Trails map (99¢) lists the trails within the Chisos Basin, gives a brief description, and marks all the backcountry campsites. There is also a *National Geographic Trails Illustrated* topographical map of the park, waterproof and tearproof, which sells for $11.95. This map is vital if you are planning to go off the trails or follow a dirt road. The bookstore also carries 7.5" pocket quads for the entire park.

How To Get There

By Car—Eighty percent of visitors enter the Big Bend National Park on U.S. 385 via Marathon. Most use I-10, turning off at Fort Stockton. Some follow U.S. 90 from San Antonio via Del Rio. Distances: Dallas to Marathon (via I-20) to Park Headquarters is 542 miles; Houston to Marathon (via I-10) to Park Headquarters is 628 miles. Marathon to Persimmon Gap, the northern entrance to the park is 40 miles. From Alpine it is 82 miles to the west entrance of the park on Texas 118. From Presidio on the River Road (FM170) to Lajitas, then to the west entrance of the park, it is 67 miles.

Airline—From Panther Junction, the nearest commercial airport is in Midland, 220 miles away. El Paso airport is 327 miles west via Alpine and Van Horn.

Car Rental—Alpine Auto Rental has a fleet of 20 vehicles, from compacts to 15-passenger vans. Rates start at $35.95 per day plus 10¢ per mile for the compacts. Cars can be picked up and dropped off at Alpine's Amtrak station or airport.

Alpine Auto Rental	
Alpine Auto Rental 2501 E. Hwy 90 Alpine, TX 79830	Phone: 800-894-3463 or 432-837-3463 fax: 432-837-5663 Web: www.alpineautorental.com

Mountain Motors—866-361-4336, 432-837-5333.

Jeep Rental—Terlingua Auto Service. 432-371-2233.

Towing—Beechies' Auto Service. Terlingua. 432-371-2362.

Rail—Amtrak's Sunset Limited connects New Orleans with Los Angeles. Eastbound trains depart Alpine 2:20P.M. Monday, Thursday, Saturday. Westbound trains depart 1:20P.M. Tuesday, Thursday, Saturday. www.amtrak.com. 800-USA-RAIL (800-872-7245) for schedule and fares.

Bus—All-American Travels serves Alpine twice daily on a north–south bound between Midland (also Midland Airport) and Presidio. Departures (north) 10:45A.M., 5:20P.M.; (south) 1:00P.M., 10:00P.M.. Bus stop and ticket office (open 6-10) 2305 E Hwy 90, next to Best Western Inn. Information: 432-837-0784. Connects in Fort Stockton with Greyhound 800-231-2222.

Taxi—Trans-Pecos Taxi, based in Alpine. Bob Brewer. Trips to/from airports, any distance, any destination. 432-294-4307, 432-837-0100.

Entry Into the Park

Entrance booths are located at the north and west entrances to the park for the purchase of entrance permits ($20 per vehicle, valid for one week). In the event that the park entrances are not staffed, proceed to Panther Junction to buy an entrance permit. Holders of Golden Age passports, Golden Access passports and National Parks Passes are admitted free of charge. A Big Bend Park Pass ($40) is good for one year from the date of purchase.

Services

Post Office—At Panther Junction Park headquarters, Monday - Friday, 8-1, 3-5, also in Study Butte.

Bank with ATM—In Study Butte, 4 miles from west entrance to park.

Towing—In Alpine: 432-837-2523 or 432-837-2653.

Visitor Center

At Panther Junction take a few minutes inside the Visitor Center to look at the large relief map of the park for an overall idea of the topography. At the desk you can book primitive campsites. This can also be done at the Chisos Basin ranger station. A daily update on the weather, river, and road situation is posted in the Center as well as the other ranger stations. At Panther Junction the daily visibility reading is posted. A well-stocked book and gift store is in one corner of the Visitor Center.

A short nature trail is immediately outside the Visitor Center. First, buy a booklet ($1.00) to the trail from the dispenser. There is no better way to get an understanding of at least some of the principal plants (names and uses) you will see later as you travel around the park. A hundred yards west of the Visitor Center is a gas station and small store.

At Panther Junction and the other ranger stations a weekly schedule of interpretive activities is posted, which includes talks, guided walks, and slide programs. Depending on the season there may be up to three of these programs daily, lasting from one to two hours, at different locations in the park. You may attend, for example, a slide show in the amphitheater in the Chisos Basin or take a guided hike with a ranger.

On a recent visit to the park, an interpretive ranger trainee led a hike into Santa Elena Canyon. He explained how these 1,500-foot limestone walls came about as well as how part of the landmass dropped dramatically due to faulting of the earth's surface. He presented the group with some thought-provoking ideas on how everything in the natural world is connected and what happens when man tries to interfere.

To illustrate the point, he proceeded down the path along the riverbank to a grove of tamarisks. This imported species has crowded out the native plants and now represents a threat to the balance of the plant

Inside Santa Elena Canyon

population. His enthusiasm for the subject was infectious, and the message he delivered to the group focused on the inter-relatedness of plant and animal life.

The trainee warned the group against feeding human food to wild animals. The animals will eat it because it is readily available, but it is likely to make them ill. Their fur or feathers lose their shine, and they get out of condition since the chemical preservatives in human food do not agree with their digestive systems. If they are large enough to absorb human food and get hooked on it, they become a menace in the campgrounds. This happens in other national parks with bear populations.

Take one of the nature walks, listen to one of the talks, or attend one of the slide shows and your understanding of the environment will increase, and with it, your enjoyment.

Where To Stay

Chisos Mountains Lodge in Chisos Basin—With seventy-two rooms, the lodge operates as a concession and provides the only motel accommodation within the park. The setting is magnificent, and the view from the dining room towards "The Window," (a break in the side of the mountain wall that permits a view out across the desert), is particularly impressive.

Chisos Mountains Lodge	
Chisos Mountains Lodge Big Bend National Park, TX 79834	Phone: 432-477-2291 800-848-2363 www.chisosmountainslodge.com

Advance reservations are definitely recommended and for peak periods during the spring, at Christmas and Thanksgiving, absolutely vital — even 1–2 years in advance. Mid-February through the end of April, when the desert flowers are blooming, is the busiest stretch. From mid-May the weather turns very hot, although there is always the elevation advantage (5,401 feet) of being in the mountains.

There are 66 rooms and 6 stone cottages. Rooms have no TVs or phones, but there is a TV in the lobby and a pay phone outside each building. The complex offers a convenience store, post office, ranger station, and restaurant in the main building, but no pool. The Casa Grande and the Rio Grande rooms have air-conditioning, but rooms in other accommodations rely on fans.

Room rates for 1-2 persons, including tax: Casa Grande (38 rooms), $119.43. Rio Grande motel units (20 total), $119.43. Emory Peak Lodge rooms (8), $116.08. Roosevelt cottages, $148.48. Each extra person $12. The Casa Grande has mostly two beds. The Rio Grande rooms all have two double beds. Emory Peak Lodge rooms have one double, one single bed. The cottages have three double beds. Rollaways are available.

If you have a choice, specify the newer units (Casa Grande), which have a balcony facing the wooded mountain slopes. Try to avoid the older rooms (Rio Grande), which look onto the parking lot. The favorite accommodation is the six stone cottages scattered among the trees, of which, Number 103 is the most popular owing to the view it offers towards The Window.

Other Accommodations (Near West Entrance)

Study Butte (4 miles from West Entrance):

Big Bend Resort and Adventures (Motel)—4 miles from BBNP at intersection FM-170/TX-118. 877- 386-4386. 432-371-2218. 51 rooms in two standard motels. Rates, excl. tax, from $99 for two persons, to $149-$169 for a small/large duplex. Arrivals after 10:00 P.M. will not be able to check in. 126 RV sites. Golf course. Café. www.bigbendresortadventures.com.

Chisos Mining Company Motel at Easter Egg Valley — 432-371-2254. One mile along FM 170 from the Study Butte intersection, this many-colored establishment provides 39 rooms, suites, cabins and condos from $57.23 (single), to $98-$153 (cabins) and $141.70 (condos), including tax.   www.cmcm.cc.

Highway 118:

Ten Bits Ranch (Bed & Breakfast)—18 miles from west entrance, 2.3 miles along North County Road. "Somewhere...Out There". 4 guest rooms, queen or double beds. Continental breakfast. 2-night minimum Rates $159-$199 per room(two persons) depending on season. $25/ night per extra person. Call 866-371-3110 or check www.tenbitsranch.com

Longhorn Ranch Motel—19 miles from west entrance (65 miles south of Alpine). 24 rooms each with two full-size beds. 1- or two-persons $75 plus tax. 432-371-2541 www.longhornranchmotel.com. Pool Restaurant. RV Park. Tent camping.

Terlingua Ghostown

See listings on page 277.

Cabins

Wildhorse Station—8 miles north of west entrance. 432-371-2526. Seven cabins, three with good views, with one- to-three bedrooms. Rates from (one bed) $80 for two, (two beds) $100 for two, $120 for four persons, plus tax. Kitchen, fully furnished.

Accommodations (Nearest to North Entrance)

The nearest accommodations to the north entrance are located in Marathon (40 miles from the north entrance). Hotel, motel, Bed & Breakfast, and cottage accommodations are available. See page 208.

Camping—Within Big Bend National Park

All campgrounds operate on a first-come, first-served basis, with no advance bookings except for groups.

Rio Grande Village RV Park—A concession operation, the only campground with hookups (25) within the park. $27/night including tax for two persons. Register at the Rio Grande Village Store. The store (open 8–8 daily, 9–6 summer) sells gas, beer, food and general supplies. It is the only place within the park with coin-operated showers ($1.50 for five minutes) and self-service laundry (open till 7 P.M.). 432-477-2293.

Note
All National Park Service Campgrounds (Class A & B) work on a self-register system. You pay upon arrival. $14 per night ($7 with a NPS pass).

Rio Grande Village—(100 sites) Provides a wooded setting adjacent to the nature trail and close to the Rio Grande. Toilets, dump station, and water—often plenty of turkey vultures looking for scraps.

Chisos Basin—Right in the center of things, close to the Lodge, amphitheater, and parking areas. Still, it is possible to get a little bit distant from the crowds in the lower section of the campground. 63 sites. All facilities except showers.

Cottonwood Campground—On the very banks of the Rio Grande, under a canopy of stately cottonwoods, some sadly no longer. 31 (Class B) sites with pit toilets, water, but no dump station. This is a no-generator campground.

Note
In the spring and during peak holiday weekends, all lodging and campgrounds can become full. Before leaving the last town closest to the park (e.g. Marathon), call 432-477-2251 and ask about the availability of accommodations or campsites. At busy periods, the National Park Service gives details of space availability on the approach roads to the park. Outside of the park, there are commercial campgrounds at Study Butte/Terlingua, Stillwell Ranch, and in Marathon.

Back Country Road Campsites—116 designated sites are scattered throughout the park on a first-come, first-served basis. All must be booked at a park visitor center, and cost $10 per group, for up to 14 days.

You must carry in your own water, remove all trash, as well as take care of your toilet requirements (dig a hole), all of which you will be briefed by the ranger who issues your permit. Most sites can be reached by vehicle with normal clearance and without four-wheel drive, but take the advice of the ranger regarding access to the site you want, particularly after any period of rain.

Backcountry Camping— For the more adventurous or for those who arrive during Spring Break to find all lodgings taken and the campsites full, there is still the chance, if you have the necessary equipment, to camp almost anywhere in the park outside of the Chisos Mountains. This is called "zone camping." Within the Chisos there are 42 designated high country sites.

As well as being permitted only in the desert area of the park, this type of camping is only allowed a specified distance from any road, trail or spring. If you are alone, the National Park Service may take an impression of your footprint, probably to persuade you to take the desert seriously when you zone camp, but also to assist in tracking you if you don't reappear. Part of the requirement for this sort of camping is that you leave a sticker inside the windshield of your car while camping, and also that you turn in your permit at a ranger station once you have completed the overnight camping.

Where To Eat

Inside the park. The Chisos Mountains Lodge has the only restaurant. 432-477-2291. The view is magnificent, the service cheerful and the food acceptable. Open from 7:00–10:00A.M. for breakfast which includes a Breakfast Buffet ($8.25) and an a la carte menu. Lunch is served 11:00–4:00 P.M., with a selection of reasonably priced burgers, sandwiches (from $6.25), a salad bar, and also a useful Hiker's Lunch (take out only) for $8.55. Dinner (5:00–8:00 P.M., til 9:00 in season) features eight entrees ($7.50–$19.95) and includes Mexican plates, ribeye steak and two popular fish dishes as well as burgers and a salad bar. Wine and beer are available.

Within the park the only other food available is groceries—at Castolon, Chisos Basin convenience store, Rio Grande Village, and the gas station at Panther Junction.

Outside of the park, the nearest restaurants are in Study Butte and Terlingua.

What To See And Do

The park's most outstanding feature is its variety. It contains mountains, desert, and the river. It reveals to the visitor fossil bones, mining remains, hot springs, homesteader and ranching history, varied and abundant flora and fauna, amazing geological formations (its strong point), and, above all, spectacular views.

To see all this, visitors can use the 123 miles of paved roads and 181 miles of unpaved roads within the park's boundaries. They can also, if they really want to make the most of their time, get out of their vehicles and use some of the 201 miles of developed and primitive trails. Just over half the visitors to the Big Bend National Park do this.

Scenic Drives

For short-term visitors the most popular route is from Basin Junction, 3 miles west of Panther Junction Visitor Center, to Chisos Basin. This 6.25-mile drive is an exciting entry into the heart of the Chisos Mountains. Because of the steep grades and switchbacks, trailers longer than 20 feet are not allowed, 24 feet for RVs.

As the road climbs through Green Gulch, the rounded, intrusive igneous rocks of Pallium Ridge are visible on the right. To the left are the blocky, extrusive rocks of Panther Peak and Lost Mine Peak. Intrusive denotes a rock formed from within, as a hardened lava flow, that only reveals itself after erosion. Extrusive rocks are those that were thrown up by volcanic action.

Desert plants give way to woodland species such as oaks, piñon pines, and junipers as the terrain rises. The road crests at 5,800 feet at Panther Pass. Here is the start of the most popular trail in the park: the 4.8 mile round trip, self-guided Lost Mine Trail.

Dropping down sharply into the Basin, a depression about three miles in diameter almost two thousand feet below the surrounding peaks, one gets the feeling of driving into a crater. Actually, the Basin was formed by natural erosion taking place over millions of years. About one mile from the pass a road leads off to the right, where the campground and amphitheater are located. Just ahead are the Chisos Mountains Lodge, a store, post office, and ranger station. It is time to get out of the vehicle.

For those visitors with only one day to spend, and who are intent on driving, there should be time to take the 32-mile Ross Maxwell Scenic Drive. This well-surfaced road winds up and down, gaining and losing elevation, affording some marvelous views and 20 different stops.

Past Santa Elena Junction, halfway between the park's west entrance and Panther Junction, the broad flank of the Chisos Mountains is visible on the left. Soon the Window comes into sight, with Casa Grande peak in the background. Shortly after, on the right side, is the trailhead for the Sam Nail Ranch House. A short trail leads to the adobe ruins of this old ranch where a windmill still pumps water, attracting birds and other wildlife. This is a peaceful, shaded spot.

The road now climbs and passes the trail to Blue Creek Ranch, which was formerly stocked with sheep. A little further on, also on the left, is a turn-off to Sotol Vista. Here, surrounded by numerous sotol plants, the visitor can learn of the edible and other uses of this prolific plant. This is one of the finest views in the whole park, across the desert lowlands to the mouth of Santa Elena Canyon, 14 miles away.

Next, the road drops steeply back to the desert floor, where a right hand turn (Burro Mesa spur road) leads to the Burro Mesa Pour-off trail head (easy walking, one mile round trip). Above is an imposing rock formation of horizontal stripes. Returning to the main road, the route winds through an area of outstanding geologic interest with volcanic features such as Mule Ears Peak, Tuff Canyon, and Castolon Peak to the right and left.

About one mile past Cerro Castellan (Castolon Peak), the road drops down further to the village of Castolon. Built and used as an army post, Castolon has been a frontier settlement since the early 1900s. Mexico is less than a half-mile away. A cool, well-stocked general store offers welcome ice cream to the hot visitor. A new Visitor Center has joined the year-round Ranger Station. Open seasonally, it has great hands-on exhibits.

The road now runs along the Rio Grande flood plain where cotton and other crops were grown until the late 1950s. Cottonwood Campground is here, directly on the banks of the Rio Grande. You can walk one mile along a dirt road adjacent to the campground, and you will arrive at the former crossing to Santa Elena, Mexico—now cut off from its previous supply of day visitors.

Eight miles beyond Castolon the paved road ends. You are now at Santa Elena Canyon, which is directly in front of you. First, go to the Santa Elena overlook and get a distant view of the canyon mouth and an explanation of the major geologic action that took place here. You will read how a fault in the earth's crust occurred here, causing part of the surface to drop 1,500 feet. In a later action, the Rio Grande wore its way through the rock formation to form the canyon into which you can now walk.

Parking close to Terlingua Creek, you now can take the most dramatic short hike in the park. Only 1.7 miles round trip, it nevertheless offers a crossing of the creek (if it is in flood, this is as far as you will get). A short, steep climb leads up some steps, followed by a gradual descent to the river, where the canyon walls close in and you can go no further.

Other Scenic Drives — Paved Roads

Maverick (West Entrance) to Panther Junction—22 miles. This route, accessed from the west, passes through desert scenery with a changing backdrop of mountain scenery. On the left shortly after the entrance station, pull over and have a look at the painted desert formations in the so-called badlands. Erosion has been the main agent here, as elsewhere in the park, revealing shapes and colors of rocks deposited in the late Cretaceous Period.

To the right, as you approach Santa Elena Junction, is the northern edge of Burro Mesa, a low, flat mountain named for a herd of wild burros that once grazed there. The mountain is interesting due to the pour-

Cerro Castellan

off on the south side that is accessible from Maxwell Scenic Drive, which you reach after 13 miles.

Continue straight on at this point. To your right, the Chisos Mountains fill the skyline; on the left you pass three dirt roads leading to campsites, at Croton Springs, Paint Gap Hills, and Grapevine Hills. Grapevine Hills, reached 7.7 miles along a good gravel road, is a fascinating rock formation of odd-shaped granite boulders piled on top of each other. The formation came about as the result of a mushroom-shaped underground lava flow, known as a laccolith, which burst through to the surface.

Returning to the main road at Government Spring, noticeable for its vegetation, you are almost at Basin Junction, the turn off for the steep, 6-mile drive into the Chisos Mountains Basin and the motel. Continue straight on. To the left you will have a distant view to the north of the Rosillos Mountains (5,373 feet). In three miles you will be at Panther Junction park headquarters where there is lots to see inside and outside.

Panther Junction to Rio Grande Village (Rio Grande Village Drive)—20 miles dropping almost 2,000 feet, from foothill grasslands through typical Chihuahuan Desert scenery to the banks of the Rio Grande. There are several turnoffs, the first of which is to the right after about 6 miles and leads (high clearance needed) to historic Glenn Spring, which is nine miles further along a dirt road. This was the site of a raid in 1916 by Mexican bandits who attacked the store at the candle wax factory, which had existed there for 5 years. Three troopers guarding the factory and the 7-year old son of the storekeeper were killed. The outcome was a call for the National Guard to patrol the border region. 10,000 troops were dispatched to the Texas and Arizona border with Mexico.

Continuing along the paved road, the next turnoff is to Dugout Wells, where a schoolhouse stood in the early 1900s. As you approach Rio Grande Village, the full magnificence of the colorful, limestone Sierra del Carmen range looms up ahead of you. Part of the larger Sierra Madre range, the peaks of the Sierra del Carmen, reach almost to 9,000 feet. Meanwhile, another turnoff on the right leads to Hot Springs (two miles on an improved dirt road). Important as an early tourism development in the first decade of the twentieth century, it remains popular with today's visitors who relish sitting in the remains of a bathhouse on the banks of the Rio Grande.

Shortly after the turnoff to Hot Springs is another of the park's roads recommended for high clearance vehicles: the Old Ore Road. This 26-mile road was developed for the wagon trains that hauled the ore (zinc, lead and silver) from the Mexican mine to Marathon where it was loaded onto trains. The Ernst Tinaja and McKinney Ranch sites are among the historical landmarks along this important backcountry dirt road.

Just east of the Old Ore Road is the Tunnel, a short cut through the limestone cliff. This provides a fine frame to the picture ahead, the flood plain of the Rio Grande, the Rio Grande Village complex, and the Mexican village of Boquillas with the Sierra del Carmen as a backdrop.

Shortly after the tunnel is an intersection. Turn left for Boquillas Canyon, 4 miles. The road dead-ends here. Read the *Hiker's Guide to Trails of the Big Bend National Park* for details of the Boquillas Canyon trail.

Persimmon Gap to Panther Junction — 27 miles. This is the best approach to the park headquarters. As you enter through Persimmon Gap, you can see the outline of the Chisos Mountains 30 miles away. Crossing the desert floor, the details of the mountains gradually become clear. It may seem a mystery, from this distance, how you are going to be able to drive right into the middle of the mighty mountain range. Don't worry, you'll soon find out.

Persimmon Gap is a cut in the Santiago Mountains, which previously afforded passage to the Comanche Indian warriors on their annual raid into Mexico and to the wagons carrying ore from Boquillas to Marathon. Today it is the northern entrance to the park and provides an entrance booth for ticket purchase and a ranger station for information.

For twenty miles the road heads more or less straight across the desert floor, passing roadside exhibits and turnoffs to other points of interest. First is Nine Point Draw, a creek that begins 40 miles to the northwest. The gravel road from Nine Point Draw leads to Dog Canyon, where in 1860, Lt. William H. Echols tested the feasibility of camel transport in the Big Bend.

The most important side trip along this approach road is to Dagger Flat, almost halfway to Panther Junction. A 14-mile round trip auto trail takes visitors to the Giant Dagger Yuccas, some 15 feet tall, which normally bloom in late March and April, a surprising sight in the apparently barren desert. Take a self-guiding pamphlet from the dispenser at the start of the auto trail.

The next exhibit is of a completely different nature: fossil bones. The fossil remains of mammals date from 50 million years ago, and a stylized panorama depicts prehistoric swamp conditions where such huge beasts once roamed.

The road starts to climb steadily and three miles before Panther Junction, on the left side, is a poignant memorial to a pioneer family. There is no marker to this sign, but simply a parking area on the side of the road and a sign, which says "Exhibit." Follow the path through the creosote bushes until, under a stand of cottonwood trees, you reach the gravesite of Mrs. Nina Hannold who died at the age of 31. The story of her life is told in *An Occasional Wildflower* by Starlene DeBord.

After 27 miles you are now at Panther Junction, park headquarters. Spend some time here looking at the exhibits and items for sale inside the Visitor Center where you also are issued camping permits. Outside, check out the Nature Trail to learn about the plant life in the park such as ocotillo, prickly pear, catclaw, and other evocative names, clearly labeled and easily learned.

Other Scenic Drives—Backcountry Roads

These roads fall into two categories: improved dirt roads and primitive roads. The problem is not so much the need for four-wheel drive (unless it has been raining), as for high clearance. The rangers will advise you—probably erring on the side of caution—according to the route, weather conditions, and your vehicle type.

Other Scenic Drives—Improved Dirt Roads

With the exception of Old Maverick Road, which is a valuable shortcut from Santa Elena Canyon and the west entrance, the other roads listed below are access roads to campsites or points of interest.

Old Maverick Road—13 miles. A frequently graded gravel road, which gets regular use and can sometimes deteriorate into washboard. It is a popular shortcut for those visitors who have traveled via Maxwell Scenic Drive to Castolon and Santa Elena Canyon. They can save 30

miles by taking the Old Maverick Road, which has points of i̇
along the route.

Starting from the Santa Elena end, the first point of interest is Terlingua Abaja, a primitive campsite along a 1.5 mile side road. It is hard to appreciate today that one hundred years ago a flourishing farming community existed here with irrigation ditches channeling water and stands of cottonwood trees providing shade. The trees have long since been cut down except for a solitary survivor. The ruins of farmers' houses can still be seen, adobe and rock structures, as well as some grave sites.

After crossing Alamo (cottonwood in Spanish) Creek and skirting by Peña (hard, slick rock) Mountain, the road passes Luna's Jacal. In this low-roofed, simple cottage, Mexican pioneer Gilberto Luna raised a large family, which he fed through his efforts in crop and vegetable raising. He died in 1947 at the age of 108.

Two geologic features can be seen along the Old Maverick Road. When the angle of the sun is just right, there are a number of places along the road where the ground appears to be covered with diamonds. This is caused by the reflection of the sun from gypsum crystals in the clay soil of Alamo Creek. Further along the Alamo Creek drainage, to the east side of the road, you can see the colored clays in the so-called Badlands, an area of broken ground where erosion of the black basalt has revealed the multi-colored clays underneath.

Croton Spring Road—Three miles east of Santa Elena Junction, a one mile dirt road leads to a primitive campsite, near which is evidence of Indian habitation.

Grapevine Hills Road—8 miles. Just west of Basin Junction. The thick vegetation of Government Spring, one-half mile along this well-maintained road, is followed by the remarkable rock formations of Grapevine Hills. A stock tank and signs of ruins mark the site of the old Grapevine Hills Ranch. Primitive Campsite. The round trip trail, which starts six miles along this road, brings you after one mile to the much-photographed balanced rock formation.

Dagger Flat Road—8 miles. Located midway between Panther Junction and the north entrance. The small valley is filled with ten to fifteen-foot high Giant Dagger Yuccas, which bloom spectacularly in late March and April. Take a pamphlet from the dispenser at the start of the auto trail.

d—2 miles. Eighteen miles southeast of Panther ande Village Drive. Winding and at times narrow, eless normally accessible to all vehicles. From the d of the drive you pass by the ruins of the store and tions built by homesteader Langford in 1909. Further aiv..g iverbank are the remains of the bathhouse, the reason for this early tourist resort.

Other Scenic Drives—Backcountry Dirt Roads

For details of the 26 mile Old Ore Road, 14.5 mile Glenn Spring Road, the 4 mile Paint Gap Road, and the 51 mile River Road, read the NPS publication *Road Guide to Backcountry Dirt Roads* ($1.95).

On Foot—The Only Way To Get Close To Nature

The Big Bend National Park is remarkably well served by its road network, allowing drivers to get to many out-of-the-way corners of the park. Having arrived there, the next step is to get out of the car. Let the senses take over and make the body do the work. Removed from the smell of vinyl seat covers or exhaust fumes, the nose can pick up the scent of a mountain pine tree. Away from traffic noise, the ear can pick up birdcalls.

Self-Guiding Trails

There are nine of these trails within the park, all with leaflets available at the start or with signs en route. Some of the most popular are:

Rio Grande Nature Trail—This .75 mile trail is unusual due to the variety of the terrain that it traverses. Starting at Site 18 in the Rio Grande campground, you proceed through dense vegetation, cross water on a boardwalk, then climb into arid desert before descending to the Rio Grande. On the way back by another route, a promontory affords a fine view along the Rio Grande and into Mexico. Sunset is a good time to be here as the rays of the sun strike the cliffs of Boquillas Canyon. Uplifting messages on the directional signs invite contemplation of nature's marvels and our own place in this changing and varied wonderland. Allow 40 minutes for a quick visit; no special exertion is required, but there is not much shade.

Santa Elena Canyon Trail—1.7 miles round-trip. A popular trail because of the dramatic entry into the mouth of the canyon. First you have to cross Terlingua Creek, which, in the unusual event it is in flood, may end the walk right there. Then you climb steeply up some steps with a handrail for a good view looking east along the flood plain of the Rio Grande. The trail drops gradually toward the riverbank, encountering vegetation as the canyon walls narrow. At this point, the trail ends and you cannot go further. Return by the same route. Perhaps you will catch sight of river rafters completing the Santa Elena Canyon trip. Medium difficulty.

Lost Mine Trail—This is a high altitude trail, which, unlike the strenuous 14-mile South Rim that starts in the Basin, begins at Panther Pass (5,600 feet). Grab (and pay for) a leaflet at the parking lot before you leave. The trail is 4.8 miles round trip on an easy surface with a gradual ascent. Benches en route. Medium difficulty because of the length and the altitude gain (1,250 feet).

This trail serves as an excellent introduction to the plants and animals of the high Chisos. Plants and trees are identified along the trail and discussed in the leaflet. The route leads upward along the northern slope of Casa Grande Mountain to a promontory high on the ridge separating Pine and Juniper canyons.

From the end of the trail at 6,850 feet, you can see Upper Pine

**Balancing Rock
(Grapevine Hills)**

Canyon to the east, and Juniper Canyon far below to the southwest. The East Rim forms a high backdrop behind Juniper Canyon. This is the spot to read about the story behind the naming of the trail and to speculate about the days long before the park was established in 1944.

If you have limited time, hike only to Juniper Canyon Overlook (stop 12 in the self-guiding booklet), one mile from the trail head, for one of the finest views in the park.

Other Self-Guiding Trails—Panther Path at Panther Junction (50-yard loop trail); Castolon Historic Compound; Glenn Spring; Chihuahuan Desert Nature Trail (at Dugout Wells); Hot Springs Historic Walk; Window View Trail (wheelchair accessible; one-third mile round-trip).

Developed Trails

Window Trail—5.2 miles round-trip. This is a popular trail because of its accessibility from the Basin parking lot and the impressive ending. It is downhill going, therefore uphill coming back. From an open area of

South Rim With Agave

grasses you move into the shaded Oak Creek canyon. The canyon narrows, and the trees give way to smooth rock. Finally, with a width of only twenty feet across, you are at the edge of the Window. The return trip uphill can be testing, and you should take water with you. A variety of plant life, plus the chance of seeing a good number of birds, add interest to the hike. Medium difficulty.

The South Rim—13 to 14.5 miles round-trip, depending on the route. This is a long loop hike with many interesting highlights and can easily be done by those traveling light and in good physical shape. An alternative hike, for those with the necessary equipment, is to incorporate this hike into a High Chisos camping trip. In either event, allow time when you get to the rim to let the panoramic views work their full effect.

Sitting on the South Rim, the escarpment drops 2,500 feet to the desert floor. Santa Elena Canyon can be seen 20 miles to the west, and Emory Peak dominates the northern skyline. In front of you is a jumble of ridges, buttes, and peaks. In the background rise the blue-hazed mountains in Mexico. Birds wheel effortlessly above you, a breeze blows up from below, your muscles are beginning to recover. It has been worth the climb.

Other Developed Trails—There are fifteen other developed trails listed in the *Hiker's Guide to trails of the Big Bend National Park* ($1.95). Emory Peak is a must for many people, a 9-mile round-trip from the Basin trail head, using the same well-graded, gradual climb of 3.5 miles (1,500 feet elevation gain) up the Pinnacles Trail to Pinnacles Pass, then taking a spur trail of one mile to the highest point in the national park (7,835 feet). The final fifteen feet require a scramble, but you will find adequate space on top among the radio antennae to enjoy the panorama.

Primitive Routes

The next step for those wishing to learn more about the desert and mountains is to try a primitive trail, of which there are seventeen in the park. For these trails, a relevant topographic map and compass are necessary. You don't need a backcountry permit for day use of these trails, but consult a ranger to get up-to-date information before setting out.

These primitive routes range from 3 to 31 miles in length, and most are rated as strenuous. Some have water, but most don't. Don't attempt any hike without sufficient water for the whole trip, right back to your vehicle. One gallon per person per day is the standard recommended quantity of water for desert use. This translates to 8 lbs of water.

Trail Rides

The nearest stables, Big Bend Stables, are in Study Butte. 800-887-4331. 432-371-2212.

River Floats

If time and budget permit, take a float trip on the Rio Grande whose three canyons are part of the 123 miles that form the southern border of the park: Santa Elena, Mariscal, and Boquillas. You can let one of four local outfitters convey you on a trip lasting from half-a-day to three days (the Lower Canyons). Many people opt for the Santa Elena trip since it is accessible and dramatic (1–2 days depending on conditions). Overnight is recommended both for the camping and dining experience, as well as allowing extra time to harmonize with the surroundings.

You can also rent kayaks and rafts and do the trip yourself; the same outfitter will arrange a shuttle for you to and from the river. A canoe trip brings you in closer touch with the river itself, and requires different skills. Consider the season when you book a trip. It can get powerfully hot inside the canyons in mid-summer. Also ask about the water level or you may find yourself pushing the boat. For a list of outfitters, turn to page 88.

Special Attractions—Hot Springs

In 1909, J. O. Langford arrived at Boquillas with his wife, daughter, dog, and all his possessions packed on mules. Seeking to regain his health, he paid $1.61 an acre for land bordering the Rio Grande with hot springs that had been used by the Indians for centuries.

With the help of a Mexican man who had been living on the site, he built a house for himself and his family on the cliff top. Later he hired a stonemason to build a bathhouse of limestone rocks over the hot springs (105°F). Alarmed by the fighting along the border (the Mexican Revolution was underway), he moved to El Paso in 1913 for safety. He did not return until 1927.

When he did return, he set to and built a store, which became a post office, and some tourist cabins. He also built a second bathhouse for unhealthy visitors downriver from the main bathhouse. Langford was thus an early developer of tourism to the Big Bend region. He wrote a moving account of his experience in *Big Bend, A Homesteader's Story*.

To see Hot Springs today, visitors can drive on a 2-mile dirt road from the Rio Grande Village Drive turnoff. A .75-mile round-trip, self-guided trail along the banks of the Rio Grande will bring you to the Hot Springs. For those using the Rio Grande Village campground, a three-mile (one way) primitive trail along the Rio Grande will bring them to the same point.

Whichever route visitors take, they will find the remains of the post office and the tourist cabins. The self-guided trail will pass pictographs and middens before arriving at the remains of the bathhouse. The structure itself was washed away in a flood, but a shallow stone tub remains in which visitors can sit, right at the edge of the river, and chat with other visitors who may have come from Houston, Germany, or just about anywhere. Jumping into the Rio Grande is not recommended by the NPS since the river carries an unknown amount of pollutants and there are sometimes tricky currents to contend with, not that this worries the hardened river guides who work the river. But crossing to the other bank and returning to the U.S. side will bring you in conflict with another federal agency—and you face a $5,000 fine.

Crossings Into Mexico

In May 2002, the unofficial border crossings, which linked the park at three points with villages on the Mexican side, were closed as a result of September 11. Now, U.S. citizens crossing to the other side at these points, where previously there was boat service, risk a fine of $5,000 upon return to the U.S. side. The closest permitted entry point from Mexico for visitors to the Big Bend area is at Presidio/Ojinaga, about 110 miles west. As a result, the economic life of the Mexican border villages, which until then depended almost entirely on American visitors, has been devastated. International Good Neighbor Day, formerly held in October to celebrate a sharing of the border, has been canceled. There are still hopes for an international park binding both sides of the river, but this plan is now much more remote.

Learning More

The Big Bend Natural History Association (BBNHA), in addition to running the bookstore in the park headquarters at Panther Junction, offers a limited number of seminars including the popular Pioneer Reunion in February. For example, the Apache Canyon Ride through History gives the participants an all-day ride within the park accompanied by an archeologist/ranger. For future seminars, on subjects ranging from Geology to Birds and Butterflies, call 432-477-2206.

The Big Bend National Park is deservedly the number one attraction in the Big Bend region. Visit it at all costs, but allow enough time for it to work its magic on you. Choose your season, and go prepared with suitable clothing, equipment, food, and water. Plan ahead, and also consult the rangers when you arrive. If you are able, walk rather than drive and camp rather than stay in motels. But go!

Entrance To Santa Elena Canyon

Big Bend Ranch State Park

History

Acquired in 1988 and opened to the public as a state park in 1994, the 311,000 acres of the Big Bend Ranch State Park (BBRSP) occupy a space as large as all the other 157 state parks combined. It comprises an area of rugged desert rangeland, mountains, and river that is significantly different in topography from the national park. At BBRSP the elevation is more constant. Water sources flowing from 116 known active springs are hidden below ground. A surprise for many visitors is the small herd of Texas Longhorn cattle, a remnant of the property's ranching history.

Two mountain ranges within the park contain ancient extinct volcanoes, precipitous canyons, waterfalls, and the Solitario, a unique geologic feature. It is an uplifted caldera (a crater from a sunken volcano) caused by a gigantic explosion millions of years ago. A diversity of animal and plant species is found here, including 14 types of hummingbird, 11 rare plants like Hinckley's oak, and even mountain lions and transient black bears.

The terrain can be easily understood when divided into six zones. The Rio Grande corridor (2200 feet) links the lowlands of the northwestern part of the park to the Fresno Canyon–Contrabando area to the east. In the center, the Bofecillos Mountains rise to 5,136 feet. In the far northwestern corner of the park, the unvisited Cienega Mountains balance the park's single best-known geologic attraction, the Solitario— a geologic window to the past—that lies in the southeast part.

Previously, relatively few visitors (9,000 a year) visited the interior of the park which looked, with its locked entrance gate, Longhorn cattle herd and corrals, more like a ranch than a park. But, following the publication of a Public Use Plan in March 2008, TPWD's policy towards Big Bend Ranch State Park changed radically and the parks' services were hugely expanded. The whole of the park is now open for visitation. Areas previously open to the public only with guides, such as the Solitario, are now accessible with a permit. A total of 66 trails have been designated covering 238 miles, 42 campsites established with additional group and equestrian campsites and 5 campgrounds. Mountain bikers may use all of the trails. Now the public can really see what this huge expanse, so different from the National Park, is all about.

Under the new Plan, the whole of the park's interior can now be visited with the right sort of vehicle and the necessary permit. To get to Sauceda Ranch headquarters involves a 38-mile journey on a dirt road. But there is plenty of interest on the way, explained via interpretive exhibits. On the east side of the park, adjacent to Lajitas, there is now a new trail system. As important as all the new trails, campsites, exhibits etc., is the realization that this unique terrain is now open for exploration.

Information

Big Bend Ranch State Park sits at an elevation of 4,149 feet. It enjoys mild winters (October–February the temperatures can his 80°F) and hot summers (up to and over 100°F).

To get to Big Bend Ranch State Park; turn off FM 170, 6.5 miles east of Presidio, 9.5 miles west of Redford. The gravel road to the park entrance is marked "Casa Piedra Road." After 6.1 miles, turn right at a sign marked "BBRSP—Sauceda." Permits to enter the park ($3 per person or free if you have a TPWD Park Pass) may be purchased at Sauceda park headquarters, the Barton Warnock Center in Lajitas or Fort Leaton State Historical Park, 2.6 miles east of Presidio on FM 170. Park Passes cost $60 (or $75 for two persons). Seniors who reside in Texas pay half price.

For more information contact the office at the BBRSP office at 432-358-4444. It is open 7 days a week from 8A.M.–4:30P.M.

Big Bend Ranch State Park	
Big Bend Ranch State Park P.O. Box 2319 Presidio, TX 79845	Phone: 432-358-4444 www.tpwd.state.tx.us/park/bigbend

Rio Grande Corridor — The River Road

The most popular part of BBRSP is the Rio Grande Corridor, known as the The River Road. The fifty miles of FM 170 between Lajitas and Presidio ranks as one of the most scenic routes in North America according to National Geographic. More exactly, it is the 34 miles east of Redford, which lies within the Big Bend Ranch State Park, that are the most dramatic. The mountains of the State Park close in, squeezing the highway against the riverbank. The narrow road twists and turns, crossing numerous creek beds, climbing up, then dropping down, revealing new views at every corner.

Most of the views across the Rio Grande are of the river's flood plain and the mountains on the Mexican side. The river itself is brown and usually slow moving, but the banks are sometimes densely vegetated and in other places cultivated. Beware of livestock when you travel this road, some of which strays from across the river. You are still in Presidio County, whose laws protect the livestock owner.

Points Of Interest Along The River Road

Abbreviated road log, in miles, starting in Presidio, going east (FM-170).

01.6 miles – Intensely cultivated farmland. The main crop is alfalfa.

02.6 miles – Fort Leaton State Historic Park. Historic adobe fort. Now BBRSP west entrance.

05.4 miles – Alamito Creek. Rises north of Marfa.

05.7 miles – Gaging Station to monitor level and flow of water by international agreement.

10.0 miles – Sierra del Centinela Mountain on Mexican side. Pancho Villa supervised the siege of Ojinaga (1913–1914) from here.

15.3 miles – Redford. Site of the Madrid family Historic Home.

24.8 miles – Hoodoos (geologists' term, of African origin). Oddly eroded rocks.

27.4 miles – Colorado Canyon. Boat access to the river.

28.6 miles – Rancherias Canyon trailhead and West Rancherias Loop trailhead.

29.2 miles – Closed Canyon.

30.6 miles – East Rancherias Loop trailhead.

35.7 miles – Big Hill, rises 451 feet coming from the west.

36.6 miles – Picnic site "The Tepees."

37.3 miles – Madera Canyon & river access.

37.4 miles – Madera campground.

38.1 miles – Rock formation El Padre al Altar (father at the altar).

39.5 miles – Grassy Banks. River access and campground.

42.6 miles – Fresno Creek. Flows from Solitario.

43.7 miles – Contrabando (Smugglers) Creek.

44.1 miles – Movie set on banks of Rio Grande.

48.1 miles – Leaving BBRSP.

48.4 miles – Site of the traditional crossing to the Mexican village of Paso Lajitas.

49.1 miles – Lajitas Resort. Once the Comanche Trail crossed the Rio Grande at this point.

The Rio Grande

Trails—Within Big Bend Ranch State Park

All are day hikes.

Prior to 2008, the total length of all BBRSP trails was 66 miles, and that included 2 lengthy trails totaling 25 miles, off the River Road. Now there are 66 trails altogether, totaling 238 miles including the Solitario Loop (12 miles) and Botella (17 miles) in the panhandle. In addition, numerous shorter trails provide access to specific sites (Ojito Adentro) or in a loop (Contrabando Dome). Cross-country hiking is allowed in all Backcountry zones for those who want something different.

Horsetrap Bike and Hiking Trail—This easy five-mile loop enjoys spectacular vistas. It begins one half mile from Sauceda on the west end of the Llano Loop road.

Sauceda Nature Trail—The trail, a one-mile loop, begins at the lodge, heading southwest across the cattle guard and onto the hill (south). Easy hike, elevation 4,200 feet.

Cinco Tinajas Trail (Five Standing Pools of Water Trail)—A 0.9 mile loop of moderate difficulty, with stunning views. 1.3 miles from Sauceda Ranch.

Ojitro Adentro Trail (The Little Spring Within Trail)—Birding, wildlife, and a waterfall. 1.4 miles round trip, moderate difficulty.

Closed Canyon

Encino Bike and Hiking Trail—A 7.5 mile loop with two back-country campsites. Easy for hikers, moderate difficulty for bikers.

Trails—Into Big Bend Ranch State Park

Accessed from the River Road (FM-170).

Rancherias Canyon Trail—A 5-mile good day hike, through typical riparian canyon flora to an impressive pour-off. Return the same way.

Rancherias Loop Trail—See under Longer Hikes (below).

Closed Canyon—An easy hike of up to two hours through a spectacular gorge (1.5 miles, round trip). Popular in hot weather because of the shade, also a good spot to take kids. The pour-offs (vertical drops) become bigger, so make sure you don't go too far since you have got to climb back up the pouroffs on your way back.

Contrabando Dome Trail—Starting from the trailhead 7.5 mile west of Lajitas, this new and well signed trail, with interpretive exhibits, covers varied terrain in a 5-mile loop. Variants of this route exist.

Trails—Longer Hikes

Rancherias Loop Trail—Approximately 19 miles long, from the desert floor to the Bofecillos Mountains. A 3 or 2-day hike. The trailhead is well signposted on FM 170.

Solitario—The signature attraction of Big Bend Ranch State Park, *el Solitario* is an eroded lava dome nine miles across, resembling from the air a series of almost concentric circles. On the ground, a well prepared hiker could spend 2-3 days examining the unique features, such as the Flat Irons and the Lower Shut Up. This area is now accessible without guides. Read more under Solitario (below).

Public Access

Vehicle Access—The 50-mile scenic drive along the River Road requires no permit for entry. But entry to the interior of the park requires a permit, obtainable from Warnock Environmental Education Center, one miles east of Lajitas, or Fort Leaton, 4 miles east of Presidio on FM 170. $3 per person. Make sure to get current, free pamphlets about the park.

The 27-mile gravel road to the Sauceda ranch house in the center of the park is fine for any vehicle. The few designated loop roads off the access road demand four-wheel drive and/or high clearance vehicles.

Points Of Interest Along The Road To Sauceda

The Old Ranch Headquarters

00.0 miles – Turn off FM 170, 2.5 miles east of Fort Leaton, onto Casa Piedra Road.

06.1 miles – Turn right off Casa Piedra Road onto the road to BBRSP–Sauceda.

08.4 miles – Entrance gate with interpretive exhibit.

08.5 miles – Terneros Creek crossing.

09.5 miles – Road to Botella. BBRSP exhibit.

10.2 miles – Canoa Large Spring with water trough, good for bird watching.

12.2 miles – Campsite Vista de Bofecillos, trail to Palo Amarillo.

13.1 miles – Rancho Viejo campsite

15.5 miles – Exhibit: Las Cuevas, Las Cuevas Amarillas, Agua Adentro Spring.

18.1 miles – Exhibit: Ojito Adentro, start of hiking trail.

18.8 miles – Exhibit: Cuesta Primo, Presidio bolson overlook.

20.0 miles – West entrance to Oso Loop jeep road; campsite Agua Adentra.

21.6 miles – Bofecillos Vents.

21.9 miles – Yedra 1 an 2 campsites.

22.1 miles – Campsite Papalotito Colorado, a wooden windmill.

24.2 miles – East entrance to Oso Loop road.

25.4 miles – Exhibit: Cinco Tinajas, start of hiking trail.

26.5 miles – West entrance to Llano Loop road.

26.7 miles – Sauceda—Ranch and Visitor Center

Recreational Activities

Rafting/Canoeing—Spectacular Colorado Canyon is a popular stretch of the Rio Grande. Bring your own gear or hire a commercial outfitter. If you are planning to continue downstream from Colorado Canyon into the National Park, permits must be obtained from the National Park Service.

Camping—Primitive campsites are located at Arenosa and at Grassy Banks on FM 170. They contain composting toilets, but no other services. Within the park are 55 primitive campsites, some with compost toilets. At Sauceda, restroom and shower facilities are now available. The fee is $8 per site for primitive campsites. Zone camping (camping at your choice) is permitted within the BBRSP. The fee is $5 per night per site. Check first for regulations concerning where you may zone camp.

Backpacking—The 19-mile Rancherias Trail is available for serious backpackers. Campsites are designated. Water must be carried in and all waste taken out. Trailheads are located at both ends of the loop trail along FM170. There is considerable elevation gain on this trail. Most people allow for an overnight. Ask for the trail pamphlet. Zone camping is permitted here as elsewhere, subject to restrictions.

Day Hiking—See the section above marked "Trails."

Picnicking—Picnic tables are available at the "Tepees," a Texas Department of Transportation rest area on FM 170 about 10 miles north of Lajitas. Also at Sauceda, the former Big Bend Ranch headquarters in the interior has tables.

Fishing—Licensed fishermen may fish only at designated locations at the campgrounds along the river.

Hiking/Mountain Bike Trails

Close to Sauceda.

Horsetrap Bike and Hiking Trail—A five-mile loop which begins one half mile from Sauceda on the Llano Loop Road. Part sandy, part rocky—moderate to challenging.

Encino Loop Bike and Hiking Trail—This 7.5 miles moderate bike trail starts one mile east of Sauceda, follows an old jeep trail through Encino Pasture, and loops back on a service road.

Mountain Bikes may be rented from Sauceda Visitor Center for $2 an hour or $12 for 8 hours.

Pets—Pets are permitted if on a leash.

Interpretive & Educational Programs

These programs take place seasonally. Here are samples of past programs.

Madrid Falls Tour—A one-day trip in January, February, March, and June to the second highest waterfall in Texas, located in a very remote part of BBRSP.

Fresno Canyon Tour—A one-day 4×4 jeep tour to this remote canyon where you will examine the flora and fauna, geology and archeology, and visit the Smith–Crawford House. February, March, May, and June.

Guale Mesa Tour—A one-day jeep tour to the remote canyon lands to see the spectacular vistas. February, March, May, and June.

Digital Photography Workshop—Bring your camera and gain access to remote view points while improving your skills. Price includes lodging, meals, and jeep tour fees. April.

Longhorn Cattle Drive — A three-day experience of helping round up, on horseback, the Texas longhorn herd. Includes horse rental, bunkhouse accommodation, and meals. April or October.

Big Bend Ranch Trail Rides—A three-day ride to remote ranch

Longhorn Roundup

land to see spectacular vistas. Limited availability. Includes trail ride fees, bunkhouse accommodations, and meals. April, May, and June.

Identification and Uses of Native Plants—Spend the weekend learning about the common plants of BBRSP and their many uses. Learn how to use plants for fibers, medicine, food, and dyes. Includes jeep fees, lodging, and food. May.

For Prices and Dates for the trip's listed above, call 432-358-4444 (Sauceda headquarters) or 432-424-3327 (Warnock Center).

Lodging

Big House—The Sauceda ranch house, built in 1904 and remodeled in the 1940s, contains 3 bedrooms, sleeping up to 8 persons. Two bathrooms. Kitchen privileges are available or arrangements may be made for meals in the Sauceda Lodge. $100 per room for two persons and $50 for each additional person. $25 for children under 12.

Sauceda Lodge—This former hunting lodge, built in the 1960s, accommodates up to 30 persons in segregated dormitories with separate showers. Married couples will be segregated. $25 per person per night. Meals by prior arrangement: breakfast $6.00, lunch $8.50, dinner $10.50.

For reservations in the Big House or at Sauceda Lodge, contact the Big Bend Ranch State Park complex at 432-358-4444. Big House and Lodge accommodation charges are stated above and carry a user's fee plus hotel tax. Meals have sales tax added.

Solitario

One of the unique features of the Big Bend Ranch State Park is the Solitario, which means "hermit" or "that which stands alone" in Spanish. It is the eroded remnant of a dome-like structure of rocks 8 miles across.

The formation of the Solitario began about 37 million years ago when an underground intrusion of molten rock between layers of sedimentary rock rose to produce a blister-like bulge. Two million years later, about 35 million years ago, new magma forced its way upward and the Solitario erupted.

The eruption removed part (but not all) of the magma that had been forcing the rocks upward. An area of overlying rocks, about 2 miles wide and 1 mile long, collapsed into the void. This depression is called a caldera. Today's Solitario was sculpted relatively recently by erosion.

Drainage from the Solitario is outward through narrow canyons in the upturned rocks of the rim. Cattle ranchers called these canyons "shutups" because, with only minimal fencing, they could "shut up" their cattle there.

The Solitario is a highly significant feature because it is one of the largest and most symmetrical lacco-caldera in the world and because it erupted (only a few other similar geologic structures have ever done so). It also exposes rock from an ancient Texas mountain range (the Ouachitas) not seen elsewhere.

Under the new Public Use Plan (March 2008) today's visitors can visit, hike and camp in the Solitario without a certified guide, as was previously required. Ask at Fort Leaton or Sauceda for maps.

There are several places in the park to experience the full visual impact of the Solitario. Solitario Overlook is a few miles past Sauceda, and is accessible by 2WD vehicles. Fresno Overlook on FM-170 between Lajitas and the Tepee Picnic area offers a great view in late afternoon. For a closer look you'll need a 4WD high-clearance vehicle, to reach the Mexicano Trailhead. A short hike will give you spectacular Solitario vistas. The interior of the Solitario can be accessed via a 4WD high-clearance road to the Tres Papalotes Trailhead. Hikes, some substantial, can then be made to all points of the interior.

Fort Leaton State Historical Park

Located three miles southeast of Presidio on FM 170 and open from 8:00 A.M.–4:30 P.M. daily, the Fort Leaton State Historical Park contains a historic structure, interpretive exhibits, a bookstore, picnic garder, and a western office for Big Bend Ranch State Park. The entrance fee is $3.

Fort Leaton State Historical Park	
Fort Leaton State Historical Park P.O. Box 2439 Presidio, TX 79845	Phone: 432-229-3613 www.tpwd.state.tx.us/park/fortleat

Nature Trails

The nature trail, provides one mile and a third of fascinating viewing, divided into two sections, the Cottonwood Trail and the Cactus Trail.

The **Cottonwood Trail** is in a shaded riparian environment which wanders through mesquite trees and under cottonwoods, ideal for the birder, the quiet thinker, and someone who simply wants an afternoon walk in the shade. Features include a bat house. Birds sighted include Northern Flickers and Golden-Fronted Woodpeckers.

The **Cactus Trail** provides a view of fauna and flora typical of this part of the Chihuahuan Desert. More than 20 types of cacti are visible, and a good selection of quail, towhees, and verdins, among other birds. Benches for resting and picnic tables under the cottonwoods give the visitor a chance to rest in comfort.

History

Fort Leaton was established in 1848 as a border trading post by former Indian bounty hunter Benjamin Leaton. Leaton married a local woman and, through her, acquired a tract of land where a Spanish garrison had once been housed.

Leaton proceeded to build a massive adobe fortress, which served as home for his family and employees, as defense against attacks, and as a trading post. He traded successfully with the Indians and soon dominated the region. Some of his activities drew charges from both the

American and Mexican governments accusing him of inciting attacks by the Indians on Mexican settlements. Resentment against Leaton persists to this day in Presidio, so much that local residents insist on calling the fort "*El Fortín*," its old Spanish name.

Leaton died of natural causes in 1851, and his widow married Edward Hall, a local customs agent. Hall was later murdered for failing to repay a debt. The lender's name was John Burgess, who had been part of a group of which Leaton was the leader. Burgess had a freighting business and furnished corn to Fort Davis under government contract. It was in Fort Davis that Burgess was killed by William Leaton, son of Ben Leaton, in revenge for the murder of his stepfather Edward Hall eleven years earlier.

The Burgess family remained in Fort Leaton until 1926 when another descendent was killed trading gunfire with a local sheriff. The property subsequently fell into disrepair until the late '60s when it was donated to the State of Texas and its reconstruction began. Today the grim history of the fort is part of the display inside and outside the building. More enjoyable are the living history reconstructions during the year—performed by students from Presidio High School—that bring life to the historic building. Visitors may also take a guided tour of the one-acre structure, including the museum, to learn about the rich culture of the region, the oldest continuously cultivated land in the USA.

Events At Fort Leaton State Historical Park

Living History Weekend—October through April. Student docents and volunteers re-enact the late nineteenth century, including cooking demonstrations and black smithing.

La Posada del Fortin—Mid-December. Borderland Christmas is celebrated through song and dance, including a solemn devotional procession and a lighthearted pinata contest.

For information on other events throughout the year call
432-229-3613.

Barton Warnock
Environmental Center

Located one mile east of Lajitas on FM 170 and open from 8:00 A.M. to 4:30 P.M. daily, the Barton Warnock Environmental Center is the eastern office for the Big Bend Ranch State Park. It houses a gift shop and bookstore, a 2.5 acre desert garden, and a state-of-the-art visual display of the geology, history, and natural/cultural assets of the whole region.

Named after Dr. Barton Warnock, the naturalist whose definitive study of plants and flowers of the area is unsurpassed, this modern structure contains the most advanced interpretive display in the region. Encompassing the Big Bend National Park, and the Mexican biosphere reserve across the Rio Grande, as well as the Big Bend Ranch State Park itself, this impressive display is the most complete and modern in the whole region.

A desert garden of 2.5 acres is the setting for periodic Desert Garden Tours, which explain how native plants have survived the harsh conditions of the Chihuahuan Desert and how the first inhabitants of the region used them for food, shelter, and medicine.

Entrance fees $3 per person (special rates for pass holders), children 12 and under free. Interpretive Guided Tours (which are well informed and fun) $2 per person. For more information, 432-424-3327.

A Big Bend Anecdote

Remembrance
Like Taking A Walk With The Creator
By Kirby Warnock

Dr. Barton Warnock spent almost his entire life in the Trans-Pecos, sharing his knowledge of the land with anyone willing to listen and learn. Along the way he became acknowledged as one of the preeminent botanists in the world, but you wouldn't have known it on your first meeting with him.

If you had to pick a poster boy for the wildflowers of Texas, Dr. Barton Warnock would have been a most unlikely candidate. Dressed in his khaki pants and jacket, a weathered Stetson atop his head, and a nose broken from playing football before face guards were required, he looked like he would be more at home in a feed lot than an arboretum. His cowboy dress and independent attitude projected an image that didn't quite fit the "tree hugger" or "nerd" stereotypes usually associated with botanists or lovers of wildflowers.

"The first time I met him, he scared me," says Tom Alex, Big Bend National Park Ranger, "he was pretty blunt and gruff, but after you got to know him, he was one of the kindest men you ever met. He probably knew more about the Big Bend country than anyone else, alive or dead," says long-time resident John Mac Carpenter. "Not just the plants, but the land, its history, and its people. He's the only man I know who has two buildings in Brewster County named after him," says Desert Sports co-owner Jim Carrico.

The author of what is considered to be the source book on Big Bend flora (*Wildflowers of the Big Bend Country*), Dr. Warnock spent his entire life cataloging just about every cactus, wildflower, and plant in an area roughly the size of New Jersey. Popular columnist and radio personality Cactus Pryor called him "the Dobie of the desert." Along the way he hiked, drove, and climbed over so much of the Big Bend, that he was widely sought to locate specific places in this rugged terrain. He discovered dozens of unknown plants, cataloging them for posterity and even has twelve plants, which bear his name, including Echino Cactus Warnocki, or Warnock's Cactus.

After heading up the botany department at Sul Ross State University in Alpine for 33 years, the university named the new science building in his honor. Author James Michener sought him out on his novel, *Texas*, and included Dr. Warnock on the dedication page. A few years later the Big Bend Ranch State Park named its visitor center after him. But while celebrity botanists such as Neil Sperry and Howard Garrett have become the Martha Stewarts of horticulture, complete with radio talk shows and magazines, Dr. Warnock remained largely unknown. "He didn't call a lot of attention to himself," says John Mac Carpenter, "and that's unusual in a field populated with large egos."

A private man, Dr. Warnock eschewed anything that might have interfered with his time in his beloved Big Bend. When noted Big Bend photographer James Evans tried to shoot Dr. Warnock, he was continually rebuffed in his efforts to get the man to sit for a photo session. In desperation, Evans signed up for one of Warnock's classes and was able to sneak a shot during a field trip.

While Warnock's attitude did not land him on the cover of Neil Sperry's Gardening magazine, he was held in the highest esteem in the circle of learned botanists. "Of the twelve plants named for Dr. Warnock, none was discovered by him," says associate John Mac Carpenter. "Most people would be thrilled to have a plant named after them, even a scummy weed, so whenever a botanist names a plant species after another botanist, you know that they truly respect him."

Born in Christoval, Barton Warnock grew up on the family farm near Fort Stockton. His father, Arch Warnock, was an alfalfa farmer who irrigated his land from the runoff from Comanche Springs. Barton's earliest recognizable talent lay in athletics, not botany. He was a star runningback for the Fort Stockton high school football team. Unlikely as it seems, it was his football prowess that got Warnock into the field of plants. He was offered a scholarship to attend Sul Ross State Teachers College in Alpine. When asked why he pursued a major in botany in the middle of cowboy country, Warnock's reply is succinct: "I wanted to chase around in the desert."

Shortly after Warnock enrolled, the federal government acquired the property that became Big Bend National Park. The first thing the feds wanted to know was: "What did we buy and what's on it?" In 1937, Dr. Ross Maxwell, the Park's first superintendent, was sent to catalog every plant, animal, and archeological site on the place. Warnock was selected to catalog the plants. Eventually Big Bend National Park was opened to the public, but Dr. Warnock's association with Big Bend did not end there. He made repeated trips to the Park and surrounding country as a graduate student at Sul Ross.

Later Warnock was picked to head up the biology department. His botany classes became some of the most popular on campus. A veritable Who's Who of botanists can lay claim to being a former student of Warnock's, including Rick LoBello, former naturalist for the National Park Service. "Dr. Warnock was my number one inspiration," says LoBello. "He was the first person to take me into the park and taught me how to learn to love it. When you know plants it's like knowing a person. You know their names so much more than just looking at cactus. Most visitors to Big Bend are more interested in plants than anything else, because the plants are always there for the visitor to look at. They don't migrate."

What separated Dr. Warnock from other catalogers and experts of the Big Bend was his access to so much private land. Although the Big Bend region is large, nearly 90% of it is private ranch land, with owners who refuse to allow outsiders to set foot on their property. The environmental movement has only hardened this attitude, with ranchers fearing that a researcher will discover an endangered species on their place, allowing the dreaded "federal intervention." Yet Dr. Warnock was allowed on almost all of the large ranches that are off-limits to others, most notably the Brite Ranch, home of Capote Falls. It didn't hurt that he was a "homebody" who grew up in the region, but it went beyond that. "He earned their trust and respect," says John Mac Carpenter. "And that is something that is hard to obtain."

Although he remained close to the ranchers of the region, Warnock occasionally came down on the side of the environmentalists. He was an early opponent of horseback riding in the Chisos Basin, feeling that horses did more damage to plant life than cattle.

A chance meeting with wealthy Houston real estate magnate Walter Mischer led to Dr. Warnock's greatest honor. Mischer had recently purchased the old Diamond A ranch and was planning a large development called Lajitas on the Rio Grande. The idea was to turn the mountainous desert country along the border into "the Palm Springs of Texas," complete with golf course and ranch style condominiums. The two men met, the upshot of which was for Dr. Warnock to put together a museum and arboretum of the area. What became known as the Lajitas Desert Museum was constructed just north of the Lajitas resort, featuring an arboretum of native plants in the museums courtyard, all collected by Dr. Warnock.

When Texas Parks & Wildlife purchased the property from Mischer to create Big Bend Ranch State Natural Area, the museum was renamed the Barton H. Warnock Environmental Education Center. Luminaries from Austin flew in for the inauguration, including the chief executive Andrew Sansom. Sansom asked Warnock: "If we name this museum after you, what do you expect to get out of it?" "I just want to go on the property whenever I want," came Warnock's reply, "And I want you to keep people out of my way.

Almost immediately after the crowds departed from the museum's dedication ceremony, Warnock was back in the desert, driving the dirt roads, looking for more plants. At age 86, despite prostate cancer and a heart bypass, he had not slowed down much. He was currently hard at work on his next book, *Wildflowers of the Big Bend*. "He had a zest for life that a lot of people envy," says former Big Bend Ranch superintendent Jim Carrico. "Most people at his age were worn out and packing it in, but he was an extremely energetic and lively person who always had that twinkle in his eye. "Going in the Big Bend with Dr. Warnock was like being with the creator," says guide Sam Richardson. "He not only knew the plants, he knew the country, the history, everything about any place that you could go."

When his wife, Ruell passed away, many people worried that Dr. Warnock wouldn't be able to carry on. But he found a new girlfriend and held a New Year's Eve party to introduce her to the community. Although somewhat slowed because of age and medical problems, he was still up early each morning, heading out into the desert country. On Tuesday, June 9, 1998, he was following his usual routine with an early breakfast, then a drive out into the countryside at sunrise. On this day he was driving back on the Fort Stockton highway. About 18 miles north of Alpine he suffered a heart attack behind the wheel of his car and died. His car rolled to a stop on the shoulder of the road without suffering any damage. They found him there, the engine still running.

It was a pretty clean getaway for a man who lived a full life, doing what he wanted. He died with his boots on, looking at the Davis Mountains. I can't think of a better way to go.

Dr. Warnock's books:

> *Wildflowers Of The Big Bend Country*
> *Wildflowers Of The Davis Mountains*
> *Wildflowers Of The Guadalupe Mountains*

Editor's note: all are out of print, but may be found in bookstores in the area.

Reprinted from *Big Bend Quarterly* (Spring 1998).

Part II
Regional Attractions

Balmorhea State Park

Located on 46 acres four miles west of Balmorhea on Texas 17, just off I-10. Open year round. The reason for the park's existence is San Solomon Spring that fills the 3.5 million gallon, 1.75 acre pool—one of the largest man-made pools in the U.S. The depth of the pool (from 3 ft.–25 ft.), the clarity of the water, and the constant 72–76 degree temperature range make this a popular spot for scuba divers who train here and for many bathers and swimmers seeking relief from the West Texas heat. The pool is open year-round from 8:00A.M. until sunset on a swim-at-your-own-risk basis. There are no lifeguards on duty. Fee: $7 per person, 12 years and younger are free, for use of park until 10 P.M.

The spring is home to eight species of fish, including catfish, crayfish, and perch. A slight nibbling sensation on your toes reminds you that, while the pool was constructed by humans, it also belongs to the fishes. The Civilian Conservation Corps built the pool and the canals in the 49-acre campground between 1935 and 1937 and the Spanish-style cottages 1938-1940. The canals are home to two rare and endangered species of small fish, the Comanche Springs Pupfish and Pecos Mosquito fish.

A recent addition to the park is the Desert Wetlands or *Ciénega*, which replicate the original wetlands that existed before the pool was built. It provides additional habitat for the pupfish and mosquito fish, as well as attracting more birds to the Park. Visitors can look through a plate glass window and watch the underwater fish activity.

Interpretive tours of the park are provided by the park staff, subject to availability of personnel.

Where To Stay

Cottages—Inside the park, close to the swimming pool and right next to one of the canals, are 18 Spanish-style cottages. All have central heat and air conditioning. TV and linens. No pets permitted. Rates: 2 cottages with two double beds ($60); 6 with three double beds ($75); 10 with two double beds and a kitchen ($80). Bring your own utensils. Each additional person $7. Maximum in any cottage is 8. For more information, and for same- and next-day reservations, call 432-375-2370. For advance bookings, call 512-389-8900. Or book online: www.pwd.state.tx.us/park/balmorhe.

Campground—34 campsites, 6 with water ($11), 16 with water and electricity, and 12 with water, electricity and TV cable hookup ($17). Open year round. Also, a trailer dump station and restrooms with hot showers. For reservations, see "Cottages" above.

Information—Entrance to the park is $7, 12 years and younger free. Park Pass holders free. Texas seniors $3. No fee for motel users.

Balmorhea State Park	
Balmorhea State Park P. O. Box 15 Toyahvale, TX 79786	Phone: 432-375-2370 www.tpwd.state.tx.us/park/balmorhe

Adjacent to the Park is Toyahvale Desert Oasis Scuba and Souvenir Shop. Outfitters, instructors in scuba diving, snorkelling and swimming. Souvenirs and books. 432-375-2572. Personable and helpful folks. Excellent web site: www.Toyahvale.com. 115-year old post office adjacent.

Chihuahuan Desert Nature Center and Botanical Gardens

The Chihuahuan Desert Research Institute (CDRI) was established in 1973 to promote public appreciation and concern for the natural diversity of the Chihuahuan Desert. As part of their educational mission, they operate the Chihuahuan Desert Nature Center and Botanical Gardens. For the visitor this is a great way to gain a quick understanding of the plant life in the largest desert in North America. 80% of the Chihuahuan Desert lies in Mexico, the rest extends north into the Big Bend region. Here at the Nature Center, the visitor can see two components of the Chihuahuan Desert region: desert in the foreground, mountains in the background.

The site is easily accessible off the Fort Davis/Alpine highway. It comprises, in addition to a visitors center, greenhouse and botanical garden, three trails—one into a hidden canyon with year-round water, one to the highest point on the 507-acre property, and the third a short butterfly and hummingbird trail near the botanical garden. The recently opened Visitors Center contains a gift shop, which carries books and nature souvenirs. Nearby, a mining exhibit, the Chihuahuan Desert Mining Heritage, shows the history, working tools and location of the many mines in the region

The entrance to the CDRI is four miles south of Fort Davis on Texas 118. Entrance fees ($5.00 per person, seniors $4, children and members are free) are paid at the Visitors Center, one mile from the entrance. Hours of operation are 9–5, Monday through Saturday, year round. Check in at the Visitors Center before starting your visit.

The first place to visit is the botanical gardens. Over 160 species of plants native to the Chihuahuan Desert are featured, each plant labeled with its Latin and common name. Highlights include the pollinator garden and the cactus and succulent greenhouse. The pollinator garden features native plants that attract hummingbirds, butterflies, moths and native bees. The garden is usually "humming" with activity during the July through September rainy season.

The cactus and succulent Greenhouse houses a collection of over 200 species of cacti and succulents, the largest such collection of Chihuahuan Desert cacti in the world. The greenhouse is spectacular in March and April when many of the cacti are in bloom. At other times of the year, visitors can enjoy the incredible diversity of the cacti and will usually find at least a few species in bloom.

Modesto Canyon Trail is a short hike into a hidden canyon to a series of permanent springs. Here, the shade of large Southwestern Choke Cherry, Hawthorn, and Madrone trees, and the crystal clear waters make for a birder's paradise. Don't forget to pick up one of the bird checklists at the Visitors Center. Visitors can purchase for $1 a trail guide at the Visitors Center.

For the more energetic, the Canyon Trail loops back via Clayton's Overlook—the highest point on the property. Here you can look north towards the Davis Mountains and see McDonald Observatory. A new geology exhibit—*Our Dynamic Landscape: Geology, Culture, History*—introduces visitors to the geological features that can be seen from Clayton's Overlook and the linkages between geology, culture and history. You can return by a short cut to the Visitors Center, Outside the Visitors Center, check out the geologic time line. This collection of rocks, described as "A path through the ages of earth", illustrates the rock types of the northern Chihuahuan Desert.

Looking at what seems to be random heaps of different shaped and colored rocks, the visitor might at first be excused for thinking this is a decorative garden display. But look again at what the signs say and you may begin to sense the enormity of what is in front of you. The rocks on the left (the display runs left to right) are from Precambrian time. Starting 4.6 billion years ago and lasting until 570 million years ago, the Precambrian period accounts for 88% of earth's time. At the other end (right hand side) there is a pile of present-day rocks (caliche), which are used for road surfacing.

For those interested in history and geology, don't miss the Chihuahuan Desert Mining Heritage Exhibit just north of the Visitors Center. The exhibit honors the long history of mining in the Chihuahuan Desert region—from paleoindians mining chert for their spearpoints to early 20th century miners using mules and donkeys to move ore to the surface. The exhibit focuses on three aspects of mining: the history of mining, the geology of mining, and the technology of mining. Samples of ores from the Chihuahuan Desert region highlight the importance of mining while mining technology is illustrated through a reproduction of an early 20th century mining operation.

CDRI has a popular annual sale of native plants in April. In July there are extended hours to enjoy the Desert at Dusk including a Saturday Sunset Hike.

Chihuahuan Desert Research Institute	
Chihuahuan Desert Research Institute P. O. Box 905 Fort Davis, TX 79734	Phone: 432-364-2499 www.cdri.org

Clayton's Overlook

Prude Ranch

Prude Ranch, located five miles north of Fort Davis on Texas 118, has been in the tourism business for over seventy years. Long before the present wave of visitors started to wash over the region, the Prude Ranch, tended by five generations of Prudes, was catering to families from Midland/Odessa. Over the years Prude Ranch has gained recognition as a destination for those wishing a taste of ranch life, not a dude ranch with hard drinking and high rollers, but a down-to-earth operation reflecting ranch family values.

It was in 1921, following the crash in cattle prices the previous year, that the Prudes first announced they were taking in guests. Some of the first visitors were construction workers at McDonald Observatory. The shift towards what John Robert Prude, who presently runs the ranch with the family, calls "the people business," was further emphasized by the introduction in 1951 of the first summer camp for kids. Since then, Prude Ranch has proved itself as a leading promoter of regional tourism. In 1989, John Robert received the Governor's Tourist Development Award as "a key figure in the whole west Texas visitor industry for decades," and in 2001 he was awarded a similar honor by the Texas Department of Transportation. In between, there were many other acknowledgments of his energetic work in promoting regional tourism.

In 1985, the ranch faced another crisis: a drastic drop in oil prices resulted in a steep decline in visitors from the Permian Basin. The upshot of this shortfall was that John Prude sold his ranch-experience idea to groups—from environmental study groups to star party enthusiasts, tour groups from overseas, church retreats, and cycling club rallies. The Prude Ranch was marketed at travel trade fairs and by video in Japan. This way, including the summer camp program and bookings by groups, the ranch kept in business—one of the few ranches in the region that moved from cattle to people.

What the visitor sees upon arrival is a people-oriented working ranch. Seventy horses provide an essential part of the experience, and trail rides to the further reaches of the ranch take place almost daily. There are no longer cattle roundups, but the rodeo arena is active during the summer, and many a chuck-wagon cookout takes place under the cottonwood trees. To have heard John G.—John Robert's father, who is well into his nineties—sing "That Strawberry Roan" at a cookout was to experience living history.

At the heart of the Prude Ranch hospitality services is the annual Summer Camp, catering to kids aged 7–15. Now into its fourth generation of camp users, it operates from mid-June to the end of July. Non-group users can still visit and use Prude Ranch during this period, as well as the rest of the year, utilizing the motel units and paying their own way at mealtime. Amenities include a heated swimming pool, hiking trails, tennis, volleyball, and basketball courts.

Accommodations

Motel units, on the top of the hill: 2 full-size beds, from $84.95/night. Family cabins $80 (1 king bed, 2 bunk beds). Bunkhouse (with linens) $80 for 1-5 persons. RV Park. Full hookup $18.50 Meals are available to visitors when the kitchen is catering to groups. For infor-mation call Prude Ranch.

Prude Ranch	
Prude Ranch P. O. Box 1907 Fort Davis, TX 79734	Phone: 800-458-6232 or 432-426-3202 www.prude-ranch.com

Davis Mountains State Park

The modest introduction in the leaflet, "Davis Mountains State Park," states that "its 2,700 acres encompass an unusually scenic portion of Texas." This statement hardly does justice to the beauty and variety of this small but wonderful park.

Description

The park is located four miles north of Ft. Davis on Texas 118 in the foothills of the Davis Mountains. Measuring 40 by 60 miles, it is the largest mountain range in Texas. The flora and fauna of the park represent a mixture of grassland and woodland species, and the vegetation offers excellent cover for birds, deer, and javelina.

The park itself is small, only 2,700 acres or about five square miles altogether. But in this compact space are the Indian Lodge, a five-mile hiking trail to Fort Davis National Historic Site, a 100-site campground, three bird viewing areas, an interpretive center, an amphitheater, and a driving route, Skyline Drive, which provides one of the finest views in the region. A 3½ mile mountain bike trail that utilized part of the original Skyline Drive has been completed.

When To Go

The elevation of the park, 4,900 to 5,675 feet, provides for cool summer nights, while the day temperatures in spring and fall can energize the visitor to take one of the hiking trails. Spring Break and Thanksgiving are the busiest times of year, and the campground is booked up well in advance. June is the hottest month, but mid-summer rains, when they happen, keep the hillsides green and fresh in July and August. The average year-round day temperature is 63 degrees, and the average annual rainfall is 19 inches.

Information

At the entrance gate on Texas 118, stop and pay the entrance fee unless you are going directly and only to Indian Lodge. The day entrance fee is $5 per person, 13 years or older (night fee is $4). There are reductions for seniors, veterans, and the disabled. Texas Park Pass holders, who pay an annual fee of $60, enter free, together with passengers in same vehicle. Seniors pay half price (eligibility depends on resi-

Century Plant

dence location). Camping rates vary from $10 a night for tent camping to $20 a night for full RV hookup. A Dump station and two well-maintained restroom and shower rooms with hot water are available.

The entrance fee to the park also permits you to hike the Primitive Area trail—first, sign in at park headquarters. But if you decide to camp on top of the mountain in the Primitive Area, you will need to pay a $6 user's fee. Horses are permitted only in the Primitive Area. Equestrian sites cost $8. The Interpretive Center, staffed by volunteers, is open year-round. Scheduled talks/slide shows take place in the amphitheater from June to August. The park office number is 432-426-3337. Campground reservations must be made at 512-389-8900.

Davis Mountains State Park	
Davis Mountains State Park P. O. Box 1458 Fort Davis, TX 79734	Phone: 432-426-3337. Reservations: 512-389-8900 www.tpwd.state.tx.us/park/davis

What To Do—Driving

A short but steep drive from the Interpretive Center up to Skyline Drive will bring you, by turning right at the top, to the Scenic Overlook. The road was first excavated in the thirties by a pick and shovel crew of the Civilian Conservation Corps. At Scenic Overlook you will have a glorious panorama. To the left, two to three miles distant, you can catch a glimpse of Historic Fort Davis. Beyond the fort, some of the buildings in Fort Davis township are visible, including those atop Dolores Mountain.

Facing south, the sharp point of Mitre Peak is visible on the skyline. In the foreground, a broad canvas of rangeland stretches to a line of low mountains. Almost a Hollywood film setting, the beauty of the desert is marred by the intrusive tomato farm on the Marfa highway. Returning to the junction with Skyline Drive and turning right, you will pass the Stone Tower and Observation Tower before coming to a dead end just before the National Historic Site (NHS) fence line. The Skyline Drive normally closes at 10 P.M., but arrangements can be made by stargazers to use this area after 10 P.M.

What To Do—Hiking

Trail to Fort Davis National Historic Site—The 4.5 mile trail (5 miles if you start from Indian Lodge) starts to the right of the Interpretive Center and passes by the Amphitheater before climbing steeply to the Scenic Overlook above the park. You are well away from traffic noise at this point, but will encounter vehicles again in the Skyline Drive parking lot a quarter mile further on. The trail descends somewhat as it crosses a road and follows the ridge towards Stone Tower and the Fort Davis NHS fence line, where it drops steeply to the fort. For this trail, you need to decide in advance if you have the stamina to do the round-trip or, if you are going one-way only, how you are going to manage the return leg (e.g., have some one pick you up, or hitchhike).

Primitive Area Trail—This nine-mile round trip trail starts from the bird banding area parking lot across Texas 118 from the park entrance. It briefly follows Limpia Creek upstream towards Prude Ranch. Leaving the creek bed and gaining altitude, the trail follows the contour of the hillside, bearing round to the right, revealing Prude Ranch below. At the top of a steep incline, you can bear right, which will bring you in one half mile to a primitive campsite and overlook, or you can bear left which will take you to the far boundary of the Primitive Area. Return by the same route.

What To Do—Birding

The Davis Mountains State Park is in one of the state's top flyways and has long been popular with birders. The Bird viewing area is at the intersection of the park road by Keesey Creek. This is a popular spot to view this protected species, which is unique to this park. If you turn at the Interpretive Center and cross the creek, you will come to the second birding feature. This is a screened viewing area where the visitor peers through holes cut into the wooden screen to watch the birds feeding and drinking.

There are so many birds around that it is difficult, once you have made a few identifications and handled one or two birds, not to get involved. The birds often come to you at your campsite. First to visit may be the curious canyon towhee. This bird is useful for picking the bugs off the radiator of your car. Uninvited, it will also venture inside your car or tent. The towhee is not harmful and is cute, but plain, except for a rust-colored crown.

The second most likely bird to spot will probably be the first one you hear. The plaintive and repetitive "Who cooks for you" sound comes from the white-winged dove. With its white wing patch and of medium size, this vocal neighbor, whose call is often mistaken for an owl's, should be easily identified. A third bird, equally easy to identify around the campground, is the acorn woodpecker, usually seen close to its nest on a telephone pole. The red cap and the yellow patch on its throat give its face the appearance of a clown.

Where To Stay—Indian Lodge

The Civilian Conservation Corps built the original part of this pueblo-style adobe lodge in 1933. The latter part was added in 1967 to form a total of 39 rooms, each with cable TV, tile baths, central air and heat, and phone. Note the decor and furnishings, especially in the older rooms that feature latilla ceilings and kiva fireplaces as well as period furniture built by the Civilian Conservation Corps.

The heated outdoor pool is a nice bonus, in season. Room rates run from $90 (1–2 adults) in the new section to $135 (for the executive suite) in the older, adobe-built part. Additional adults are charged $10 each. Children 12 and under stay for free. Handicap-accessible rooms are available, and all rooms are non-smoking. No pets. Book early, particularly for popular periods.

Indian Lodge	
Indian Lodge P. O. Box 1707 Ft. Davis, TX 79734	Phone: 432-426-3254 www.tpwd.state.tx.us email: Indian.Lodge@tpwd.state.tx.us

Where to Stay—Camping

Primitive Sites.—Hike in 4 miles. $6 for 4 persons.

Primitive Equestrian Sites.—Ride in 4 miles. $8 for 4 persons.

Campground.—33 sites with water (sometimes sharing) $10; 34 sites with electric and water hookups, $15; 10 sites with electricity, water, sewer and cable TV, $20. For same and next day reservations, call 432-426-3254. For advance reservations call 512-389-8900 or book online: www.reserveamerica.com

Where to Eat

Black Bear Restaurant — Open for breakfast from 7:00A.M., also for lunch and dinner, up to 8:00 P.M. Sunday through Thursday, and to 9:00 P.M. Friday and Saturday. If you're driving the Scenic Loop, this might be a good spot for a breakfast such as a breakfast burrito with salsa. At lunch you might try the salad bar or the CCC sandwich, named for the builders of the lodge. In the evening, you might be tempted by something more hearty like the chicken fried steak, ribeye, or the sizzling fajitas for two. There is a useful section on the menu "For Smaller Appetites," a buffet on Sunday (12-2:30 P.M.) and dinner specials on Friday and Saturday (call 432-426-3254 for details). Afterwards, you may choose to stroll along Keesey Creek below the lodge and try to identify some of the many birds that frequent the park.

Fort Davis National Historic Site

Open daily, except for Thanksgiving, Christmas, New Year's Day, Martin Luther King's birthday, and Presidents Day, 8 A.M.–5 P.M. Entrance fee: $3 per person. Educational groups, individuals under sixteen, and various pass holders (Golden Passport, National Parks Pass) enter free of charge.

Located on Texas 118/17 one mile north of downtown Fort Davis, this fort is easy to spot and even easier to visit. From the highway, the restored barracks, the officers' quarters and the parade ground with its tall flagpole stand out clearly against the backdrop of cliffs.

Visitors enter by a short driveway, which passes a stand of enormous, ancient cottonwood trees. A marker stone at the fort's parking lot gives a summary: "Fort Davis. Established by Lt. Col. Washington Seawell with 6 companies of the 8th U.S. Infantry in October 1854 to protect travelers on the San Antonio–El Paso road. Named in honor of the then Secretary of War Jefferson Davis, it was abandoned by federal troops in April 1861 and reoccupied in 1867. The fort was deactivated in 1891."

Next door to the Visitor Center, where permits are issued, is the auditorium. Take 15 minutes to watch the video, which plays every 30 minutes, except for 11:00 A.M., 2:00 P.M. and 4:00 P.M., explaining mainly through illustrations, the fort's history. The fort's layout is compact and the restored buildings are easily identified, so 1–2 hours is usually enough time to get a feel for the fort including a visit to the museum. More time can be taken exploring the trails around the fort, enjoying the view from the cliff top overlooking the site and listening to the Dress Retreat Parade (11:00 A.M., 2:00 P.M. and 4:00 P.M.) and bugle calls which issue from the loudspeakers.

Following the Civil War in 1867 when the fort was rebuilt, black troops of the Ninth U.S. Cavalry were assigned to Fort Davis and to other posts in west Texas. Reportedly nicknamed "Buffalo Soldiers" by the Indians, these troops served until 1885. Under the leadership of Colonel Grierson, they played an active part tracking and skirmishing with the Apaches until the demise of the Apache leader Victorio, which in turn foretold the end of the fort's usefulness.

During the first 50 years of the twentieth century, the Fort remained in private ownership, its buildings gradually deteriorating. In the early 1950s, Malcolm "Bish" Tweedy, a schoolteacher, lived in one of the officer's quarters as his home. Tweedy had a vision: a restoration of the Fort to its original condition as a memorial to the soldiers and to the early history of the region. His actions led to the founding of Fort Davis Historical Society whose activity over the years culminated in the authorization by the federal government in 1961 of a National Historic Site and the purchase of the Fort. The work of the Society continues today.

The Fort's buildings may be visited in any order. Since the enlisted

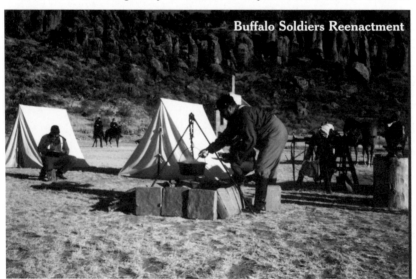

Buffalo Soldiers Reenactment

men's barracks is next to the visitor center, this is usually the first stop on the tour. In the squad room, the two rows of bunks, blankets neatly folded, hats and helmets placed on top, would satisfy any sergeant. There is also an Artillery exhibit featuring a Gatling gun, a 12-lb. Mountain Howitzer and a 3-lb. Ordnance Rifle, together with exhibits on transportation and "Life in the Field."

In the commissary, the provisioning order forms list "baked beans, 3-lb. can; Worcestershire, 1 pint bottle;" and other basic food items that give an idea of the soldier's diet. Across the parade ground, the officers' quarters show a more homey, feminine touch with fabrics, pictures, and soft chairs. This post was a major establishment in its time. Two hundred men were employed to rebuild the second fort, and, at its peak, ten companies (600 men) were assigned here. The careful reconstruction, the background of military music and the display of small everyday items combine to create a vivid impression of life on the frontier.

In the small museum, the history of the Buffalo Soldiers is displayed, including the fateful career of Henry O. Flipper, the first black graduate of West Point. Flipper was assigned to Fort Davis in 1880, but his career was cut short when he was accused of dishonesty and he was dismissed from the service. His record was belatedly exonerated when in 1999 President Clinton posthumously pardoned him.

Elsewhere in the museum, old faces stare out from the pictures on the walls, including that of Victorio, the Warm Springs Apache leader, who, according to W. W. Mills, a prominent businessman and politician from El Paso, was "the greatest commander, white or red, who roamed these plains." The military purpose of the fort is clearly stated: "forcing the Indians from the region and keeping them from it" (Major General Ord, 1879). With this task accomplished, the fort's purpose was achieved, and in 1891 it closed for the second and final time.

Today, the fort continues to attract visitors through events like Living History Activities. In March and throughout the summer, you can see live soldiers in the barracks wearing the uniforms from the 1880's, sometimes talking about conditions and duties of those days, at other time giving weapons demonstrations. Each fall, the Friends of the Fort celebrate their work with Frontier Day. Restoration work continues, most noticeably with the Fort Hospital, a substantial challenge, still in the early days of restoration.

Fort Davis National Historic Site	
Fort Davis National Historic Site P. O. Box 1379 Ft. Davis, TX 79734	Phone: 432-426-3224 www.nps.gov/foda

McDonald Observatory

One of the major astronomical research facilities in the world, possessing three major telescopes ranging from 82 to 433 inches in diameter, McDonald Observatory is open to the public. Enjoying one of the darkest sites in the world for astronomical viewing, the site also provides the visitor with unequaled daytime views across the Davis Mountains.

History

In 1926, a wealthy banker from Paris, Texas died at the age of 81. William Johnson McDonald, a bachelor, had other interests besides making money. He studied zoology, geology, biology, and also owned a telescope. When he died, he left one million dollars to the University of Texas to build an astronomical observatory. Since apparently he never attended class at the university or had even visited the campus, the gift

McDonald Observatory

seemed curious, especially to his heirs who challenged the will in a legal battle with the university.

The heirs, who were only distant relatives, claimed that McDonald did not have a sound mind when making his will. The university, anxious to proceed with the project, settled for about $840,000, which was still plenty of money in those days, to build a first class observatory. However, since the university did not have a practicing astronomer on its faculty, an agreement was reached with the University of Chicago, which had been looking into building an observatory of its own, to provide astronomers. Then the search for the location began.

Dr. Otto Struve, who had once built an observatory for the Czar of Russia, was hired as director. He picked Mount Locke in the Davis Mountains as the site. Named after Mrs. Violet Locke McIvor, who donated the land, Mt. Locke at 6,791 feet provided plenty of elevation. The vegetation of the mountainside kept dust and radiation to a minimum. Struve said, "the clear night skies were possibly greater than any other location in the United States." Far from the lights of the large cities or the clouds of coastal Texas, with only 40 days of cloud or rain a year, and an 80% chance of clear visibility year-round, Mt. Locke was clearly the first choice.

In 1939, the 82-inch reflecting telescope, devoted solely to research, was dedicated. In 1956 and 1969, further telescopes (36 inch and 30 inch) were added and then, in 1969, the 107-inch Harlan J. Smith telescope, the third largest in the world and the largest open for public viewing, came into use. In July 1999, a massive new telescope, the Hobby-Eberly Telescope, was dedicated. Unlike traditional telescopes, this 11-meter (433 inch) wide telescope is a spectroscopic survey telescope or SST and it purpose is to measure, through its collection of 91 separate computer-controlled hexagonal segments, the amount and composition of wavelengths (or colors) of light from astronomic objects. The Hobby-Eberly Telescope is for research only.

In 2002, a much larger Visitors Center was opened, offering visitors a 90-seat theater, expanded gift shop, Telescope Park, and a new exhibit hall. The hall, featuring the "Decoding Starlight" exhibit, allows visitors to explore "Spectroscopy," the technique used by many explorers around the world to determine details about stars, planets and galaxies.

Location

16 miles north of Fort Davis, 40 miles from Alpine on Texas 118. Alternatively, visitors traveling on I-10 from the west can exit at Kent and drive south on Texas 118. I-10 travelers from the east can exit at Balmorhea and take Texas 17 to Fort Davis. The MacDonald Observatory Visitors Center is the check-in point for visitors and is open from 10–5:30 daily, except for Thanksgiving, Christmas, and New Year's Day. Access for RV's and trailers is limited. If you have an RV, you may ride the shuttle bus for the fee-based guided tours only. A free, self-guided tour is also available.

Information

Astronomy is the study of light and is a non-tactile science. Videos shown inside the Visitor Center touch on the mystery of the sky, the enormous distances involved, and the potential we have to learn about the vast universe of which we are a part. The premise to all the public programs at the Visitors Center is simply that astronomy is accessible to everyone. The sky is one of the things that has not changed much in our world, and you don't need a degree in science to appreciate its beauty or to learn about the layout of the night sky. Kids generally love star parties.

The Center guides are entertaining as well as knowledgeable, drawing participation from the group. You will easily locate the moon, work out which way is north, and start to identify planets and star clusters. In these clear conditions, with this expert yet low-key advice, one's own eyes or a pair of binoculars are sufficient for a major part of the enjoyment even before looking through a telescope.

During Star Parties, 3 nights a week, various telescopes are situated outside of the Visitors Center. Depending on the number of visitors, several of the telescopes may be visited and peered through under staff guidance. In winter, hot drinks are available inside the Center. The best advice of all during those months is to dress warmly. The Stardate Café is open daily and on Star Party nights. Located in the Visitor Center, this spot is open 10-5:30 daily with an creative menu (sandwiches, salads) with a Southwestern and international flavor. On Star Party nights, it is open for dinner 8:30-11:15. Phone 877-984-7827 for tour times/prices. or visit the website: www.mcdonaldobservatory.org. For other information, call 432-426-4102. McDonald Observatory Visitors Center, 3640 Dark Sky Drive, Fort Davis, TX 79734.

McDonald Observatory	
McDonald Observatory Visitors Center 3640 Dark Sky Drive McDonald Observatory, TX 79734	Phone: 432-426-3640 www.mcdonaldobservatory.org

Guided Tours of the Observatory

This is the recommended way to get the most out of your visit. The daily tours usually include the 107-inch and the 433-inch telescopes and last about 80 minutes. Guides explain the telescopes' history, operations, and research. Reservations are not required, but arrive early to ensure a seat. Daytime Passes are $8 for adults, $7 for children, family rate $30. Tour times are 11:00 A.M. and again at 2:00 P.M., beginning with the Solar Viewing. Plan to arrive 30 minutes before the tour leaves. Call 877-984-7827 for recorded message of seasonal program times and ticket prices.

Solar Viewing at the Visitor Center

View live images of the Sun and observe solar activity such as sunspots, prominences, and flares live in the 90-seat theater. Viewing times are 11:00 A.M. and 2:00 P.M. daily. The programs lasts about 50 minutes. Solar viewing is included in the Daytime Pass admission fee. The Pass can be applied towards a discount for the Star Party. Discount combination passes are available.

Star Parties

On Tuesday, Friday, and Saturday. The most fun and certainly the most popular activity. Attendance can vary from a couple of dozen to many hundreds, depending on the month. After checking-in and paying the fee of $10 per adult, $8 children 6–12, family rate $40, visitors are taken by the interpreter/guides outside of the Center to study the present night sky conditions with the aid of a bright laser flashlight. Viewing is through telescopes from 22-inch to 8-inch, and lasts up to 2 hours. Kids especially enjoy star parties. Dress warmly; the mountain air can cool quickly.

Twilight Program

November–March 7:30 P.M., March–April 9:00 P.M., May–August 9:30 P.M., September–November 8:30 P.M. For those wanting a more enriched star party experience, a new class called the Twilight Program is offered 90 minutes before the public star party, for an additional charge. Subject matter changes with the season, and astronomical occurrences. 432-426-4102. www.mcdonaldobservatory.org

Special Viewing Night

(On the 107-inch Harlan J. Smith Telescope)

In this program, a professional astronomer shows how this large telescope is used for research. He/she discusses the research in progress, and, if conditions permit, you will get you look through the 'scope at two celestial objects. However, you'll learn that this large telescope was not designed to "look through." Instead, scientists attach gadgets to the telescope, which gather data about the universe. Programs occur once a month and times vary. There is a 40-person limit, so reservations are required. See the website for fees, times and availability. Due to its length this program may not be suitable for children under 10.

Special Viewing Night

(On the 82-inch telescope)

This is different in that there is no lecture by an astronomer. It is primarily intended to permit visitors to look through the telescope. This program also includes dinner. There is a limit of 15 persons, so reservations must be made in advance. See www.mcdonaldobservatory.org. for fees. Available nights are posted on the Observatory website. Low light conditions, elevated platforms, and late hours make this program unsuitable for children under 10.

Special Viewing Night

(On the 36-inch telescope)

This is the most casual viewing program. Not only will you get fabulous views through a large telescope, but you will also have more opportunity to marvel at the dark skies, since you will not be in a large dome that obscures most of the sky. The program does not include dinner, but snacks are provided. There is a limit of 15 persons, so reservations must be made in advance. See webpage for fees.

Ranching, The Early Days

Retrospect
Cattle Drive 1885

"Had one stood on the Capote Mountain October 12th, 1885, and viewed the surroundings, he would most likely have been impressed with the thought that the country was just as God had made it, not a trace of man was visible. Not a house in sight; no fences, no windmills, no watering places, not even a road and no livestock of the domestic order.

"The beautiful valleys bordered by the mountains were untouched by man. As far as we know, this spot had been in waiting since the dawn of creation for development that it might contribute to the support and dominion of man.

"Beneath the horizon there appeared a great cloud of dust which seemed headed toward Capote peak; slowly but steadily it moved like a great reptile as it wormed its way across the broad stretches of valley.

"The dim outlines of a covered wagon could be seen. Following the wagon was a 'remuda,' the horses could be seen marching leisurely forward frequently lowering their heads into the luxuriant gramma grass that waved its welcome to the new adventurers. Following in the rear was herd of cattle of many colors: reds, roads, whites, blacks, duns, brindles, and spotted.

"Months of hardships and exposure had been experienced during the drive to the west. Traveling through rain and mud, sleeping on wet bedding spread on the wet ground, standing guard at night over the herd, bracing the storms as the lightning flashed and the thunder rolled.

"The herd consisted of 730 cattle in which were interested half a dozen owners. The procession moved with perfect order. The cook drove the chuck wagon in front toward some mount or object across the broad valley as directed by the 'Boss.' The wrangler followed with the 'remuda,' and closely behind was the advance guard of the herd. The dun steer, which had so closely and gallantly led the herd the whole way, could be seen marching with regular step, his head erect, and seemingly undaunted by the long test of endurance.

"Close to the lead of the herd on either side rode the pointers, Louis Open on one side and Bud Musgrave on the other, whose respective duties were to keep the herd going straight. Further back on either side rode New Bowls and Sandy McDonald who kept the herd in line. Directly behind the herd with a helper on either side the writer, a youth just past his teens, rode the 'Boss' who, with the procession spread out before him, could see and direct every movement.

"Before me was a new and untried country...an experiment. I wondered what the future held in store for me. I fully realized whether successful or unsuccessful that I would necessarily have to endure many hardships, living an isolated life in camp, preparing my own meals, consisting of the plainest variety of foods, sleeping on the ground, exposed to all sorts of weather, and piercing winter winds as well as the scorching rays of the summer sun. I realized that the task before me required not only days of this isolated life, but weeks, and months, and even years.

"Luke Brit lived in a canyon camp up on the Rimrock, several miles from the Capote headquarters which he built ten years later. He lived out in the open, down in the bottom of a canyon off the beaten path. People didn't know where Luke Brit's camp was. He had the advantage of seeing and hearing anything that approached. After a time he built a rock shelter with two rooms and a fireplace. A spring surrounded by cottonwoods flowed nearby.

"There was good grass, free land, water, and he was secure. He worked alone tending his cattle. Every month or so he took a pack mule into Valentine for supplies. Canned tomatoes and sardines were delicacies to him. He used to make canned tomato cobbler. Luke Brit lived in this manner for ten years. During the first year of his ordeal the area was stricken by drought. He raised only nineteen calves and most of his mother cows died of starvation. But, after five years he had paid off his indebtedness, had increased his herd and had started accumulating land. L.C. Brit built an estate of 125,000 acres, which is still intact. From this humble beginning, L.C. Brit accumulated a fortune which enabled him to become a philanthropist."

From *The History of Marfa and Presidio County*, by Cecilia
Thompson (Nortex Press, 1985).

Part III
Adventures

The following eight Adventures provide the chance to get to places and do things that the average visitor does not. Some of the trips are for special interests (e.g., birding); others are sedentary like driving—your driving skills may be tested on back-country dirt roads—and some may be physically demanding, like the Solitario hike.

Usually, you can do these trips on your own and at the end of each section, under "or" or "alternatively," you will be given a guideline of how to do the trip yourself.

Of course you pay more for guided trips, specifically for the personnel, equipment and overhead of the outfitter. But you gain from the outfitter's expertise. You also gain precious time to get in harmony with nature. Someone else does the chores, plans the route, and takes care of the details, while you gaze upward at a soaring falcon or into a star-filled sky. Whichever way you go, remember this is the Chihuahuan Desert, so take plenty of water. Have a great trip!

Hiking Through Time

Where

The Lower Shut-up canyon of the Solitario basin. Big Bend Ranch State Park (BBRSP).

What

A two- or three-day hike through a remote area of outstanding geologic importance and great beauty. Intermediate level, requiring 6-8 hours hiking on Day Two. Note: Texas Parks & Wildlife (TPWD) require visitors to hire a guide/outfitter for this trip.

Location

Big Bend Ranch State Park, 311,000 acres, is located off FM 170 6.5 miles south of Presidio.

A 26-mile, well-graded dirt road leads to Sauceda, the old ranch headquarters. From Sauceda it is a further 14 miles over rough roads to the campsite at Tres Papalotes ("Three windmills.")

Special Attraction Of The Area

Thirty-five million years ago, a remarkable explosion erupted in this area. The resultant caldera, the name given to the collapsed volcano, is a basin eight miles in diameter. It is called the *Solitario*, Spanish for "hermit" or "he who stands alone."

A distinctive feature of the Solitario is the circular shape of the basin, which until the eruption was a dome. Some of the rocks exposed by this upheaval are from a 330-million year old mountain range. The collapse of the caldera caused a tilting of uplifted rocks, known as "flatirons" that through erosion became much more visible.

Hiking

This hike is a state park classic. It begins with the drive from the historic Terlingua/Lajitas mining district, along the Camino del Rio and into the state park's interior road system. With interpretive and scenic stops along the way, we'll make our way to our camp inside the ancient caldera of the Solitario. The Lower Shut-up canyon is one of three drainages from the Solitario into Fresno Creek. It takes us through millions of years of geologic history on this out and back excursion. The name derives from when ranchers in the old days used to "shutup" their cattle in the drainages to prevent them from straying.

The hike takes 6-8 hours and is of intermediate difficulty. It goes downhill, passing along a sandy wash to a series of drop-offs (steep, boulder-strewn gorges) which require some agility as well as stamina. Wading or even swimming across in the pools at the bottom of the drop-offs may be necessary.

The remoteness of the location, the changing geologic nature of the trail, the coloration and shape of the rock formations and the realization that this is a walk through millions of years of geologic history are the high points of the trip.

When To Go

Fall or Spring, with advance booking.

Outfitters

Desert Sports in Terlingua offers a 2-day, 1-night package for $475 and, recommended, a 3-day trip for $600. Camping is inside the caldera. 888-989-6900. www.DesertSportsTX.com.

An alternative hike inside the Big Bend Ranch State Park is the 20-mile Rancherias Trail which starts and ends on the River Road This trail does not enter the Solitario, but provides a demanding route over varied terrain. Contact BBRSP for a trail pamphlet (432-229-3416) and to pay a fee. There are other, shorter hikes in the park and many new routes and campgrounds within the state park including the Solitario, open to visitors without a guide. See page 41.

Mexico—Just Across the River

Ojinaga (pop. 30,500)

Ojinaga ('OJ' to many Texans) is one of the most remote and least used crossings along the Texas/Mexico border, and the only one for almost 600 miles between Fort Hancock and Del Rio. The traffic congestion now common at other border crossings is largely absent here. Other factors absent in this regional center are urban pollution and commercial sleaze.

The first impression for the visitor is of pickup trucks, mariachi music, shop fronts painted in bright colors, and dusty streets. The wild days of drug gang shoot-outs in the late 80's are largely a thing of the past although the recent increase in narco-related violence is worrisome. Caution needs to be taken. Daytime visits are still routine, avoid travel after dark. In the past 10 years Ojinaga has seen a slow if steady improvement in its infrastructure. The rumor of a new factory and the completion of a supermarket are positive signs. Despite this, Ojinaga still has the feel of somewhere remote, a struggling border town.

Orientation

There are no longer any maps of Ojinaga available at Presidio Chamber of Commerce. But, if you can get a copy of Mexico, Unofficial Border Crossings & Copper Canyon (by Jim Glendinning, Alpine Press Company, 2000) there is a map of Ojinaga on page 57. More easily, check the Ojinaga web page, www.ojinaga.com. This well-packed web site is out-of-date, but still contains useful information. Check the maps to give you orientation.

Ojinaga is cut in two by Free Trade Boulevard (Blv. Libre Comercio) which runs clear across town three miles from the Port of Entry. At that point, (traffic lights), it becomes Mexico 16 and continues west to Coyame and Chihuahua City (145 miles). Turning left at the lights will take you onto Chihuahua 49, heading southwest to Camargo (161 Miles). After thirty miles along this highway, at an army check point, the highway divides, left going to Camargo, and the right hand route becomes a toll-way, the faster way but longer road to Chihuahua.

Half way along Libre Comercio, to the right is the second main street (Trasvines y Retes) which leads to the plaza in one mile. The two bus stations are nearby: Transportes Chihuahuenses bus station is close to Libre Comercio and Trasvines y Retes; the terminal for the other bus line, Omnibus de Mexico, is half way along Trasvines y Retes on the right side. For bus schedules to Chihuahua City, see later in this section.

Crossing to Ojinaga

By car: Quick and easy. Crossing the International Bridge your vehicle may be randomly stopped by Mexican customs officials. If this happens, say comer (to eat) or dentista (dentist) and you will have hit upon the two most likely reasons to go to Ojinaga. No tourist card is needed unless you proceed further than 18 miles into the interior. For most vehicles, no extra insurance is needed in Mexican border towns; your US policy will cover you. At Mexican Customs, either drive straight through, if the light is green, or be prepared for a token inspection if the light is red. Do not bring in guns.

By taxi: Call Presidio Taxi 432-229-2959 or American Taxi 432-229-2525. Coming back you will need to catch a local taxi. There is a taxi stand at the plaza, and taxis are usually parked outside the bus stations.

On foot: It will take you 40-50 minutes to reach the bus stations from the bridge, longer to the plaza. Avoid walking at night.

Returning To The USA

This is when you may experience a delay, depending on the day of the week and the time. Sunday evenings, traffic going back to the U.S. can get seriously backed up, and vehicle searches on the U.S. side longer. But, by the standards of the crossings at El Paso and Laredo, this remains a quiet entry point. You need a passport or a passport card for re-entry.

Restaurants

A fancy new hotel, *Cañon de Peguis*, is located on Libre Comercio (Free Trade) Boulevard heading towards Chihuahua and, while you may not have reason to stay there, (rooms from US $51) the restaurant is attractive and the menu well priced (entrees from US $6). Three or four restaurants are favored by U.S. visitors: *Los Comales*, near the plaza, *El Bucanero* on the Camargo highway, *Lalo's* and *Lobby's*, which are near the intersection Libre Comercio and Trasvinas y Retes. It is a surprise to visitors, this far from the sea, to find two of the above restaurants (*Lalo's*, small and family run; *Bucanero*, flashy, with a new thatched roof, following a suspicious fire) serve excellent seafood and bass. *Las Cazuelas*, near *Lobby's* is recommended by a Presidio resident for its "smothered pork chop".

Bars

Colorful Bikini Bar on the plaza used to have bullet marks in the walls. Jumano's Bar next to Lobby's is more comfortable. The bar at the Cañon de Peguis hotel is at the top end of the comfort scale.

Shopping

Big Bend area residents visit Ojinaga for prescription drugs, and produce, as well as for dental visits and to eat out. Now, a large supermarket (El Super) has opened with a pharmacy, coffee shop and a wide range of food from fresh bass to mountains of fruits. The staff will know what you can bring back to the USA.

Most visitors head for Fausto's Gallery, on Juarez Street, one block from the plaza, shop offers Tarahumara items, craft products from elsewhere in Mexico, clothing, toys and religious art. Don't miss a visit to Fausto's. Try his web page (www.ojinaga.com). This site is an alternative to the local tourist office, which doesn't exist. Colorful and lively, combining restaurant reviews, bus schedules, folklore, local history including Pancho Villa's victory at the Battle of Ojinaga (1914).

What To Do

City Hall—Located in the plaza, City Hall shows dramatic historical murals so typical of Mexico. At the other end of the plaza, the eighteenth-century, red tiled church has a surprisingly simple interior.

Museum—A new museum has opened on Libre Comercio Boulevard just after the international bridge but exhibitions are few in number. A museum in the private home (Dinosaurs) exists just off Juarez Street, where Fausto's Gallery is located. Look for a sign, then follow some steps downhill. Should be fun just trying to find it. Leave a small tip.

La Junta de los Rios (The Junction of the Rivers)—Find your way by driving 1.5 miles west along the southern bank of the Rio Grande to the point where the Rio Conchos flows into the Rio Grande, and see the difference in the two rivers. The tributary, the Rio Conchos, has a much larger and cleaner flow of water.

Cañon de Peguis—Those with a couple of hours to spend might take the 'old' highway (Mexico 16) to Chihuahua and drive towards the mountains. After 27 miles you will arrive at the impressive Cañon de Peguis, a 9-mile cut in the mountain through which the Rio Conchos flows. Park at the top of the pass near a concrete sculpture and take a path towards the canyon edge. Peer over the rim down the vertical, calcareous walls to the stream 1,200 feet below.

Going Farther into Mexico

Information—Buses leave every two hours for the 145-mile trip to Chihuahua, either via Coyame over the mountains or on the toll road which follows the old railroad line. Journey time about 3 hours on either route.

Omnibus de Mexico departures: 7:30 A.M., 12 noon, 2 P.M., 4 P.M., 8 P.M. Check times 011-52-626-453-0061.

Transportes Chihuahuenses departures: 6 A.M., 10 A.M., 2 P.M., 6 P.M., 10 P.M. Check times: 011-52-626-453-1183).

Drive your own vehicle—To drive yourself (an easy drive, made easier by a new toll highway part of the way), you will need an import sticker ($30) for your vehicle, obtainable at Mexican Immigration at the International Bridge. To get the sticker you will need to show vehicle registration papers, tourist card, and a credit card.

Insurance can be purchased from La Junta/Mexico Insurance in Presidio 432-229-4621 just before the bridge, or on the Mexican side. Short-term liability insurance within Mexico will cost you about $18 a day.

Tourist Card—You will also need a tourist card if you are going beyond the border zone. Tourist Cards are issued at Mexican Immigration at the International Bridge. You need a passport or birth certificate (or certified copy). For 7 days or less, no fee. For more than 7 days US $20

San Carlos, Chihuahua

Fifty-five miles from Ojinaga on a new paved road is the small town of San Carlos (formally known as Manuel Benevides). Between the Sierra Rica Mountains and the Santa Elena Protected Area, at the entrance to the impressive San Carlos Canyon, San Carlos gives the impression of remoteness, yet is only 17 miles from the Rio Grande. A fort was built here in 1772 to protect the northern border of the Spanish empire; the ruins are still visible today. Later, marauding Comanches passed through San Carlos on their annual raids into the interior of Mexico. Mining (zinc, lead, and copper) flourished in the early part of the twentieth century, leaving as evidence the San Carlos mine. Water from the canyon is channeled to the town, flowing down the sides of the streets, irrigating the fields as well as the orchard of La Gloria Bed & Breakfast, immediately adjacent to the canyon.

La Gloria Bed & Breakfast—a modern villa with a wide veranda and a red-tile roof is the brainchild of Gloria Rodríguez. Gloria offers three rooms and baths, each with two beds. The price of $100 per person ($65 May—August), depending on size of group, includes dinner, bed, and breakfast. Guests can easily drive themselves on a paved road from Presidio/Ojinaga, without needing a tourist card or vehicle import permit. Or, she will drive them to San Carlos and back to Presidio in her own car at a cost of $275, round trip per group. This trip is ideal for a small group or a couple that wants some quality time together, with the chance to explore the nearby canyon or stroll through the village. In either case, it is the chance to explore borderland Mexico of mountain and desert—www.lagloriabb.com or call Gloria (cell phone) 432-294-4137.

Horseback Across the Rio Grande

Where

From Paso Lajitas (across the Rio Grande from Lajitas, Texas), to San Carlos, Chihuahua.

What

A five-day, four-night ride across the Chihuahuan Desert inside Mexico. Rough going, rugged terrain. One night's camping and three nights luxurious Bed & Breakfast. Deluxe meals.

Note: A passport is required for return to USA. The group will re-enter the US at Presidio, Texas.

Location

Lajitas Stables are 80 miles from Alpine on TX 118, and 67 miles from Presidio on FM 170, "The River Road." The whole area is part of the Chihuahuan Desert, the largest and highest of the five North American deserts, which extends north into the Big Bend region.

Special Attraction

A boat ride into Mexico and a horseback ride across the desert to a different culture. A chance to witness Mexican village life.

The Ride

We cross the Rio Grande by rowboat. It is a short hop by boat but a giant step culturally as we mount our horses and ride into a Mexican way of life. We will encounter vaqueros, goat herders and *candelilla* gatherers as they go about their business. We ride for half a day along Los Mongos creek past deep *tinajas*, stopping to view some well preserved pictographs at an archaic Indian site. Our campsite is at a small rock house on Milagro Creek. We sleep under the stars.

The next day is longer, perhaps 7 hours in the saddle, as we follow an ancient trail through La Mora Ranch, noting the roots of giant cottonwood tress which form a dam for the water that is the life blood of this harsh desert country. After rounding San Carlos mountain, we drop down to the 300-year old community of San Carlos. We ride along cobblestone streets to Gloria's Bed & Breakfast. Outside, terraced gardens and a veranda overlooking San Carlos Creek complement the comfortable rooms inside and the tasty local food. We will stay here for three nights.

Day 3 is more leisurely. In the morning we spend exploring the canyon by foot, passing by hanging fern grottos and deep limestone pools. In the afternoon we can choose between relaxing on Gloria's patio or riding to another canyon to see more waterfalls. In the evening, some more of Gloria's fabulous cooking.

On the fourth day we saddle up and head up the canyon, turning into a twisting side canyon—not a ride for the faint of heart! At last we top the ridge and view La Mina Grande (the Big Mine). This community was once home to 4,000 people. Now only the shells of homes and mine buildings remain, high on a mountain. After a scrumptious saddle bag lunch, we investigate the dusty, windblown site and marvel at the energy and ingenuity of its inhabitants

Day 5. We have a choice between a short energetic ride along the creek or a relaxed morning in hammocks or wading in warm pools.

Riding To San Carlos

Lunch is taken in a small restaurant in town, followed by a tour of the town. Our shuttle leaves at 2:00 P.M. for the quick 55-mile drive on a new road through the Sierra Rica mountains to Ojinaga, from where we cross into Presidio, Texas. A further 50-mile drive along the River Road bordering the Rio Grande brings us back to Lajitas around 5:00 P.M.

This extraordinary trip, called the Milagro Trail lasts five days and costs $1,000 per person. The price includes all meals, horse and guides, one night's camping and three nights B & B, transportation back to Lajitas. The October trip enables participants to witness the Day of the Dead celebrations in San Carlos. This trip costs $1,150. The terrain and time in the saddle requires fitness from participants but, those up for this adventure will see a slice of rural life in Mexico not experienced by others. In addition to a Lajitas Stables CPR-trained wrangler, each trip is staffed by a Mexican citizen whose insights and interpretations provide a unique window into another way of life.

Lajitas Stables also offers a 4-day riding trip costing $850, called *Rancho Picachos* which is based at a small working rancho across the border. Rancho owner Israel Tercero will accompany the group to nearby sights of interests and encourage participation in daily chores. Prior horseback experience is suggested. This is a flexible trip, depending on the interests and energy of the participants.

Lajitas Stables, the exclusive horseback outfitters, also provides short and longer trail rides in Big Bend, ride and rafting combinations, and trips to Big Bend Ranch State Park. wwwlajitasstables.com. 800-887-4331 or 432-371-2212.

Off-Road Self-Drive Driving Tours

Where

Tour #1—Marfa/Pinto Canyon/Hot Springs/Presidio/Ojinaga/ Fort Leaton/Casa Piedra/Marfa. A 181-mile circle trip, part blacktop, part gravel (70 miles). See page 118 for detailed itinerary.

Tour #2—In Big Bend National Park (BBNP) paralleling the Rio Grande. "The River Road," a 51-mile east-to-west dirt road. See page 123 for detailed itinerary.

What

Self-drive tours in your own vehicle. High clearance vehicle required for the second itinerary. Jeeps can be rented from Terlingua Auto Service 432-371-2223. See page 91.

Duration/Conditions

Tour #1—Presidio County. Seven hours including lunch and crossing into Mexico. Check that you have Mexican insurance coverage for your vehicle, and your passport. If not, stay in Presidio for lunch. Blacktop and gravel.

Tour #2—Within Big Bend National Park in South Brewster County Four to six hours depending on number and length of stops. Take advice at Panther Junction park headquarters regarding the condition of the all-dirt road. Normally 4-wheel drive is not necessary for this trip but high clearance is.

Special Attraction Of The Trips

Tour #1—The rugged terrain of Pinto Canyon; then a surprise contrast at Chinati Hot Springs. Cross the border to Ojinaga, Mexico (optional), return to Presidio and continue four miles on FM 170 to Fort Leaton State Park. The trip back is a 2 1/2- hour drive to Marfa across stark rangeland. The route passes the tiny community of Casa Piedra and crosses the no longer used rail line at La Plata before joining US 67 just before the Border Patrol checkpoint.

Tour #2—The Chisos Mountains viewed from the southern side and to follow the northern bank of the Rio Grande passing Mariscal Mine—the Chihuahuan Desert at its remote best.

When To Go

Choose the cooler months so you can get out of your car and enjoy the scenery.

Off-Road Travel

Allow plenty of time and take plenty of water. In the BBNP, you are free to take any side trip or backcountry road, but elsewhere, on county roads crossing private ranch land, drivers should be careful not to stray off the road or cross any fence line. In Presidio County, be aware of the livestock law, which says the driver is responsible for hitting any stray animal.

Rafting The Rio Grande

Where
Through Santa Elena or Mariscal Canyons in BBNP.

What
A two or three-day guided or self-guided float trip by canoe, kayak or raft.

Note
Decide whether you wish to be a passenger and have all your time available to enjoy the river by letting someone else organize the camping/eating services or if you wish to navigate, paddle, and take care of all those chores yourself.

Location/Description
The Rio Grande acts as the southern boundary of Big Bend National Park, as well as the international border with Mexico. BBNP is anchored in Mariscal Canyon, which forms the right angle bend of the river as it changes direction.

Santa Elena Canyon is the better known and more easily accessed canyon (20 miles). Mariscal Canyon (10 miles) is more remote, requiring a 3-hour shuttle. Both canyons have sheer 1,500-foot limestone walls, and one or two navigation challenges depending on the water level.

Special Attraction Of The Trip
From the glare of the desert you enter the cool, quiet of the canyon. Light softens, and noise intensifies. The craft is dwarfed by the soaring limestone cliffs. The visitor can actively explore side canyons or sit back and identify bird life. Allow an overnight for the quiet and grandeur of the setting to work their magic.

On The Rio Grande

River Trip

The main differences between a guided trip and a do-it-yourself passage through the canyons are in the interpretation and the logistics. In the first case, your river guide will explain the geologic and wildlife features of the canyons and describe past history along the Mexican border. He will also set up camp and cook all meals.

The water level affects how quickly you travel, how much time you have on shore and whether the occasional rapids ("Rockpile" or "Tight-squeeze") present a challenge. In recent years, low water has been the norm and the rafting companies have had to react creatively to put guests on the river.

When To Go

Historically, rains occur in late summer making September/ October a good time to go due to increased water flow and moderate temperatures. In mid-summer, the canyons can become like ovens, in mid-winter, like refrigerators. Get the water level reading and a weather forecast before deciding when to go. Avoid Spring Break, if possible, when local services can get overstretched.

Outfitters

The three local outfitters which use the same stretch of river, the same equipment and often share river guides are:

Big Bend River Tours
www.bigbendrivertours.com. 800-545-4240.
Desert Sports
www.DesertSportsTX.com. 888-989-6900.

Far Flung Outdoor Center
www.farflungoutdoorcenter.com. 800-839-7238.

Trip prices, per person , which vary slightly from outfitter to outfitter, range from $72 for a half-day through Colorado Canyon (2-3 persons), $310 for the overnight Santa Elena Canyon trip, and from $1,250 for the 7-day Lower Canyons float. Or do it yourself by renting a two-person canoe ($50/day), kayak ($59/day) or raft ($35 per person, per day). The outfitters also provide shuttles only (for example, $60 for Santa Elena Canyon put-in, $145 take-out).

Sample 2-day itinerary for Santa Elena Canyon:

Day One. 8:30 A.M. Meet at your outfitter's office and transfer to the river bank at Lajitas. Instruction of safety measures. Board your raft. Morning highlights may include visiting a candelilla wax processing plant, the ruins of an old Spanish fort or a hike into an interesting side canyon. Your guide will serve lunch. Continue in the afternoon until the guide finds a comfortable spot for your overnight camp. While the guide prepares your evening dinner, you are free to explore or simply take a nap to the soothing sounds of running water.

After a filling and tasty dinner, enjoy the warmth of the campfire. Lie back and look up, where you will see more stars than you thought possible. You may sleep under the stars or in one of the tents provided.

Day Two. You may want to explore along the river bank to perk up your appetite while your guide prepares a pot of camp coffee and a hearty river-style breakfast. After breaking camp and repacking the rafts, you will float into the canyon entrance. As you drift deeper into the canyon, the sheer walls gradually rise. The level of excitement rises as well when you approach the Rock Slide. This rapid was created millions of years ago when a portion of the cliffs above you broke off and crashed into the river. It left behind house-sized boulders creating a great obstacle. But your guide will find a way to circumnavigate the boulders as you proceed downstream.

In the afternoon you may well take a hike into beautiful Fern Canyon. With sculptured walls and cool, clear pools the canyon makes a refreshing stop along the way and provides a unique contrast to the desert. Continuing downstream you will exit the canyon into the bright desert light, to find your transportation ready to carry you back to Terlingua late afternoon, with plenty of time to plan your evening activity.

Combination Trips—Hiking, Biking, and Paddling

Where

Big Bend National Park.

What

Big Bend Multi-Sport, South Rim through Mariscal Canyon.

A 3-day program of hiking (17 miles), biking (23-28 miles) and paddling (10 miles), from the South Rim of the Chisos Mountains down to Juniper Canyon, and through Mariscal Canyon of the Rio Grande.

Location

Assemble at Desert Sports in Terlingua.

Note
There is a minimum of 4 and a maximum of 8 persons allowed per group. An intermediate level of experience is required for this trip. Part of the trip is SAG wagon supported.

Special Attraction of The Trip

Experience the different types of terrain: mountain, desert and river with appropriate means of locomotion: hike, bike and paddle. Or perhaps you might like to try a new activity while engaging also in your favorite sport.

Cost

$550 per person. Contact Desert Sports 888-989-6900.

www.DesertSportsTx.com.

Desert Sports is unique in Big Bend in its willingness and ability to outfit and guide combination trips. In addition to the trip described above, Desert Sports offers Solitario Combination in Big Bend Ranch State Park. This 3-day trip combines a mountain bike ride (39 miles) with a 6-8 hour "Hike through Time" in the Solitario, $600 per person. The 3-day Glenn Springs/Mariscal Canyon combines mountain biking and paddling ($550). The Mesa de Anguilla/Santa Elena Canyon 2-day trip ($290) offers hiking and paddling. For all of these trips a minimum of 4 persons is required.

Jeep Tours

Where

South Brewster County on Terlingua Ranch.

What

Camp 360 Tour. A three-hour trip with interpretive guide to a mountaintop with one of the best views in the whole of Big Bend.

Location

Study Butte, at the intersection of Texas 118 and FM 170 is the start for this tour. Our destination is Terlingua Ranch. This 200,000-acre property was subdivided, starting 25 years ago. Today, approximately 170 families live on the ranch year-round. Far Flung Outdoor Center has arranged access to one of the private areas to the west of Texas 118.

Special Attraction Of The Trip

The unique feature of this half-day trip is that you go to remote places where other vehicles are not able or permitted to go. Secondly, you are going up high and will enjoy a 360-degree panorama of the whole area including the Chisos Mountains in Big Bend National Park, and the mountains inside Mexico.

Jeep Country

Third, on the way there you will stop and view 80 million year old fossils, old mining sites and rare Big Bend cacti.

A more general point is that you are not just driving around in mountainous desert terrain. Your driver acts as your eyes; he will show you plant life growing among the rocks which you would not have seen yourself. He will tell you about the general history of the border region, and the natural history of the immediate vicinity with some local tales thrown in.

Jeep Tour

After assembling at Far Flung Outdoor Center headquarters, we drive north on Texas 118 for eight miles before turning left on to a county road. Shortly after, we pass through a gate onto private property and begin our ascent.

A rough, winding track takes us sharply uphill for 30 minutes, passing an abandoned mine and crossing a creek. Soon, we have gained sufficient altitude to gather an impression of the terrain. To the south, peak after peak recedes into the distance—a layering of mountain ridges. The jeep finally stops, and we dismount and clamber to a pile of rocks, the summit. After enough time for contemplation, asking questions or taking photographs, it is time to return.

When To Go

The cooler months are generally better, although a cold day in January or February or a windy day in April is no fun. Remember, you are sitting in an open-sided vehicle with a canvas roof.

Outfitters

Far Flung Outdoor Center pioneered jeep tours in the area. This 3-hour trip costs $64 per person. Other short trips (Apache Trail–2 hours; Lone Star Mine–3 hours; Ten Bits Tour with paleontologist as guide–7 hours) cost from $49–$135. The all-day Round the Bend tour cost $129. Tours start at 9 A.M. and (some) also at 2 P.M. 800-839-7238. 432-371-2489. www.farflungoutdoorcenter.com.

Birding

Where

The Trans-Pecos. 500 species, which is over half of all North America's bird species, have been recorded there. Birding enthusiasts can search for as many of those species as possible, or search for some of the rarer endemic species. Or just sight-see while birding along the way.

What

A few birding forays will require long hikes (Boot Springs in Big Bend National Park) or a high-clearance vehicle (Pine Canyon, also in the park). Most of the trails are well-maintained and well-marked. Much good birding can be done with little effort or walking, such as Davis Mountains State Park, or Cottonwood Campground and Rio Grande Village at BBNP.

Area birding hotspots are:

Lake Balmorhea, a spring-fed lake, can be a gold mine of wintering waterfowl as well as a good place to find Sage Sparrows and Sedge Wrens. There is a small charge to bird the lake area. While there, pick up a checklist for the location to give you an idea of what to expect and when to expect it.

Fort Davis area, including the state park, is an excellent place to seek (and hopefully find) the elusive Montezuma Quail. While there, don't forget to look for Hepatic Tanagers, Acorn Woodpeckers, and whatever other goodies you can find.

Big Bend National Park is the prime hotspot for a major variety of species. It is traversed by madrone-dotted forests in the Chisos Mountains' sky-island habitat, an abundance of lowland desert, plus the riparian corridor of the Rio Grande River. Diversity of habitat means diversity of avian species. Be sure to check out the sightings reports at the Panther Junction headquarters. You will have to ask to see them.

Specialties

This is the only nesting site in the US for the Colima Warbler. This neotropic migrant can best be located along the trail to Boot Springs in

Big Bend National Park. Other specialties along that trail are Hutton's Vireo, Painted Redstart, and any number of hummingbird species. In fact, the Big Bend is host to as many, if not more, hummingbird species(15) as anywhere else in the U.S. (Worldwide, hummers occur only in the Americas.) This phenomenon is celebrated by an annual hummingbird festival at Fort Davis every August. Information on the festival can be found at www.cdri.org. The rare Lucifer Hummingbird, which nests in the Trans-Pecos, is a much sought after species by birders as well as bird photographers.

Lucifer Hummingbird

The world's tiniest owl, the Elf Owl, is a denizen of the Chihuahuan Desert, as is the nation's only Silky-flycatcher, the Phainopepla.

When

Winter is the best time for birding Lake Balmorhea, whereas spring is the best time to see the most number of species in the Trans-Pecos, in general. Summer afternoons are too hot to bird in the lowlands. Best to head for the Chisos or Davis Mountains, or take a siesta then. Summer mornings are a good time to observe the endemic nesting species. Whenever you come be sure to carry plenty of water and wear a hat. Please note: Light colored clothing is immensely cooler than dark colors.

Who to Contact

For more information on birding tours to the Davis Mountinas and Big Bend, go to www.dmectexas.org.

Ranching Today

Ranching In The Big Bend

"Davis Mountains and Trans-Pecos Heritage Association." This sign appears at the entrance to almost every ranch in the Big Bend area, an indication how local ranchers have united to fight for their property rights and protect their livelihood. The Association, whose office is in Alpine, aims to send a message to the government that "it will not stand by and see private property use restricted by undue governmental regulations." It conducts on-going, defensive action against encroachment on members' property by the government, environmentalists, and anyone else perceived as a threat to the ranching way of life.

The ranchers' mood of activism stems from 1986 and a now famous meeting in Fort Davis. It was rumored at that time that the U.S. National Park Service had a plan to establish a new national park in the Davis Mountains. The aim was to fill in the missing link between the Guadalupe National Park to the northwest and the Big Bend National Park to the southeast. A meeting in Fort Davis was called by the Park Service to determine local opinion. The ranchers turned out in force, effectively took over the meeting, and told the visiting officials in no uncertain terms that they wanted no part in any national park.

Eleven years later, in 1997 in Alpine, a more modest proposition by the Texas Department of Transportation to establish Scenic Routes in the area as a means of encouraging tourism received a similar response from local ranchers. Again, the ranchers dominated the meeting and informed the audience and the hapless Transportation Department personnel that they opposed encouraging more tourists to visit the area. The tourists left litter, trespassed on private property, and did damage. The ranchers' sentiments were clear and their tone was hostile.

To understand why local ranchers, normally correct in manners and easy-going in attitude, were still so riled at what seemed to be a simple question of encouraging tourism and promoting local jobs, it is useful to see how the cattle raising industry in this part of West Texas is doing. The answer is: not well at all. Everything seems to be going wrong for these hard-working and hard-pressed custodians of the pioneer tradition:

the climate, the economics of the beef industry, and even general eating habits, which have shown a steady move away from beef over recent years.

In addition, governmental regulations at all levels and perceived threat of encroachment by officialdom onto their properties has further antagonized ranchers, already suspicious of outsiders. On top of this, businessmen from elsewhere, called "hobby ranchers" by the Association, have been buying up local ranches and turning them into non-productive, recreational parks to provide hunting for their clients, thereby inflating the price of land and with it the appraisal and taxes on the ranching properties.

The present drought, of several years' duration, is just the latest of a cyclical pattern of droughts in the region. But it is seen, when joined by other factors, to be worse than the infamous drought of the fifties, which drove many ranchers to the wall. Since then there has been a sorting out

Rancher Ike Roberts

and redistribution of ranches. The larger, family-run properties with good pastureland are still hanging on, but the others are being sold off to hobby ranchers. A few ranchers, usually in areas close to communities where there is a demand for building land, have subdivided and sold plots of land, but they are very much in the minority and disparaged or envied by the others. The rest of the ranchers soldier on, hanging on precariously to a living passed down from their pioneering forebears.

Understandably, ranchers are suspicious of outsiders encroaching on their property. Sierra Club activists are a traditional enemy, but government in its many forms is seen as a bigger threat. An event in 1990 galvanized the ranchers once more. It stemmed from an apparent find of an endangered species of pondweed, supposedly discovered by U.S. Fish and Wildlife Service researchers on a local ranch. Action by the ranchers' association contained this threat, but deep suspicion remains. Previously, geology and other students from Sul Ross State University in Alpine had been allowed on to ranch property to do field trips. Now none of this is permitted anymore as the ranchers retreat into defensive mode.

Visitors to the Big Bend area today should look to the parks to provide their recreational enjoyment. Ranchers, preoccupied with their economic problems to which there does not seem to be an easy way out, turn reluctantly to tourism as a source of income. A few ranches have gone into the tourism business: Prude Ranch is the oldest; Woodward Ranch mixes some cattle raising with access for rock hounds; Cibolo Creek Ranch offers a luxury guest ranch experience. But for the vast majority, cattle raising is the only way despite a gloomy consensus regarding the future. "The ranching business is sliding away," according to one of the former officers of the Davis Mountains and Trans-Pecos Heritage Association.

Part IV
Scenic Routes
Big Bend & River Road Loop

Alpine, Terlingua, Lajitas, River Road, Presidio, Marfa, Alpine

Miles: 230 (all paved) — Stops: 5–6

✓ = Must See, ♦ = Food Stop

Start—Head south out of Alpine on Texas 118 after stocking up with coffee/snacks at Bread & Breakast downtown at 113 W. Holland Avenue. Adjust odometer at intersection of US 90/TX 118. Three miles south of town the road climbs steeply up Big Hill.

We are now running through Double Diamond country, as the entrance gates to the right of the highway indicate. Double Diamond Ranch is one of the few ranches that has sold off lots for residential development. The views looking west towards Cathedral Mountain are spectacular, and Alpine is only 20 minutes away.

16.3 miles—Woodward Ranch, open to visitors for rock hunting, sales of polished stones, and camping. A 1.7-mile dirt road brings you to the ranch house and rock shop. Here you collect a bucket and take off to collect plumed agate or other rock specimens. When you are finished, you pay according to weight. Alternatively, you can buy uncut or cut-and-polished stones in the rock shop, as well as pieces of opal, pendants, and other jewelry items. This exploration is great for kids—keeps them busy and provides a sense of achievement. The area has been well picked over during recent years, but there are still some fine specimens around the ranch house if time is taken to locate them. An RV Park at the ranch house and a primitive camping area 2 miles further along a bumpy track by the edge of Calamity Creek provide camping.

17.8 miles—A shaded picnic site. A second one follows at 27.2 miles.

27.3 miles—Entrance (left side) to the vast bulk of 6,200 foot Elephant Mountain. This 23,000-acre property of Texas Parks and Wildlife is used primarily for research, particularly into the life of the herd of 150 big horn sheep that roam the mountain. It is also used seasonally by hunters, birders, hikers and campers.

The general public is admitted to part of the reserve. Check in at the registration booth at the entrance to the property (no fee) and follow the signs indicating Self Driving Tour, along which you will find interpretive signs, as far as the viewing area. From May 1–August 31 the viewing site for Bighorn Sheep is open to those holding a TPWD Limited Public Use Permit ($12). Bring binoculars since the sheep are difficult to spot. A 15-site campground, with shelter shade, picnic tables, and one pit toilet is available. Call 432-364-2228 for information.

The terrain now flattens out and takes on a desert character. On the right side, you will see a line of cliffs, which marks the southeast limit of the Marfa Plateau. Farther on (36.1 miles, right side) is a sign that reads "02 Ranch." This 264,000 acre ranch is the property of Lykes Lines Shipping Company. To hear how Lykes Line, misinformed about annual rainfall, bought the property in 1941, and what subsequently developed, read *Below the Escondido Rim* by David Keller who traces the ranch's history.

43.1 miles—To your left in the distance is the solitary Santiago Mountain, a 6,521-foot truncated cone of volcanic rock. The origin of the name Santiago (St. James) is told by Hallie Stillwell in her book *How Come It's Called That?* There are two different explanations. One is that the peak was named after Don Santiago, chief of the Chisos Indians. Perhaps so, for it is a matter of record that the Spanish General Juan de Retana fought an all-day battle against Don Santiago who finally surrendered. An alternative tale is told by Natividad Lujan, a survey chainman, who claims his uncle Santiago was killed by Apaches and was buried at the foot of the highest peak of the range.

In the freewheeling days of the early 1900s, a particularly infamous scam involved the sale of lots in a township to be called Progress City. The unsuspecting buyers little knew it was on top of Santiage Peak. A plan of the proposed city is displayed in the Brewster County courthouse in Alpine.

47.8 miles—Directly ahead, on the skyline, and later to the left as the road bends, the outline of the Chisos Mountains in Big Bend National Park becomes visible. In the middle distance are other peaks, giving a look of layered mountain ranges that is typical of the Big Bend region.

54.8 miles—Cowhead Ranch. Horseback riding by the hour or overnight, bunkhouse accommodation. A cluster of old west buildings (bar, church etc), some corrals, goats and dogs wandering around—this is the unusual Cowhead Ranch, self-built by cowboy visionary Chris Calvin who describes the place as the "Home of the free spirited American dream." Strong on atmosphere, good for kids. 432-371-2142.

60.6 miles—To your right is Agua Fria Mountain, named after the cold-water spring at the base of a 600-foot cliff. Pictographs on the cliff tell that the Indians used this spot as a camp. This is private property, however, and you may not visit.

63.4 miles—Entrance (left side) to Terlingua Ranch, a 200,000-acre property, owned by the 4,600 property holders. Around 10% have built houses on the ranch. Eleven hundred miles of dirt road connect these seasonal and year-round homes. The houses range in style from straw bale constructions to conventional ranch-type houses to primitive cabins, reflecting the tastes of the many types of people attracted to the desert location. The Resort also has tourist cottages for overnight visitors, a restaurant, RV park, and swimming pool at the end of a 16-mile road. These are temporarily closed. Look for signs on Hwy 118 that the facility has reopened before driving in

The Grub Shack, a burger joint with shade seating, at the intersection. Open daily except Sunday & Monday, 7:30–10:30 A.M.; 11:30–3:30 P.M. Great place to meet locals. Betty serves up great food, and offers insights into local life. Bestseller is the lunch burrito ($6), and cheeseburger ($6). Full breakfast menu.

68.1 miles—The Longhorn Ranch Motel and Tivo's Place restaurant offers well-priced, clean motel accommodation in a remote desert location. 24 spacious rooms, each with two double beds. Rates $75 per room, plus tax. An RV Park has been added, $22 for hookup.

Tivo's Place is open daily except Monday 5–9 P.M. Previously in Study Butte, they have kept their popular, mainly Mexican menu.

Longhorn Ranch Motel & Tivo's Place Restaurant	
Longhorn Ranch Motel & Tivo's Place Restaurant P. O. Box 177 Terlingua, TX 79852	Phone: 432-371-2541 www.longhornranchmotel.com.

74.7 miles—Wildhorse Station (left side), a grocery store/gift shop, has seven furnished mountain cabins for rent, by the night or longer. Excellent views from the higher cabins. 432-271-2526.

80.4 miles—Study Butte (Stewdy Beaut), formerly an active mining town, was named after Will Study, early prospector and mine manager. Debris from the old mine overlooks the scattered village of haphazard buildings, old and new. Turn right onto FM 170.

♦81.4 miles—Kathy's Kosmic Kowgirl Kafe. One mile west of the Y, on Hwy 170. Very Terlingua in decor and style, the Pink Place offers burritos, burgers and BBQ, served up by its spirited owner, Kathy. Shade, comfy seating, magazines to read. Open Thursday–Monday, 6:30–3:00. Popular with river guides. An outdoor fire is lit in winter. Movies are shown from time to time.

✓85.2 miles—Terlingua Ghostown. Until the mid 1900s over 2,000 miners toiled here extracting cinnabar from the ground for conversion to mercury. The old mine shafts and abandoned mine buildings and housing, including the two-story manager's house, are clearly seen. The Ghostown has evolved over recent years into a tourist destination with a famous restaurant, a well-stocked gift store, and the porch where the locals sit and talk. Go to page 271

89.8 miles—(right side) Site of the major chili cook-off operation, Chili Appreciation Society International (CASI), which attracts thousands each November to taste and party.

91.0 miles—Badlands Fossil Museum (right side). Local paleontologist Ken Barnes' remarkable fossil collection including duck billed dinosaur and mosasaur (marine lizard) remains. If the gate is open, he is at home.

✓96.8 miles—Lajitas, 2,364 feet. The Barton Warnock Environmental Center, a museum of the Texas Department of Parks and Wildlife. A must-see museum for the whole area, with a desert garden adjacent. Open 8:00 A.M.–4:30 P.M.

A little over a mile farther on (98.0) is Lajitas Resort. Steve Smith from Austin bought the lackluster resort in 1999. Determined to make it a top-class destination resort ("The Ultimate Hideout") with championship golf course, spa, a choice of restaurants, and a runway capable to taking jets, Mr. Smith has spent $100 million to achieve his aim, in vain. The project stalled, Smith ran out of money, and the property was auctioned. The new owners have lowered the prices and changed the elitist tone of the resort, hoping to attract a new, larger clientele.

98.8 miles—We now pass into Presidio County, which has different live-stock laws. If you hit a stray animal the responsibility falls on you, the driver.

103.2 miles—Movie set for one of a variety of Western movies filmed locally in the 90s. We are now in Big Bend Ranch State Park.

104.5 miles—Contrabando Trailhead. One of the new trails in the Big Bend Ranch State Park. Well designed and marked, offering varied terrain, this 5-mile circle route passes close by the abandoned Buena Suerte Mine.

107.8 miles—"Grassy Banks" campground and river access point.

109.4 miles—To the right, the Hoodoos or Penguin Rocks, formed by the erosion of the limestone and volcanic ash deposits.

110.8 miles—Teepee Picnic Site. Next is "Big Hill," a 15% gradient, the steepest public highway in Texas. Stop at the top for a view.

✓**118.7 miles**—Closed Canyon. This hike through narrow canyon is easily accessible and makes a nice break from driving. The narrow, shaded passage along the sandy bottom is a pleasant change from the heat and glare of the open country. There are periodic drop-offs; make sure you can climb back up before going down!

120.6 miles—Colorado Canyon river access. A good place to stop, walk down to the river.

133.2 miles—We exit the state park and come to the village of Redford, which has a small store, gas station, and school. The tragic shooting in 1997 of local teenager Esequiel Hernandez by U.S. Marines on anti-narcotics patrol left a deep scar on the Redford community and outraged many in the region. A $1.9 million payment from the U.S. Government to the family effectively acknowledged responsibility for the killing. The subsequent removal of the Marines admitted the error of the policy. Esequiel Hernandez's gravesite is in the cemetery, signposted from the main road. A memorial is planned.

Nine miles west of Redford a cable is stretched across the river. It is used by the International Boundary and Water Commission to take flow measurements in the center of the stream to determine how much water is allocated to each country for irrigation—a contentious issue.

✓**146.5 miles**—On the left is Fort Leaton, open to the public. This historic fort serves as park headquarters for Big Bend Ranch State Park and has a museum and shop.

♦**150.3 miles**—At the "Y", downtown Presidio (pop. 5,900), the hottest town in Texas and the center of the oldest continuously occupied and cultivated area in North America. This border town, whose population is 80% Hispanic, is linked by the International Bridge to Ojinaga (30,500 inhabitants) in Mexico. In 1915, following the defeat of the Mexican army by Pancho Villa, the whole of the federal force fled across the Rio Grande to safety. For ✓El Patio Restaurant, go straight-ahead 100 yards from the "Y". The Enlightened Bear, almost opposite, is a new coffee shop with a good menu. Return to FM 170.

152.5 miles—After crossing Cibolo Creek, we leave FM 170 and bear right onto U.S. 67 heading north towards Marfa. We now begin to ascend steadily towards the volcanic mass of the Chinati Mountains. We head uphill for 19 miles before dropping down slightly to the ghost town of Shafter. Formerly a silver mining town, production closed in 1952. Turn right, cross the creek and drive to the cemetery where there is an outdoor exhibit of the history of Shafter on display boards. Allow ten minutes.

170.5 miles—Shafter. Formerly an active silver mining community. The simple museum across the creek documents Shafter's social hey day. Now home to some teachers from Presidio and a few others.

178.2 miles—We pass on our left the entrance to Cibolo Creek Ranch, a luxury guest ranch formerly the home of early cattle baron Milton Faver, who lies buried at the top of the hill overlooking the ranch and surrounding orchards. See page 228 for more information on Cibolo Creek Ranch.

The highway continues to climb steadily until mile 190.2 where it tops out at the entrance to the Shurley Ranch. This is the highest point on U.S. 67 between Presidio and Chicago, IL. Straight ahead is the broad panorama of the Marfa Plateau with the Davis Mountains behind. To the east is the Del Norte Range. To the left in the distance may be spotted the tethered aerial balloon packed with electronic devices for detecting illegal air and ground movements.

208.6 miles—The Border Patrol inspection point. Three miles farther on the left is a row of ten open-sided concrete sculptures in front of two large, glass-sided buildings. This is the main showcase of the Chinati Foundation's display of minimalist artist Donald Judd's work. People visit from all over the world to view this unusual collection.

213.4 miles—Marfa. 4,668 feet. At U.S. 90 turn right. If you want to visit the easily visible Presidio County Courthouse, continue straight ahead. Built (1886) in Second Empire style for $60,000 in the confident days shortly after the arrival of the railroad, this courthouse outshines all others in the region. In 2001 it underwent a complete refurbishment costing $2.6 million.

222.2 miles—Nine miles east of Marfa on U.S. 90 is the Marfa Lights viewing area. Since humans arrived in the region, unusual lights moving in irregular patterns have been seen south and west of this point in the desert. They only appear when it is dark, and they don't appear every night.

226.4 miles—The highway passes over Paisano Pass, the highest point (5,074 feet) on the Union Pacific Railroad between Los Angeles and Miami.

234.4 miles—U.S. 90 traverses a caldera (a collapsed volcano) dominated by Twin Peaks Mountain, which guards the approach to Alpine. Passing the Ramada Ltd. Hotel we re-enter Alpine (population 6,560), having driven 240.3 miles.

Big Bend National Park Loop

Alpine, Marathon, Big Bend National Park, Study Butte, Alpine

271 miles (all paved, except for Old Maverick Road in the
National Park—13 miles, normally passable by all vehicles)—5 or 6
stops

✓ =Must See, ♦ =Food Stop

Start—Downtown Alpine. Going east on US 90, we pass on our left
the campus of Sul Ross State University, founded in 1916 as a teachers training college. As we leave Alpine (2.3 miles), we see two
additional parts of the Sul Ross campus—on the right the Range
Animal Science complex, and on the left an experimental vineyard.

8.3 miles—The highway divides. U.S. 67 goes left towards I-10; we
proceed straight ahead on U.S. 90. Take a moment to read the historical
marker at the picnic site. It reflects on the geological importance of the
area. Five miles further on, the Glass Mountains appear on the left, so-
named for the reflection of the sun on the limestone rock.

✓♦31.4 miles—Marathon. Population 800. Stop at The Gage Hotel, an historic landmark and the most important hotel between San
Antonio and El Paso. Enter the older, red brick part of the hotel, which
opened in 1927. The lobby and adjoining rooms are decorated with all
the trappings of a frontier hotel: chaps, lassoes, Indian fishing nets, and
Mexican pots. Have a quick look, if the timing is right, at some of the
older rooms down the hall. Proceed out of the back door of the lobby,
cross a courtyard and pass the swimming pool before entering the new
section, Los Portales. Peek into one of the rooms and admire the shaded
courtyard, green lawn, the Mexican elder tree, and the flowing fountain.
Then exit the courtyard directly onto the highway and find your vehicle.

Continue east on U.S. 90 for a half mile, then turn right (31.9
miles)on U.S. 385 heading for Big Bend National Park. The entrance
at Persimmon Gap is 40 miles to the south.

36.8 miles—Pass the Border Patrol checkpoint. Vehicles heading
south do not have to stop.

✓42.4 miles—Los Caballos. A picnic site and an historical marker.
This is a unique geological place, where the Appalachians bump into
the Rockies.

The sign describes the rock formations of whitish rock to the right and left of the highway which resemble galloping horses, *caballos*. These outcroppings are part of a northeasterly trending range, dating back 270–295 million years, connecting to the Appalachians.

On the southwest skyline, flat-top Santiago Peak is visible, part of the Del Norte range, dating 40–60 million years. Thus the fusion of young and old mountains, unmatched at any other site in North America.

55.9 miles—Santiago Peak is to your right. Anchoring the Santiago Range, which forms a continuation of the Del Norte Mountains, a spur of the Rockies, this flat-topped 6,524 foot peak is the most visible landmark for miles.

68.4 miles—Double Mills. There was water here since prehistoric times. More recently, rancher George Miller dug two wells and put up two windmills. Hence the name. It was a stopping point for horses and cattle being driven from Mexico, also for the wagon trains of ore heading for Marathon from the mine in Mexico.

72.2 miles—Intersection with FM 2627. Turn left.

78.0 miles—Stillwell Ranch store, RV Park and Hallie Stillwell Hall of Fame. This three-room display of artifacts, awards, photographs, and memorabilia commemorates the remarkable life of Hallie Stillwell who died in 1997 at the age of 99 years. A look at her long and varied life is a good way to appreciate the early days on the frontier. Hallie Stillwell epitomizes the strength, courage, and resilience of the pioneers' life. Visitors will see the coffee pot she scrubbed so zealously when she was a rancher's wife and the typewriter she used when Justice of the Peace. An inscription in the Visitors Book said: "We felt her presence."

Paintings and photographs crowd the walls: Hallie with a mountain lion she shot, Hallie dancing when in her nineties, James Evans' famous photograph of Hallie and her daughter Dadie, and Hallie with the governor of Texas. The recognition of Hallie Stillwell across the state and around the country are an indication of the high regard in which she was held. Entry to the museum is free; ask for a key at the Stillwell store. Inside the small store, which carries snacks items and gifts, visitors may talk with Hallie's family and show appreciation of her life story by buying her best-selling book, *I'll Gather My Geese.*

The Stillwell Ranch RV Park is adjacent. Full hookup is $18.50, also tent camping. Showers, with towel, $4. Rock hounds are welcome;

you can search for all colors of agate and samples of petrified wood, then pay 50¢ per pound for their collection. 432-376-2244.

FM 2672 continues another 22 miles. This is an optional side trip, leading to a dead end, only recommended to those with time to see how and where the road ends.

90.2 miles—On the left is Black Gap Wildlife Management Area (WMA) comprising 107,000 acres, the largest such area in the Texas Parks & Wildlife Department (TPWD) system, including 25 miles of Rio Grande river bank. The primary concern of the WMA is wildlife research and demonstration, such as trapping and collaring the black bear population of nine, and monitoring the herd of 60 desert big horn sheep. The area is also open to hunters who come to hunt quail, javelina, mule deer, and dove.

In recent years WMAs have been opened to non-hunters, called "non-consumptive users" in the department's language. 250 miles of road connect sixty-one primitive campsites, with shade shelter and picnic tables. These are available to tourists who carry a $13 Limited Use Permit from an authorized dealer. You cannot buy the permits on site; the closest place to purchase one is at Morrison True Value hardware store in Alpine. Visitors are then free to hike, go birding, and explore Horse and Maravillas Canyons.

TPWD seeks to maintain a balance between their primary concern of wildlife management and their income-producing services aimed at hunters while opening the areas up to the general public. On a few occasions each year, the area is closed completely except to hunters. On other occasions, certain parts are closed. For information call 432-837-3251 or 432-376-2216.

100.2 miles—Heath Canyon Ranch and Stillwell Bridge—the end of the road. On the far side of the Rio Grande is La Linda, whose ruins testify to a prior industrial life. A one-lane bridge spans the river, but a few years ago it was blocked by a brick wall put up by Mexican authorities and later by a mesh barricade on the U.S. side. This was done to prevent crossings by Mexican trucks carrying produce, seeking to avoid customs payment. Think twice about wading the river and crossing into Mexico; you face a $5,000 fine upon return since this is an unauthorized crossing. Better, observe from a distance on the U.S. side.

On the U.S. side, is a cluster of buildings. This is Heath Canyon ranch, previously the VIP guest house for the mining corporation which operated across the Rio Grande. Now privately owned, and until recently a café and bunkhouse accommodation, the enterprise is now shut. Across the Rio Grande, the desert wilderness of Coahuila stretches into the distance, bordered by the Sierra del Carmen to the south. In the foreground is a small chapel. Beyond it the desert wilderness of Coahuila stretches into the distance, bordered by the Sierra del Carmen to the south. Fortunately, from this angle you cannot see the mangled, rusting remains of the crushing plant, which sorted and reduced the ore.

From 1968–90 this was an active mine owned by The DuPont Corporation, extracting and crushing fluorspar. Among other uses, fluorspar is an ingredient in freon. The finished product was then transported to Marathon and trans-shipped by rail. All of this provided jobs and profit until 1990 when a new supply of fluorspar became available in China, and the Mexican/U.S. operation became overpriced.

The few visitors here are river users. This is the starting point of the 7-day Lower Canyon stretch of the Rio Grande. It is the end of the Mariscal Canyon river trip. Now drive back 28 miles along FM 2627 until you intersect with US 385 half a mile west of the entrance to Big Bend National Park.

The majority of travelers who turned back at Stilwell Ranch, will find they rejoin US 385 at 85.0 miles.

86.0 miles—You are now in the Big Bend National Park and should stop at the booth next to the ranger station at Persimmon Gap. (87.5) The entrance fee is $20 per vehicle, good for seven days. Stop at the ranger station for brochures or wait until you get to the park headquarters.

Persimmon Gap, named for the native Texas persimmon trees that grow nearby, is a pass through the mountain range to the south. It was used by Comanche Indian raiders on their way to Mexico, by the Marathon–Boquillas stage, by ore trains hauling minerals from the Boquillas mines to the railhead, and by the U.S. Army carrying supplies to garrisons along the border.

You have 27 miles to cover before reaching Panther Junction park headquarters. You may pause at any one of the several roadside exhibits or take a driving or hiking detour. Remember the speed limit inside the park is 45 mph.

On the left, approximately 5 miles from the park entrance, is the first turn off, to Nine Point Draw, a primitive campsite. In the distance, a cut in the mountainside indicates Dog Canyon also known as Camel Pass. The first name remembers a dog that was discovered guarding an abandoned ox-wagon. The second name arose later when Lt. Echols brought his camel troop through the canyon during the experimental camel expedition of 1860. The Civil War ended the experiment.

101.2 miles—Dagger Flat. An improved gravel road winds eastward for 3.5 miles to a small valley called Dagger Flat. Here, in late March and April when the plants are blooming, you will see a profusion of white-flowering stalks of the Giant Dagger Yucca, some of them as much as 15 feet tall.

106.0 miles—Fossil Bones. A short side road takes you to this exhibit where you will find bones of 29 species of forest-dwelling animals dating back 50 million years to the Eocene period. Where you now see deserts there were once swamps and rivers.

Also visible at this point are Tornillo Creek and Flat. This flat area has not recovered from overgrazing during the early years before the National Park was established and remains one of the most barren areas of the park.

110.4 miles—Pioneer Grave. A parking spot and a 4-mile marker (from Panther Junction) indicate this moving and serene site. A short walk brings you to the grave located by a stand of cottonwood trees. This is the resting place of Mrs. Nina Hannold who died aged 31. Her family story is told in the book *An Occasional Wildflower*, sold at Panther Junction bookstore. A faded card "To Grandma and Grandpa" and some flowers show that the family is not forgotten.

✓**114.5 miles**.—Panther Junction. Visitor Center, post office, park offices, and meeting room. The Visitor Center has a large topographical map, a visibility register, and a compact, well-stocked bookstore. Information on trail and road conditions, camping permits, and details of ranger-guided walks and talks are available. Immediately adjacent is a short nature trail. Take a 25¢ pamphlet and follow it. You will find it easy to identify the most common desert plants and understand their uses. Return to your car; check if you need gas or snacks since there is a service station just 100 yards west. Turn left outside the parking lot, and head three miles to the next junction.

117.7 miles—You are now at the start of the Basin Drive. Turn left. This seven-mile drive will take you up Green Gulch to Panther Pass and drop you down into the Chisos Basin. To the left of the road you will see Panther Peak, and to the right is Pulliam Ridge, which is named after a pioneer ranch family and resembles the profile of a reclining face. This is Alsate, the ancient chief of the Chisos Indians.

Notice as the highway climbs how the vegetation changes. You will leave the Chihuahuan Desert plant zone and move into the woodland community where trees such as piñon pine, oak, and juniper flourish. It is easy to see why the Chisos Mountains are called an island in the middle of a desert.

Panther Pass and the Lost Mine Trail. After a twisty ascent reaching a 10% incline, the road tops out at 5,679 feet at Panther Pass. Panthers, or mountain lions, are residents of the park, but not generally seen. This is the Lost Mine Trailhead with a parking lot and a dispenser of

Big Bend National Park

trail pamphlets. This popular 4.8 mile round trip trail goes steadily uphill on a well-maintained path. Physical features on the trail are identified and numbered, corresponding to the same numbered explanation in the pamphlet.

✓◆**123.7 miles**—Chisos Basin. The road now drops sharply with some sharp curves before straightening out as it arrives at the Chisos Basin. The Lower Basin campground and amphitheater are to the right, and the main or Upper Basin is straight ahead. Here you'll find the Chisos Mountain Lodge, the post office, ranger station, and store. From here you can look up to Casa Grande (Big House) Mountain behind the lodge, or prepare to hike up Emory Peak, the highest in the park at 7,835 feet, or to the South Rim. Buy some snacks at the grocery store or a meal at the Lodge, take the shortest hike (The Window View Trail, 0.3 miles) then return 7 miles to the Basin Junction.

At Basin Junction (130.4), turn left and head west, passing signs to Grapevine Hills, where wild grapes used to grow, and Croton Springs. After ten miles you will arrive at the Ross Maxwell Scenic Drive junction. You are now at 140.3 miles along your drive and have the option either of taking a 44-mile diversion to Santa Elena Canyon, or continuing straight on nine miles to the west entrance. If proceeding to Santa Elena Canyon, turn left.

Santa Elena Canyon Detour—Via Ross Maxwell Scenic Drive and Old Maverick Road (44 miles Total)

Summary—Heading south, the road skirts the western flanks of the Chisos and climbs to a panoramic overlook, Sotol Vista. It then drops down sharply to the old army compound at Castolon, where it follows the Rio Grande upstream for eight miles to Santa Elena Canyon. At this point, you can backtrack 30 miles to where you started, or take a shortcut (14 miles) on a gravel road (Maverick Road), which will bring you to the west entrance of the park.

✓**140.3 miles**—Ross Maxwell Scenic Drive. Named after the first superintendent of the park, this 30-mile route reveals a varied landscape, some sites of the area's early occupants, and a variety of classical geological structures.

Old Sam Nail Ranch—Adobe structure, built in 1916 on Cottonwood Creek, home of the Nail brothers. These early pioneers kept chickens and a milk cow, planted pecan and fig trees, and put up two windmills.

Fins of Fire—On the left side of road, these rock outcroppings, called dikes or walls, are visible on the mountainside. Formed by molten material squeezing through cracks, this extra hard material is left standing when the softer rock around it erodes.

Homer Wilson Ranch—A trail leads down to the ruins of the ranch house and bunkhouse of what was a working ranch prior to the establishment of the park in 1944. 4,000 sheep and 2,500 goats grazed here prior to the ranch being abandoned in 1945—a fearful toll on the vegetation.

✓*Sotol Vista*—Stop here for a distant view of the entrance to Santa Elena Canyon (17 miles as the crow flies) and the mountains of Mexico. The ridge you are on contains a large number of sotol plants. A sign explains the properties and uses of this plant, a member of the lily family. Another sign identifies the geographic features in the distance.

Mule Ear Peaks—One of the most prominent landmarks easily identified from a distance. Erosion has left the dikes revealed, creating the peak's two ears.

Tuff Canyon—On the right side of the road, this small canyon offers a fine example of compressed volcanic ash, called tuff, layered and then exposed by erosion. Read the explanatory sign at the start of the trail, or if you are feeling energetic, follow the trail to the bottom (20 minutes.)

Cerro Castolon—Before the road drops down to Castolon village it passes through an area of white tuff beds and black basaltic boulders. Above, like a layered cake, Cerro Castolon dominates the scene.

Castolon—(163.7). Old army fort and trading post catering to locals, visitors, and residents from across the Rio Grande in the Mexican village of Santa Elena. For more details of the active history of this military compound, ask at the adjacent ranger station for a pamphlet. The store does a big business in cold drinks and ice cream.

A road to Santa Elena boat crossing, and one to Cottonwood Campground, next appear on the left. On the right are the remains of Old Castolon, the oldest building in the park. The road flattens out and turns towards Santa Elena Canyon 8 miles away. We are now on the floodplain where in past years irrigation farming produced substantial crops of cotton.

✓**170.5 miles**—Santa Elena Canyon Overlook. Instead of going immediately to the mouth of the canyon, park and enjoy the view from a short distance and read about the geologic happenings that caused such a dramatic drop in part of the landscape as well as the formation of the canyon itself. Cliffs rising to 1,500 feet mark the entrance, which also is the exit for those river runners who have rafted 22 miles from Lajitas through the canyon. Drive one mile to Santa Elena Canyon trail head.If time and conditions permit, cross Terlingua Creek (you may need to take your shoes off if it is muddy) and climb the steps into the canyon mouth. Follow the trail down and along the riverbank until the canyon walls prevent any further progress. 1.7 miles round trip, classified as "medium difficulty" by the park service.

You are now at the end of the Ross Maxwell Scenic Drive, at the Santa Elena Canyon trailhead, with 172.8 miles completed on the Big Bend National Park Loop. You can now retrace your route 30 miles to the Maxwell Scenic Drive Junction and turn LEFT to reach the west entrance (9 miles). Or you can drive directly on the Old Maverick gravel road to the west entrance, a distance of 13 miles. It is wise to check with a park ranger about the state of this road if you have any fears about your vehicle.

Old Maverick Road (173.3)—This short cut runs through flat, barren country best seen early in the morning or late in the afternoon when the desert colors are less harsh than at midday. The road roughly parallels Terlingua Creek and after two miles a sign to the left points to Terlingua Abaja (Lower Terlingua). Once a farming community on the fertile banks of the creek, it is now a primitive campsite.

When the angle of the sun is right there are certain places along this route when the ground appears to be covered with thousands of diamonds. This is caused by the reflection of the sun off gypsum crystals in the soil.

Where the roadway crosses Alamo Creek and turns north, it passes beneath a dark cliff. This is Peña Mountain. Two rock house ruins may be seen near to the cliff, the home of a farmer in bygone years.

The low-roofed cottage (*jacal*) of Gilberto Luna, a pioneer farmer, next appears on the right of the highway. After a lifetime of primitive living, hard work in farming crops, and raising a family of 58 children from six marriages, he died in 1947, at age 108.

186.4 miles—Maverick Junction. West Entrance to Park. The paved road comes as a welcome relief. Turn left and exit the Park.

You are now back to the west entrance to the park. Four miles down the road is Study Butte.

♦**177.1 miles**—Study Butte ("Stewdy Beaut"). Named after Will Study, early prospector and mine manager. Like Terlingua, four miles to the west, Study Butte was an active mining town in the early years of the century extracting cinnabar from the ground.

Various places are worth noting in this scattered settlement. The Study Butte Store reflects the attitude of some of its inhabitants through the inscription on the wall of the entrance porch: "This is the place where brilliant minds assemble to willfully pool ignorance with questionable logic in order to reach absurd conclusions."

In case you want a meal before heading back to Alpine, in the immediate vicinity of TX 118/FM 170, are two Mexican restaurants: Los Paisanos and Chili Pepper Café. Next to the Big Bend Motor Inn is a cafe/gas station/convenience store, 6 A.M.–10 P.M. daily. Going towards Terlingua (2 miles) is La Kiva steakhouse.

You are now on TX 118 heading north. It is 78 miles directly back to Alpine, or 156 miles via the River Road, Presidio, and Marfa.

196.3 miles—Wildhorse Station. Cabins on the mountainside above a grocery/gift store. On each side of the highway along this stretch are gates to Terlingua Ranch, the 200,000-acre residential ranch, which spreads across South Brewster County.

203.4 miles—Longhorn Ranch Motel and Tivo's Place. Only 12 miles from Study Butte, enjoying a desert setting with fine mountain views.

207.4 miles—Entrance to Terlingua Ranch Resort. The ranch headquarters is 16 miles to the east. Tourist facilities (cottages for overnight rental, a restaurant, pool, and airstrip) are closed at the time of writing. This development, which started in the late 60s, has seen a slow but gradual buildup. It is owned by the Owners Association and appeals to those wanting a second home in a desert setting, those who want to retire to a remote area, and to those experimenting with a new lifestyle. Their homes, connected by 1,100 miles of dirt road, range from substantial ranch houses, to straw bale constructions, to dilapidated cabins.

210.3 miles—Agua Fria Mountain. 4,828 feet. Named after the cold water spring at the base of a 600-foot cliff. Pictographs on the cliff are evidence that Indians used this place as a camp. This is private property and you may not visit.

227.7 miles—Santiago Peak, to the right. Previously seen from the other side on US 385 from Marathon. A 6,511 foot truncated cone of volcanic rock. It was probably named after Don Santiago, chief of the Apache Indians. A bold scam was launched in 1910 to sell lots on top of Santiago Peak to unsuspecting buyers. The township was named Progress City, and thousands of lots to this phantom town were sold to naive buyers before the fraud was revealed.

234.7 miles—On the left, the entrance to the 02 Ranch, now owned, like other ranches which were previously in family hands, by a corporation—in this case, Lykes Lines. *Below the Escondido Rim* by David Keller traces the ranch's history.

243.1 miles—Entrance to Elephant Mountain. This Texas Parks & Wildlife property is operated as a Wildlife Management Reserve. The research includes monitoring the herd of 150 big horn sheep that graze the mountainside. It is open seasonally to hunters and to the public who may use the campsite. A year-round self- driving tour with informational signs leads to a viewing point. Bring binoculars and self register at the entrance station.

244.0 miles—On the right, a picnic spot under some trees. Another follows nine miles farther on.

254.5 miles—Woodward Ranch. 1.7 miles to your left down a dirt road is Woodward Ranch, open to visitors for rock hunting and camping. Check in at the ranch house/gift shop. You can pick up a bucket and take off to collect plumed agate and other rock specimens. When you are finished, you pay according to weight. Alternatively, you can buy uncut or cut-and-polished stones in the rock shop, also pieces of opal, pendants, and other jewelry items. This exploration is popular with kids, keeps them busy and gives them a sense of achievement. The area has been well picked over during recent years, but there are still some fine specimens around the ranch house if time is taken to search. An RV Park at the ranch house and a primitive camping area two miles further at the edge of Calamity Creek.

256.2 miles—Border Patrol Checkpoint.

259.3 miles—On your left is the south entrance to South Double Diamond Ranch. This is one of the few ranches that have sold off lots for building. Lots cost up to $25,000 for 5 acres; the views toward Cathedral Mountain are magnificent and it is only a 20 minute drive into Alpine.

264.5 miles—From the top of the hill Alpine is clearly visible. Twin Peaks Mountain fills the horizon to the west; the Davis Mountains can be seen to the north. Sul Ross University campus clings to the hillside east of town. In the center of the picture, and extending west to the residential community of Sunny Glen, the residential and commercial buildings of Alpine are silhouetted against the trees. After 271 miles the trip is over.

Canyon & Border Loop

Marfa, Pinto Canyon, Ruidosa, Presidio, (Ojinaga),
Casa Piedra Road, Marfa

181 miles total. 63 miles of gravel and dirt roads, sometimes narrow, with steep inclines going down.

✓=Must See, ♦=Food Stop

00.0 miles—From downtown Marfa head west on US 90 half a mile, then turn left on to FM 2810. Passing former Fort Russell, now the Chinati Foundation, on the left, the road proceeds southwest over rolling rangeland, with fine views to the south towards Chinati Moun-tain (7,730 feet). This is a good spot for morning photography.

29.0 miles—Chinati Peak is ahead. Good photograph stop.

33.9 miles—The pavement ends here. At Mile 34.5, the road passes some "No Trespassing" signs and drops steeply on a rough surface into Pinto Canyon. Becoming one-lane, it crosses one or two creek beds and passes an abandoned mine on the left. This is a remote area and little traffic uses the canyon road. It is passable without 4-wheel drive or high clearance, but caution is needed. It should not be attempted after rains.

43.8 miles—This is the Judd Ranch, noticeable because the fence line is close to the roadside. The road now widens before climbing out of the canyon. At Mile 45.5, the panorama of the Rio Grande valley, with the Mexican mountains as a backdrop, is in front of you. At Mile 46.7, we exit Pinto Canyon Ranch.

50.2 miles—A sign points right to Chinati Hot Springs, 6 miles.

53.1 miles—Turn right and proceed uphill for a further three miles before dropping down into Chinati Hot Springs (56.7 miles).

Remote, peaceful, therapeutic. This oasis on the south-facing flank of the Chinati range is open to the public for day use or overnight stays. Wedged into a small canyon, surrounded by mature tress, and facing Mexico only 8 miles away. 109 degree Fahrenheit water flows from a spring in the small canyon and is piped into the bath houses and the outdoor tub.

Rates: Day Use: $12.50, children under 6: $5. Overnight Camping: $15 per person, includes baths. Cabins and Rooms from $75-

Canyon & Border Loop Map

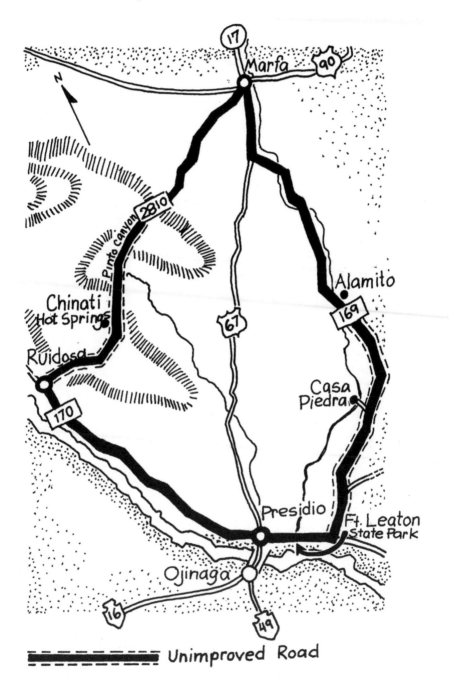

Unimproved Road

$115: *El Corazón* and *Dos Amigos*; Triple Rooms (3): *El Presidente* and *El Patrón* (private bath). No meals. Use of kitchen. Bring your own food. Use of mineral baths included. Outdoor tub. Cool pool. For further details check www.chinatihotsprings.com.

After the drama of the canyon drive and the stark surroundings of the desert, the shade of the cottonwood trees and the flow of spring water into the creek make for a soothing break. Depending on the season, this can be a brief stopover and walk around during the day's drive, or a longer soak in a tub, or an overnight. Book in advance. 432-229-4165.

56.7 miles—Follow the improved gravel road that heads straight downhill to intersect after 7 miles at Ruidosa with FM 170. You can make a detour here to Candelaria (24 miles), where the blacktop stops. Candelaria, a U.S. Cavalry post in the early 1900's, previously the crossing point, by pedestrian bridge, to the Mexican village across the Rio Grande and the site of a famous local school presided over by Johnnie Chambers for many years. Now left with 25 inhabitants, with the children being bused to Presidio.

64.7 miles—Ruidosa means "noisy" in Spanish, but today is anything but. The store and bar have closed. The adobe mission church ruins have been stabilised to prevent erosion. A few local residents make this their home. A sign, "Marfa 54 miles", in the middle of the settlement points to the start of Farm Road 2810 which heads directly back through Pinto Canyon.

From here the narrow, bumpy blacktop road runs due south for 37 miles, following the north bank of the Rio Grande, to Presidio. There is little evidence of activity here except for an occasional ranch sign or a private residence. There is no substantial riverside cultivation until Presidio.

102.0 miles—If you now feel like a bite to eat, head for Escondido Restaurant just before you enter Presidio. Where FM 170 meets US 67, just before the creek, turn sharp right, go 100 yards, then left and follow the road. Here under shade trees, with a bar adjacent, is outdoor and indoor seating and a well priced menu.

After crossing Cibolo creek into Presidio, the visitor needs to decide whether to make a detour into Ojinaga. Unlike other Mexico border crossings that often involve delays on returning to the U.S. side, the Ojinaga/Presidio crossing is usually quick. A passport is required for reentry into the USA. See page 77 for a description of Ojinaga.

102.4 miles—After crossing Cibolo Creek turn left at the sign "Presidio founded 1683". Near the "Y" one mile ahead are the Chamber of Commerce, El Patio restaurant and The Enlightened Bean coffee shop. From the Y, head south on FM 170, the famous River Road, to Lajitas

107.2 miles—Fort Leaton. Well worth a stop. This massive adobe fortress was previously the home and headquarters of trader Ben Leaton and is now a museum belonging to Texas Parks and Wildlife. See page 43.

111.4 miles—Stay on FM 170 for 4 miles, then turn left towards Big Bend Ranch State Park and Casa Piedra. This is also the entrance to Big Bend Ranch State Park. Follow the wide gravel road, passing two private adobe homes on the right. These majestic buildings, with domes and vaults constructed according to Nubian designs, are the work of pioneer adobe architect Simone Swan who teaches a course in adobe construction annually. For more information, see www.adobealliance.org.

117.6 miles—Bear left towards Casa Piedra, the right fork leads to Big Bend Ranch State Park. The improved dirt road now gains altitude and runs through desert terrain with little sign of livestock or homesteads for 18 miles, except for the nearly abandoned communities of Casa Piedra and Alamito. Alamito (135.8 miles) used to have a store and

Chianti Peak

post office when trains passed this way. If you should catch Mr. Armando Vásquez at his home in Casa Piedra, which used to be the old post office, he would be happy to give you a private visit to this very local piece of history. The rail line which the highway crosses, formerly the South Orient Line, ran from Fort Worth to Presidio, connecting with the Mexican rail system in Ojinaga, but ceased operations in 1999. Its future use has been further complicated by the collapse of the rail bridge crossing the Rio Grande at Presidio/Ojinaga.

147.7 miles—The pavement (RR 169) resumes at the former supply point of La Plata (Alamito community). Here the steam locomotives were filled with water from a tall tank, now empty. Half a mile further is a Historical Marker giving the history of Alamito Creek. The road continues past scattered ranches and a telephone relay tower with red lights on the right. At mileage 173.8, US 67 is reached. From there, after passing the Border Patrol checkpoint, you arrive back in downtown Marfa, the conclusion of our 181.4 mile trip.

River Road—East To West

Big Bend National Park—Backcountry Road, All-Dirt

51 miles east-to-west following the southern boundary of the park.

Note that the floods of September 2008 washed out some riverside campsites: Woodson I and II, and Jewel I which were not replaced.

Check at Panther Junction park headquarters regarding the condition of the River Road before setting out. You have the option of exiting the River Road via Glenn Spring or joining it from Glenn Spring. After that point (10 miles from the start), there are no escape routes—you either continue or turn back.

Note
This road may be traveled in either direction, but east-to-west means the sun is behind you when you start. Consult with Park personnel about road conditions before starting out and whether you vehicle can make it.

Start—15 miles from Panther Junction and 5.1 miles before Rio Grande Village. Turn off onto a gravel road that later becomes dirt.

2.6 miles—Turn off to La Clocha, a fishing camp. The name is Spanish for "crusher" since there was once a rock crusher here.

3.3 miles—You now approach the Old San Vicente Crossing. San Vicente, Coahuila, Mexico lies across the river, a farming community of around 200 persons. A fort, or *presidio*, was built here in 1774 to protect the northern frontier of New Spain from Indian raids. As with other similar forts along the river, it was abandoned shortly afterwards.

5.2 miles—New San Vicente Crossing. A spur road leads to a parking area, and a track continues through the riverside vegetation to the riverbank. Pre- 9/11, there was a boat crossing here for day visitors. South of San Vicente village is the high, rounded mountain range Sierra San Vicente, an anticlinal fold (arched strata formed by the folding of layered rock).

8.8 miles—A walking trail leads 0.4 miles to Rooney's Place, another riverside rock house.

River Road — East To West Map

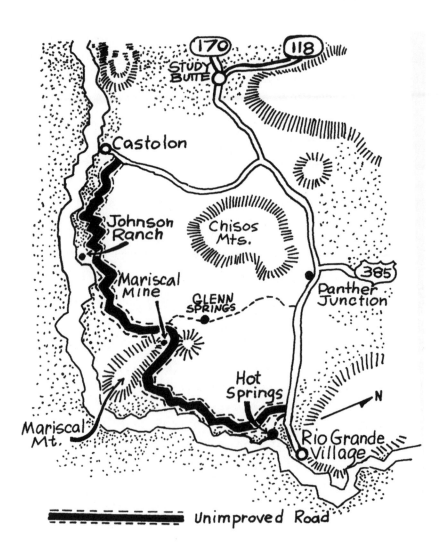

Unimproved Road

The River Road now angles away from river and begins its circle of Mariscal Mountain.

9.6 miles—The Glenn Spring road joins from the northwest. Next, a side road turns east leading to a fishing camp called Compton's. In half a mile a large draw or wash, called Glenn Draw, is crossed. Look for mesquite, seep-willow, and desert-willow bushes.

11.6 miles—The narrow, rocky wash will slow you down, but also give you the chance to notice lechuguilla, chino grass, and purple-tinged prickly pear as you pass.

13.7 miles—The remains of the Solis farm border the side road that runs for 1.4 miles to the river bank. The Solis family ranched from 1900 to 1926 in this area. Others worked this particular riverside farm until 1950 when the National Park Service purchased it.

18.6 miles—Mariscal Mine was a mercury (quicksilver) mine, comprised of two dozen structures along the valley flats and on the hillside above. Near the road are the remains of residences and the company store. On the hillside above are the processing plant and other mine buildings. Ore was discovered here in 1900, but it was not until 1916 that the refining sections of the mine were completed. The end of the First World War (and the subsequent drop in demand for mercury as a detonating agent) saw a drop in demand for mercury. The mine closed down in 1923.

19.5 miles—Piles of rubble west of the road are waste material from the old kiln where the bricks were made from local clay for the furnace at Mariscal Mine.

21.0 miles—At the north end of Mariscal Mountain watch for Black Gap road, which runs 8.5 miles north to Glenn Spring. This road is no longer maintained.

23.2 miles—Turnoff to Talley, six miles south on the river. This is a put-in point for rafts entering Mariscal Canyon.

25.6 miles—Midway point. A side road leads towards Woodson Place on the river, 4 miles away.

27.5 miles—Dominguez Trailhead. A 14-mile strenuous round trip to a well preserved rock house at Dominguez Spring.

29.8 miles—Another road leads off south to Jewel's Camp on the Rio Grande.

32.0 miles—Notice the thick growth of the flood plain again. The road is now close to the Rio Grande, and the thick stands of tamarisk and mesquite are the evidence.

32.9 miles—This wash is an easy access point to the river, a short distance away.

35.3 miles—Ruins of the Elmo Johnson Ranch house, possibly the largest adobe ruin in the park. A few of the outbuildings and a graveyard lie just to the east of the turnoff. These were part of a cotton farm, goat ranch, and trading post that operated here until the 1940s.

36.7 miles—Gauging Station. The Boundary and Water Commission have taken weekly measurements of river flow here since 1936.

37.9 miles—A picturesque area of tuff – compressed, volcanic ash. The high wall to the north is Red Dike, formed by lavas that filled a crack in the earth's surface millions of years ago. The outer layers have since eroded away, exposing the soft tuff and the hard dike.

39.9 miles—On the south side of the road are the remains of a threshing circle used by the Mexican people who once farmed small plots along the river.

41.4 miles—Smoky Creek drainage—one of the major drainages in the southwestern section of the park.

43.4 miles—A forest of ocotillo plants.

44.2 miles—Look west towards Santa Elena Canyon, 13 miles distant, and the Sierra Ponce escarpment will be on your left, in Mexico.

46.0 miles—Turn north to reach the paved road to Castolon. This is a rerouted section of the road. You are now facing the Chisos Mountains. Emory Peak at 7,835 feet is over one mile above your present location. East of Emory Peak is the outline of the South Rim. Further east, the tips of Mule Ears Peak are visible above the brownish hills of the Sierra Quemada.

47.1 miles—The break in the rock face to the south is known locally as Smuggler's Canyon, a reference to past smuggling from the U.S.A. into Mexico.

48.3 miles—If you look carefully to the north along this wash, you will see the remains of a rock house at the old Román De La O ranch site, where there is a natural spring.

50.6 miles—You are now at the west end of the River Road, just north of Cerro Castellan. The colorful bands of the peak are lava flows that at one time covered the whole area. The stack forming this peak is all that remains.

Two miles south lies Castolon, formerly a military post, now a ranger station. A store provides snacks, cold drinks and ice cream. A Visitor Center with hands-on exhibits is open November–April. To exit the park from Castolon, you can drive eight miles upstream to the mouth of Santa Elena Canyon, then take the Maverick Road (dirt road 14 miles) to the west entrance—22 miles total. Or you can turn right and follow the Maxwell Scenic Drive 22 miles toward Santa Elena Junction, from where you turn left to exit the park—35 miles total.

Davis Mountains Scenic Loop

Fort Davis, McDonald Observatory

78 miles (all paved).

✓=Must See, ◆=Food Stop

From *The Fort Davis Visitor Guide*

Before starting your trip along the Scenic Loop, we offer a few words of caution. There are no gasoline stations, so make sure you have enough gas in your tank. There are numerous low-water crossings and during the summer months flash floods are possible and potentially dangerous. At dawn and dusk deer ignore road signs and frolic merrily wherever they choose. They are fun to watch and expensive to hit. As you drive through open range ranches expect to see cattle grazing alongside and sleeping in the middle of the road. Excluding the Davis Mountains State Park, all land fronting the Scenic Loop is private property and generally working ranches. Please do not trespass.

✓**Start**—Start at the Courthouse in Fort Davis. One mile north on TX 118/TX 17 you will find the restored Fort Davis National Historic Site. The site sprawls on the grassy plain at the foot of, and is protected by, Sleeping Lion Mountain.

1.6 miles—As you proceed north on TX 118/TX 17, look to your left. You will see the rock remains of the fort's old water pump station that supplied water for the Post from the 1880s to 1891. Cottonwood-lined Limpia Creek is easily seen to your right. If you are a bird watcher, it is time to take out your binoculars.

✓◆**4.3 miles**—The Scenic Loop now ascends into the Davis Mountains, passing on the left the Davis Mountains State Park that abounds in wildlife. Indian Lodge, a southwestern pueblo-style hotel and restaurant, is set in the rolling hills of the park.

6.0 miles—Now, mosey on down the road a couple of miles. On the right is Prude Ranch, where you may enjoy the ambiance of a true, western vacation. This facility has been a home to five generations of the Prude family and has received international acclaim.

7.9 miles—As the highway climbs you will see to your right Limpia Crossing, one of the very few residential areas developed in this ranching country. Ahead of you on Mt. Locke (nearly 6,800 feet) is McDonald Observatory, and, atop nearby Mt. Fowlkes (6,500 feet), is the Hobby-Eberly Telescope.

✓♦**15.8 miles**—When you approach the sign to the observatory, turn and head for the Visitor Center to enjoy a few hours (day or evening) of celestial entertainment (see page 68). You are now at the highest point in the Texas highway system, elevation 6,791 feet. The valley below is at 5,289 feet. After your stop at the observatory, your drive will take you through grassy rangeland. (If stopping, add 0.5 miles to each mileage figure below.)

To the northeast of the observatories, some 20 miles distant, is the extinct Buckhorn Volcanic Caldera. Higher elevations reveal piñon and ponderosa pine trees. As you enter Madera Canyon, you will pass picnic areas and flowing creeks during the summer months.

25.0 miles—The large roadside park in Madera Canyon is named after Lawrence E. Wood, the highway engineer responsible for most of the highways in the area. He acquired this beautiful site by a bit of horse-trading. Stop here, stretch your legs, and enjoy the towering trees.

The Nature Conservancy, which recently established a nature reserve close to here (see Mile 25.4), opened the Madera Canyon Trail in one corner of the picnic area. This 2.4 mile, moderate difficulty, roundtrip takes the visitor through piñon, ok and juniper woodlands with views to Mt. Livermore (8,378 feet). This is well marked, has an easy surface and has an altitude gain of 175 feet.

25.4 miles—Entrance (left) to the Nature Conservancy's 32,000-acre Davis Mountains Nature Preserve, open periodically through the year. 432-837-5954.

30.7 miles—As TX 118 continues straight ahead to Kent, take Texas 166 to the left to continue the Scenic Loop.

36.7 miles—Keep your camera ready for the awesome Rock Pile on the right. It is located on private property and has been fenced off due to vandalism. Sawtooth Mountain looms directly ahead.

37.6 miles—Further ahead on your left you will experience the wonder of the famous 7,746 foot Sawtooth Mountain closer up.

Davis Mountains Scenic Loop Map

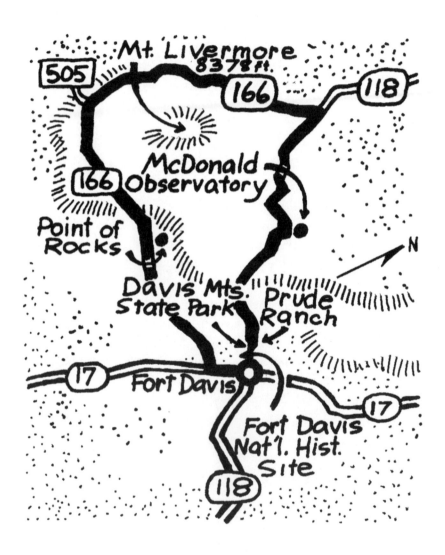

39.2 miles—A smaller rock pile, accessible on the right side of the road. The road now descends, affording distant views ahead of rangeland.

40.6 miles—Picnic site.

44.0 miles—Look for Mt. Livermore to your left. This mountain peaks at 8,382 feet.

51.6 miles—This is the junction with TX 505, the cutoff to Valentine (16 miles), and to US 90. Continue on TX 166 (Fort Davis 25 miles) around the loop. Much of this highway parallels the Old Overland Trail, as it leaves Fort Davis. You will start to see red and white rocks that dot the landscape and form volcanic mountains.

55.2 miles—To your left was the site of Barrel Springs Stage Stop. Stout wooden barrels were placed in the reeds to catch the slow drip of the water. *Barilla* means "reedy," and reeds grew in the area of the spring. This was a welcome sight to the travelers on the Overland Trail, who would drink from this clear spring water. This is private property although it is not fenced. Please do not enter. Continue for another mile and notice the tanks on top of the white rock mountain.

56.2 miles—On the ridge to your right, tall structures support modern wind turbine generators. A part of the CSW/WTU Renewable Energy Project, these twelve turbines supply six megawatts of electricity to the West Texas Utilities grid.

Double Windmills

60.4 miles—Crow's Nest RV Park and Campground is on the left. This campground derives its name from the crows that nest in the cliffs nearby. Behind, the transmitter aerial of KRTS, Marfa Public Radio, beams its message across the region, 93.5 FM. Outside of the area, you can listen via www.marfapublicradio.org.

61.1 miles—You will drive through Skillman's Grove, elevation 6,000 feet. Here in 1890, Reverend W. B. Bloys established Camp Meeting, a yearly encampment to minister to far-flung ranch families and cowboys. Notice on the right the "tin city" of approximately 400 metal buildings, a tabernacle and several chapels. Read the Historical Marker. However, you are welcome to enter only during Camp Meeting in August.

63.9 miles—A little further on, to your left, you will notice the mailboxes of Fort Davis Resort, a sprawling mountainside development. A few years ago, Rick McLaren announced the self-proclaimed Republic of Texas at this spot, took a hostage, killed a dog, and caused an army of law enforcement officials and media types to besiege his "embassy" before he surrendered.

66.0 miles—If you are ready to take a break, stop at Point of Rocks picnic area, a welcoming site only a few miles ahead on your left. This shady stop has a plaque secured to a huge boulder describing how the wagon trains halted here for water.

69.2 miles—Continuing on the Scenic Loop, Blue Mountain looms on the left. Look for the pronghorn antelope that often graze on these plains. They are usually seen in herds close to the fence. To your right you will see a large glass and metal structure, a tomato farm. There are now three of these hydroponics operations in the area.

75.4 miles—At the intersection with US 90, TX 166 ends. Going left takes you back to Fort Davis, passing on your left the community park and the Fort Davis Veterinary Services. Further on, to your left, is Sleeping Lion Mountain. First you notice its haunches, then its head, which points towards the center of town. As you approach the "Y" intersection with TX 118, the speed limit drops to 25 mph and the Scenic Loop is complete at a total of 78.0 miles.

Desert Survival

Desert Survival Basics
By David Alloway

It is unfortunate that many people equate deserts with a hostile environment that conspires against human life. In the popular media, desert areas seem to be considered to be at the top of the wilderness danger list. The historical fact is, however, that the human race was cradled in arid lands and people are well adapted to survive in deserts. Learning to be part of the desert's ecosystem and not viewing it as an antagonist is the first step of desert survival. I teach desert survival classes and our class philosophy is not to fight the desert, but to learn how to live with it.

Being prepared is an obvious benefit and that starts with how you dress. People stand upright and receive only 60% of the solar radiation that animals on all fours do. By adding a proper hat, with a wide brim and closed crown, the head and body are further protected. A common mistake made by new desert visitors is wearing shorts and sleeveless shirts. Loose fitting long sleeves and pants provide good air circulation and much better protection than sunblock. Sunglasses that exclude ultraviolet light are a good idea and some studies claim they can help prevent cataracts later. Other areas of preparation include proper vehicle maintenance, carrying sufficient water, first aid and survival kits for desert environments, a sturdy sharp knife, and some useful knowledge.

The Panic Factor

The biggest killer in any emergency situation is panic. Panic blinds a person to reason and can cause them to compound the emergency with fatal results. Controlling panic is a matter of focusing the mind and operating in an organized manner. My Australian counterpart, Bob Cooper, teaches the ABC's of survival to ward off panic and start the person on a constructive course of action.

ABC's of Survival

A: Accept the situation. Do not blame yourself or others. Do not waste time contemplating "What if I had...?"

B: Brew up a cup of tea. This is a typical Aussie approach to the solution of everything. What you are actually doing is starting a fire, which is needed and completing a familiar calming chore. You can brew coffee or just build a fire.

C: Consider your options. Take stock of items at hand, such as water reserves, survival kits, etc.

D: Decide on a plan. Look at the alternatives and decide on a plan that best ensures your health and safety. Thoughts such as "I have to be at work tomorrow" are not relevant.

E: Execute the plan and stick with it unless new conditions warrant a change.

The brain is by far the best survival tool we have. Survival is much more a mental than physical exercise and keeping control of the brain is necessary. The large size of the human brain requires a high metabolic sacrifice in water and temperature control. Keeping the brain hydrated and in the shade will be more beneficial than all the gee-whiz survival gizmos in the sporting goods store.

An additional psychological factor is the will to survive. It may sound odd, but some people have just given up due to what they felt was hopelessness, impending pain, hunger, etc. I keep a photo of my two sons in the lid of my survival kit to remind me of who needs me. Women should not be discouraged in these situations on the basis of their gender; they have several physical advantages over men in high stress situations. I participated in a 200 kilometer survival trek in Western Australia in 1996 with two women in our group and they did as well as the seven men.

Survival Kit

I am a believer in a well-planned survival kit. On the Australian trek each of us had a pocket sized survival kit that fit in a soap dish. That, along with a knife, two one-liter canteens, a medical blanket, and a compass were all we needed to cross the finish line at the Indian Ocean. A survival kit must be small enough to carry at all times in the wild. By cramming them full of unnecessary items they get too bulky and tend to get left in the car, backpack, or elsewhere, which is the same as not having one at all. See the sidebar for the contents of such a kit. You'll be surprised at what can fit in a 4"×3"×1" box.

Desert Survival Priorities

While there are exceptions to the rule, desert survival priorities usually fall in the order of water, fire, shelter, aiding rescuers, and food.

Water

Deserts are defined by their lack of water. Learn to ration sweat, not water. By staying in the shade, limiting activity to cooler times such as night, and using your available water, your chances for survival increase greatly. Sipping water does not get it to the brain and vital organs. Take a good drink when you need it. People have been found dead from dehydration with water in their canteens. Also, do not rely on "parlor tricks" such as solar stills as a primary source. These will often produce more sweat digging the hole than is obtained from water gained. Learn to locate water through areas of green vegetation, flights of birds, converging animal trails, and digging in the outside bends of dry creek beds. Javelinas and burros are excellent at finding water and digging it up in

Abandoned In The Big Bend

creek beds. Best of all, plan ahead and allow one gallon of water per person a day. This does not include your needs for cooking, pets, or auto maintenance.

Fire

Fire may seem odd to have so high on the list of desert survival priorities, but there are reasons to consider other than warmth, which may also be needed. Fire can be used to signal, cook food, and purify water. Fire also provides psychological comfort. People do not feel so lonely with a fire. It makes the night less frightening, and, while there are few large animals dangerous to people in North American deserts, fire will keep them at bay. It is important to know how to start a fire under severe conditions with means other than matches. Friction methods such as the bow and drill take much practice and should be learned before they are needed.

Shelter

Aside from your clothes, additional shelter may be needed. In desert areas, shelter from the sun is usually the main consideration, but cold, rain, hail, and even snow can also be factors. It is important to keep the skin temperature under 92 degrees to keep from sweating away precious water. Draping a sleeping bag over a bush for shade but allowing for breezes may be the best bet. Try to make your shelter visible to searchers. Build in a safe place—not in creek beds, which can be subject to flash floods.

Signals

Signaling for help will hasten rescue. Signals, whether visible or audible, must be distinguished from nature. A signal mirror is best for most desert conditions and can be seen for miles. Flash at aircrafts, dust clouds (which may be vehicles on dirt roads), and periodically scan the horizon. Burning a spare tire will put up a huge column of black smoke, but the tire must be punctured or have the valve core removed first to prevent it from exploding and injuring those nearby. Flares are good at night if there is reason to think they will be seen. Put the hood up on your car and tie a rag to the antennae. Wearing bright colored clothing will help aircraft see you better.

Audible signals should be done in rhythmic bursts of three. A long whistle blast sounds like a hawk from a distance, but three timed short blasts sound like a signal for help. Gunshots and car horns also should be timed in groups of three. Yelling is the poorest alternative.

Food

"What did you eat?" is the question I get asked the most about my Australian trek. Most people think of survival in terms of lack of food. In hot climates, however, food is not as important as other factors. If water is in short supply it is important not to eat anything because it increases your water needs to digest the food. On my Australian adventure I had a six-inch perch, a handful of wattle seeds, and six cattail shoots. I lost twenty pounds, but after day three I did not feel really hungry. Water was our biggest worry. Most people today can go three weeks without eating. I think more people are afraid of the pain of hunger than starvation.

The basics of desert survival? Prepare for the worst. Control panic. Use your brain. Use energy and water wisely. Be ready to signal. Don't listen to your stomach. Most of all, do not fear the desert. For many of us, it is home.

David Alloway, author of *Desert Survival Skills* (UT Press, 2000), died suddenly in April 2003 of complications following an injury, and will be greatly missed by those who benefited from his great knowledge of the desert.

Contents Of The Author's Pocket Survival Kit

Soap dish container	2 Bouillon cubes
1 Mark III knife	1 Condom ✦
1 Strip magnifier	Sterile scalpel blade
1 Signal mirror	Sugar tablets
1 Flint striker	1 Vial potassium permanganate *
1 Small lighter	1 Signal whistle
(childproof to prevent leaking)	Micro-flashlight with spare battery
Fish hooks & Sinkers	1 Button compass
Tweezers	1 Tea bag ☆
Snare wire	2 Alcohol wipes ★
Fishing line	3 Band-Aids
1 Large needle	2 Plastic bags
Cellophane fire starters	Instructions with blank side for
1 Pencil stub	notes

Picture of the kids and a card with a prayer of comfort by Saint Francis.
Add: Benadryl, Tylenol, and any other personal medications needed.

✦ *Traditionally included as a water bladder, but better to store items that need to be kept dry such as tinder.*

* *Used for water purification, anti-septic, anti-fungal. When mixed with crushed sugar tablet it can be friction ignited to start a fire.*

☆ *Use black tea cooled down for sunburn relief.*

★ *Besides being antiseptic, they will ignite with sparks from flint striker.*

Part V
Towns & Communities

Alpine

Elevation: 4,481 feet   **Population: 6,200**

History

Alpine, the major town in the tri-county area of Big Bend, is the county seat of Brewster County (6,139 square miles), the largest in Texas. Its development followed a pattern similar to other towns in the area: the existence of a local spring, the arrival of the railroad needing water for its steam locomotives, and rapidly expanding herds of cattle requiring shipping to market.

Families of the Mexican-American railroad workers laying the track eastbound in the early 1880s were the first permanent settlers of what was to become Alpine, Texas. A silver spike was driven into a railroad tie in January 1883 near the Pecos River, marking the joining of the two construction groups of the Southern Pacific Railroad. Shortly after, on January 12, 1883, the first train rolled through Osborne (Alpine's first name) headed westward towards California.

Osborne was later changed to Murphyville, after Daniel Murphy, a land developer who had leased his nearby spring to the railroad company. The first schoolhouse was built three years later and the courthouse and jail were completed the following year. Around that time of rapid expansion the city leaders, feeling that Murphyville was too personalized a name for their growing township, voted to change the name to Alpine.

Alpine developed as its position on the railroad tracks enabled ranchers to ship their cattle to markets. Its population and prosperity increased in turn. In 1887, Alpine was named county seat of the newly created Brewster County, named for Henry Percy Brewster, lawyer and personal secretary to Sam Houston. Benefiting from a central geographical position and a railroad link, Alpine expanded steadily during the first twenty years of the 20th century. The construction of the

Holland Hotel in 1912 and of a teacher's training college in 1919 gave added emphasis to Alpine's position as the major town in the area.

The teacher's training college was named after H. Sullivan Ross. Following a successful military career that culminated in promotion to Confederate Army general, Ross was elected governor of Texas in 1886. While in office, he signed the bill that created Brewster County and advocated many pro-education changes. Later, he was appointed President of Texas A & M University (1891-98).

Sul Ross Normal College developed into Sul Ross Teachers College and finally into Sul Ross State University (1969)—a four-year institution—the only university in Big Bend country. SRSU, as it is known, has a current enrollment of around 2,200 and has recently benefitted from a $100 million extension to the library, a new Student Center, 600 new rooms for students, and the addition of an events center. The on-campus Museum of the Big Bend has also benefitted, now re-housed in its original stone-built premises, with striking new exhibits reflecting the rich culture of the region.

Alpine also is home to Big Bend Regional Medical Center, a small airport, and the only Amtrak stop between El Paso and Del Rio. Its source of employment is government service at all levels, followed by retail and service jobs in the one hotel, eleven motels and 16 restaurants and five fast food places in town. Together with the other towns of the tri-county region, it is experiencing an increase in people migrating to the area: retirees, artists and entrepreneurs.

Access/Orientation/Information

U.S. Highway 90 runs east–west linking Alpine with Marfa and Marathon. TX 118 connects Fort Davis 26 miles to the north with Study Butte/Terlingua, 80 miles to the south. The shortest route to I-10 is via U.S. 67 which branches off eight miles east of Alpine and turns north towards Fort Stockton (67 miles).

Mileage to: Midland 160, El Paso 220, San Antonio 367, Austin 402, Dallas 497, and Houston 580.

Public Transportation

Rail—At the present time, Amtrak provides service three times weekly on the Sunset Limited from New Orleans to California. Call Amtrak for schedule and fares: 800-USA-RAIL.

Bus—All-American Travel bus service between Midland (including the airport) and Presidio stops twice daily in Alpine. Northbound to Midland: 10:45 A.M., 5:20 P.M. Southbound to Presidio: 1:00 and10:00 P.M. Alpine bus stop, 2303 E. Hwy 90. 432-837-0784.

Taxi—Trans-Pecos Transport. 432-837-0100 / 432-940-1776. Tours and Shuttles 432-837-0897 / 432-386-2015.

Car Rental—Alpine Auto Rentals has a fleet of 23 vehicles, from compacts to 15-passenger vans. Rates start at $35.95/day plus 10¢/mile for compacts. Travelers with reservations will be met, regardless of time, at Amtrak or the airport, and the vehicle can be dropped off at either place. This agency also does U-Haul.

Alpine Auto Rental	
Alpine Auto Rental 2501 E. Hwy 90 Alpine, TX 79830	Phone: 800-894-3463 or 432-837-3463 www.alpineautorental.com

Midland Airport has a good choice of car rental companies. Check for seasonal discounts. Expect to pay around $30/day for a compact, with unlimited mileage (from Alamo). Other car rental agencies are: Avis, Budget, Enterprise, Hertz and National.

Air—There is no commercial air service to Alpine at present. The nearest airport is in Midland/Odessa (MAF), (150 miles northeast), that has about 30 flights daily by Southwest, Continental and American Airlines. El Paso Airport (ELP) is 220 miles west

Tow/Wrecker Service—Highland Automotive, where your car is loaded on a truck: 432-837-2523. Bud-N-Nita: 432-837-2653.

Local Publications

The Alpine Avalanche is published weekly on Thursday as are the award-winning *Big Bend Sentinel* from Marfa and the *Jeff Davis County Mountain Dispatch* in Fort Davis. *Big Bend Gazette*, a regional newspaper, comes out monthly. Free publications include *The Cenizo Journal*, a quarterly literary magazine, and the region's tourist guide *Big Bend and Texas Mountains*.

Information

The Alpine Visitor Center, at 106 N. 3rd Street, is the main information point for visitors. Open Monday–Friday from 9–5, Saturday from 9–4.

Alpine Visitor Center	
Alpine Chamber of Commerce 106 N. Third Street Alpine, TX 79830	Phone: 800-561-3712 or 432-837-2326 www.alpinetexas.com

Other websites: Big Bend National Park: www.nps.gov/bibe/

Brewster County Tourism Council: www.visitbigbend.com

When To Visit

As its name suggests, Alpine has a mountain climate with an average temperature of 71°F. In summer, daytime temperatures may sometimes go above 100°F, particularly in May–June, but this is dry heat. In the evenings, the temperatures drop considerably, usually to the mid-60s. In fact, at the outdoor summer theater in Kokernot Park, visitors are advised to bring a light sweater.

Sunshine is abundant and the infrequent periods of cloudy weather occur mostly in the winter months. Sunny Days 247. The average annual rainfall is around sixteen inches, although this has dropped in recent years. The rainy season traditionally is in late summer.

In winter, Alpine is partly protected from the cold air masses that move south across the plains. Most of these fronts turn east before reaching Alpine. Snow falls occasionally (3 inches annually), but most often it is light and remains on the ground only a short time. Equally, cold spells rarely last for more than 2–3 days. Average January temperature 33°F.

Relative humidity is low, averaging about 50 percent annually. The Davis Mountains to the north block the northerly winds, so that the prevailing wind direction is westerly November–May, sometimes fierce. A southeasterly flow prevails throughout the summer and early fall.

Where To Stay—Top End (Motel)

The Maverick Inn—Opposite campus. Tasteful and comfortable conversion from a historic trailer court. Luxury bath linens, Egyptian cotton sheets, tile floors, and many amenities including wireless internet, also a small, pleasant pool. 20 rooms come with king and/or queen beds, some adjoining, some with full bath, some with kitchens, one with a garden tub. Discounts for students, seniors, and bikers. Continental breakfast. Rates, low season, from $90 (One queen bed) to $140 (One king, one queen bed) to $150 (One queen bed with kitchenette).

The Maverick Inn	
The Maverick Inn 1200 E. Holland Avenue Alpine, TX 79830	Phone: 432-837-0628 www.themaverickinn.com

Where To Stay—Top End (Hotel)

Holland Hotel—a Texas Historic Landmark. The only Downtown hotel, located in the central shopping and dining area. Built in 1928, for decades it was the social and cultural center of the region. The Holland Hotel was purchased in August 2009 and is undergoing a major revitalization and historical rehabilitation, dining and additional services being added. 24 guest rooms and suites from $129–$300 (one-three

Alpine & Twin Peaks

persons). Amenities: Wi-Fi, flat screen TV, fridge, microwave, coffee maker and breakfast snack. No pets.

Historic Holland Hotel	
Historic Holland Hotel 209 W. Holland Alpine, TX 79830	Phone: 800-535-8040 432-837-2800 www.hollandhoteltexas.com

Where To Stay—Top End (Motels)

Best Western Alpine Classic Inn—Modern, two-story structure with a Southwest look. Well placed for Sul Ross State University and eating-places on the east side of town. Outdoor hot tub, swimming pool, full hot breakfast included, non-smoking area. Recently renovated. 63 rooms. Rates for two persons from $89.99–$140.95, plus tax. Discounts.

Best Western Alpine Classic Inn	
Best Western Alpine Classic Inn 2401 E. US 90 Alpine, TX 79830	Phone: 800-528-1234 or 432-837-1530 www.bestwestern.com

Hampton Inn—Alpine's newest motel. On the west side of town. 64 pleasantly decorated rooms with king or two queen beds ($109). Also studios, with choice of beds and a living area ($139), three with jacuzzi. Pool and fitness center. Full hot breakfast. Nice touches in the rooms such as the lap desk.

Hampton Inn	
Hampton Inn 2607 W. US 90 Alpine, TX 79830	Phone: 800-426-7866 432-837-5805 www.hampton.com

Oak Tree Inn—Brand new at the time of writing and part of an expanding hotel chain that ties in with Union Pacific Railroad. Exercise room and outdoor hot tub. The Inn owns the 24-hour, classic 50s-style diner, Penny's, immediately adjacent where guests check in. 40 rooms.

$79 plus tax. 100% non-smoking. Extra quiet, with light-proof draperies.

Oak Tree Inn	
Oak Tree Inn 2407 E. US 90 Alpine, TX 79830	Phone: 432-837-5711 www.oaktreeinn.com

Ramada Ltd.—Recently-built, two-story motel on the west edge of town. Fine views towards Twin Peaks Mountain and no train noise. Non-smoking rooms. Accepts pets ($25 fee). Full hot breakfast. Restaurant adjacent. Indoor jacuzzi. 58 rooms/suites. Rates for two persons from $89.49 (standard room)–$104.49 (deluxe suite), plus tax. Discounts for AAA, etc.

Ramada Ltd.	
Ramada Ltd. 2800 West US 90 Alpine, TX 79830	Phone: 800-272-6232 or 432-837-1100 www.ramada-alpineTexas.com

Where To Stay — Medium Level

Antelope Lodge — 1940s-built compact cottages surround a shady park on the west edge of town, all with porches and kitchenettes. Even some pink tile still to be seen! Rates from $40 for one, facing highway, to $74 for two persons. $89 for four in the suite. Pets ok. Fascinating rock & gem museum in the lobby. Tours available with the owner.

Antelope Lodge	
Antelope Lodge 2310 W. US 90 Alpine, TX 79830	Phone: 800-880-8106 or 432-837-2451 www..antelopelodge.com

Highland Inn — Opposite Sul Ross State University and Museum of the Big Bend. Older property with 44 rooms and 6 suites. $55 for one or two persons, including tax. $5 for each additional person. The medium-size rooms are in fair condition. Max the cat is in attendance.

Highland Inn	
Highland Inn 1404 East US 90 Alpine, TX 79830	Phone: 432-837-5811 www.highlandinn.net.

La Loma Motel—Small, recently built motel on the west side of town. 13 standard rooms. TV, fridge, coffee maker but no phone in rooms. $50 for one person, $60 for two, includes tax. 432-837.9567.

Sunday House Motor Inn—This 80-room property is on the east side of Alpine. Large rooms. Property undergoing renovations. Pool. Discounts. $59.95 (one bed)–$69.95 (two beds).

Sunday House Motor Inn	
Sunday House Motor Inn 2010 East U.S. 90. Alpine, TX 79830	Phone: 432-837-3363 www.sundayhouseinn.us

Where To Stay—Budget

Bien Venido — Two floors of budget rooms set around a courtyard, near to intersection of U.S. 90 and Texas 118. Old property with fresh paint job. Some traffic noise, but a value for the price. Casual service. Elvis stayed here in 1953! $35 (1 person), $38 (2 persons), plus tax.

Bien Venido	
Bien Venido 809 East Holland Ave. (US 90) Alpine, TX 79830	Phone: 432-837-3454

Alpine Inn—$35 (one bed) including tax. $40 (two beds). Check your room carefully before taking possession. There have been complaints. Internet access. 432-837-3417. 2401 E. US 90.

Where To Stay—Guest Rooms

The Alpine Guest Lofts—Four loft-style accommodations fronting onto a quiet courtyard. Set in an historic building, renovated to a high standard and within walking distance of all downtown shopping and landmarks. $105-$195. Ask about discounts.

The Alpine Guest Lofts	
The Alpine Guest Lofts 117 N 6th Street Alpine, TX 79830	Phone: 877-298-5683 432-837-1818 www.alpineguestlofts.com

Wright Building Guest Quarters—Very central and stylishly remodeled, in the old hospital, this accommodation comprises one single unit ($79/night) and an apartment sleeping up to four ($179/night) plus cleaning fee. "Sweet, cozy and efficient" describes the small unit which has a twin bed. The larger unit, with TV, has a queen bed and sofa bed. Keen weekly rates. Wi-Fi.

Wright Building Guest Quarters	
Wright Building Guest Quarters 208 W. Avenue E Alpine, TX 79830	Phone: 432-837-4244 www.brewstercountylodging.com

The White House Inn —Two efficiency apartments in a separate building behind the house. Queen bed, kitchenette. Longer rentals preferred. $89/night

The White House Inn	
The White House Inn 2003 State Highway 118 Alpine, TX 79830	Phone: 432-837-1401

Where To Stay—House/Cottage

Casa Vida—604 E. Gallego. Two-bedroom, two bath remodeled adobe home. Satellite TV and wireless internet. Seven can sleep comfortably. From $145–$175/night. www.vrbo.com/230912. Or call 210-394-8103.

Stone Rose Cottage—610 E. Avenue E. Sleeps four comfortably. Two bedroom (one double bed, one set adult bunk beds), one bath. Fully equipped kitchen Chiminea. Walking distance to downtown, and campus.$125/night, two nights minimum. 281-265-9898 or 713-553-1924. www.stonevillagecottage.com.

Where To Stay — RV Parks

BC Ranch—On TX 118 N, three miles from center. Fine views. 20 spaces $25 full hookup. 432-837-5883. www.bcranchrvpark.com

Lost Alaskan—Large, well equipped site, on TX 118 N., two miles from downtown. Rec. room, gift shop, laundry. Swimming pool. Wireless internet. 91 sites, $26.95. www.lostalaskan.com. 800-837-3604. 432-837-1136.

Pecan Grove—US 90 on the west side of town. Shady, compact. Laundry and showers. 31 sites, $27. Wireless internet. Tent camping available. 800-644-7175, 432-837-7175.

La Vista—6 miles south on Hwy 118. 5,400 feet. 14 sites. $23/night. Wireless internet. Common House with laundry, bathrooms. 432-364-2293. www.lavistarvpark.com.

Where To Eat — Top End

Reata — Downtown. Open 7 days a week for lunch, 11:30–2:00, and dinner from Monday–Saturday 5–10 P.M. Totally cowboy from the stylish, professional decor to the menu that is described as Texas cuisine. Look for the wall mural in the shady garden out back depicting the Reata story. Well-priced lunches (packsaddle combo $9.95) give way to a substantial evening menu. Best sellers are Carne Asada topped with cheese enchiladas, and Herb Crusted Mahi Mahi with roasted tomatoes and crawfish. Entrees generally run $16–$32. Desserts ($6.95) are rich and yummy. Bar ($5 membership required for guests) with a large selection of tequila. Reservations suggested.

Reata	
Reata 203 N. Fifth Alpine, TX 79830	Phone: 432-837-9232 www.reata.net

Where To Eat—Middle Range—Italian

La Trattoria — Espresso Bar and Ristorante. Now in its 10th year in a new spot with much more space. Open 6 days. weekdays at 7:30 A.M. and 'til 9:30 P.M. on Friday and Saturday. The comprehensive menu ranges from salads (e.g. Hunter's Salad) and deli sandwiches, to pasta and the popular thin crust pizza. In the evening the dining room becomes more sophisticated, the menu also, with dishes like pistachio encrusted salmon. Espresso, Italian sodas and a sophisticated wine list.

La Trattoria	
La Trattoria 901 E. Holland Ave. Alpine, TX 79830	Phone: 432-837-2200 www. latrattoriacafe.com.

Primo's—Italian. Open Monday–Thursday 4-9, Friday–Saturday 4–10, and Sunday 12–8. The sign outside says Pizza but inside the menu lists Appetizers, Salads, Pasta and Desserts. The 14" pizza starts at $8.25, and the pasta dishes the same price. Other dishes, such as Mediterranean Salad with Tabouli, and Tiramisu, provide variety to the pasta and pizza in this small eatery.

Primo's	
Primo's 501 W. Holland Alpine, TX 79830	Phone: 432-837-9400

Where To Eat—Steakhouse

Longhorn Steakhouse—Open Monday–Saturday, 11–2, 5–9. Tables and booths, with a substantial salad bar. Menu based mainly on beef, but with options for other tastes. For visitors this might be the place to try chicken fried steak, or the brisket plate ($7.99). Burgers from $5.99.

Longhorn Steakhouse	
Longhorn Steakhouse 801 N. Fifth Alpine, TX 79830	Phone: 432-837-3217 www.longhornsteakhouse.net

Buffalo Rose Saloon—2010 E. Hwy 90. Full service restaurant on east side of town plus a bar with hard liquor. In addition to steaks, the restaurant gets good reviews for a juicy hamburger (from $5.95), Sunday brunch (Eggs Benedict $6.99) and chicken fried steak with the house ranchero dressing. Open Tuesday–Sunday from 11–midnight. Monday opens at 4 P.M., Sunday closes at 10. 432--837-9700.

Where To Eat — Mexican

La Casita — Open 6 days 11:00–8:30, Closed Sunday. A location on the south side of town does not stop savvy tourists from seeking out the most popular Mexican food restaurant. Set in the front part of the home of the family who has run it for years, La Casita combines business with friendliness and remains very consistent. Student and senior discounts. Chicken enchiladas and de luxe campechanos are frequently mentioned by regulars

La Casita	
La Casita 1104 East Ave. H Alpine, TX 79830	Phone: 432-837-2842

Alicia's Mexican Restaurant—Open Monday–Friday, 8–8. Saturday and Sunday, 8–3. Now with more seating space in addition to the counter. Try the trashcan burrito ($3.99) or the Mexican Plate ($8.99).

Alicia's Mexican Restaurant	
Alicia's Mexican Restaurant 708 East Avenue G Alpine, TX 79830	Phone: 432-837-2802

Talgar's—New. Great space, Juliana Johnson's fine art on the walls. Outdoor patio. Talgar learned to cook in a family kitchen in Sonora, and is inspired by Mexican cooking traditions. Real Mexico cuisine. Fish tacos ($10.95) are popular. Sopa Azteca ($4.95) and Kahlua Flan($5.95) are exotic. Green tomatillo Shrimp and Cheese Enchiladas are also a hit. Open Tuesday–Saturday 11:30–2; Thursday–Saturday 5–9.

Talgar's	
Talgar's 102 W. Murphy Alpine, TX 79830	Phone: 432-837-5101

Where To Eat — 24-hour Diner

Penny's Diner — Owned by the adjacent Oak Tree Inn. (You check in for the inn at the diner). Classic 1950's-style diner, decorated with nostalgic memorabilia from that era. Breakfasts, burgers, sandwiches and Mexican dishes. Open round-the-clock.

Penny's Diner	
Penny's Diner 2407 E. U.S. 90 Alpine, TX 79830	Phone: 432-837-5711

Where To Eat—General (Burgers, BBQ, Mexican)

Texas Fusion—200 W. Murphy. Open Monday–Friday 11–8, Saturday 11–3. Now with added seating due to demand. The fusion refers to a mix of mesquite-smoked BBQ (plate from $9.99), Mexican dishes such as the enchilada plate ($6.99) and burgers, including Pulled Pork on a Bun ($5.39). 432-837-1215.

Gulf Station Café—Opposite Holland Hotel, downtown. Open Monday–Saturday 11–9 for food, later Thursday–Saturday. Outdoor and inside seating. Upscale menu from owner chef Jonathan Boyd who grew up locally then learned his trade elsewhere. The French Dip sandwich is popular at lunch, together with salads; in the evening a more ambitious menu lists pork loin, chicken breast and crab cakes. ($ 15-

$16). Much of the produce is local, and the desserts are a specialty of the house. Wine and beer. 837.5754.

Gulf Station Café	
Gulf Station Café 202 W. Holland Avenue Alpine, TX 79830	Phone: 432-837-5615

Magoo's Place—905 E. Avenue E. Opposite McDonalds. Open Monday–Friday 6–2; Saturday and Sunday til noon. Basic and popular. Try at breakfast the Huevos Rancheros and for lunch the Magoorita burrito. 432-837-9951.

Where To Eat—Chinese

Oriental Express—Open Monday–Saturday, 11–8:30. Chinese menu, also corn dogs etc. on the kids' menu. The Noon Buffet ($6.95) appeals for its all-you-can-eat value. Now a weekend evening buffet, also. From a lengthy a la carte menu ($6.95–$12.95) Sesame Chicken and Black Pepper Beef on Sizzling Plate sell well. Also vegetarian dishes including tofu for the careful eaters. 432-837-1159.

Oriental Express	
Oriental Express 3000 W. Hwy 90 Alpine, TX 79830	Phone: 432-837-1159

Panda's Buffet— 106 E. Holland. Formerly Alexander's Cantina, this large yellow downtown building is now Alpine's second Chinese restaurant. Open 7 days, from 11:00 A.M. until 9:30 or weekends 10 P.M. The buffet is the main draw, but any of the 115 menu items, including diet items and vegetarian dishes, can be ordered from your waitress. The all-day buffet is substantial (11 mains) and Bluebell ice cream one of the desserts. Daytime price $6.99; evening buffet price $8.99; weekend (which includes oysters) $12.99. 432- 837-5668.

Where To Eat—Bakeries / Coffee Shop

Bread & Breakfast —Open Monday–Saturday (7–2) for breakfast and lunch, Sunday (8–12). Popular with locals, convenient for visitors. Large space with local art on the walls. Pastries and bread baked daily on the premises. The Cowboy Breakfast is popular, and the Rueben and BLT sandwiches at lunch. There's lots more, including daily specials, wraps, burgers and salads.

Bread & Breakfast	
Bread & Breakfast 113 W. Holland Alpine, TX 79830	Phone: 432-837-9424

Mural Café—New and timely. Open Tuesday–Friday 10:30–7, Saturday 10–3. Shaded outdoor seating available. Artisanal breads and housemade butter, grilled panini wraps and sandwiches. Soups and salads. Vegetarian and Gluten Free options. Lunch specials. Great coffee.

Mural Café	
Mural Café 104 N. 5th Street Alpine, TX 79830	Phone: 432-837-3400 www.themuralcafe.com

Murphy Street Raspa Company—A touch of Mexico across the tracks. Big Bend Roasters coffee. Opens at noon. (Saturday /Sunday at 11) daily except Tuesday. Also raspas (shaved ice), try the blue coconut flavor. Blue Bell and Henry's Homemade icecreams. 432-837-5556. www.raspaland.com.

Where To Eat—Fast Food

Dairy Queen—E. US 90. 432-837-2420.

Pizza Hut—2300 E. US 90. 432-837-5819.

McDonald's—900 E. Avenue E. 432-837-3640.

Sonic—602 E. Holland. 432-837-5521.

Subway—1002 E. US 90. 432-837-2533.

Where To Eat—Alternatives

Sunshine House — 205 E Sul Ross Avenue, offers $4.00 lunches for visiting seniors. 11:30–12:30 Monday–Friday. 432-837-5402.

Big Bend Hospital cafeteria — 2600 TX 118 N. Open to the public 11:30 Monday–Friday serving tasty lunches ($7.00) supervised by Fran Voigt, the hospital dietitian. Popular with local residents. 432-837-3447.

Cow Dog—Next to Thrift Store (Avenue A & 5th Street). A renovated trailer with outdoor shaded seating sells 100% beef hot dogs and soft drinks. Basic dogs sell from $1.75 with free toppings, and more elaborate dogs (The Mexican, The Hangover, The Vegomatic) for $3–$4.50. A good place to meet local folk. Open Thursday–Saturday 11:30–3:00 pm. 432-386-0616.

Sul Ross State University Cafeteria—In the Student Center. Well-priced, fast food in a modern comfortable setting. Sunday brunch, 11–2, an all-you-can-eat offer with made -to-order omelets is popular with local residents.

Where To Drink — Bars/Nightlife

Harry's Tinaja—412 E. Holland. Open 12 noon to 2:00 A.M. 7 days. Indoor and beer garden. Beer and wine. Pool and darts. Live music at weekends. Brewmaster Harry Mois presides. 432-837-5060.

Railroad Blues—Big Bend's premier live music venue, featuring a changing slate of local and visiting bands, of many styles but consistent quality. Open 4 P.M., Monday–Saturday. Cover charge depends on the band performing, usually $10–$15. Wine and beer (largest selection in the region). Pool. Good place to meet the locals.

Railroad Blues	
Railroad Blues 504 West Holland Alpine, TX 79830	Phone: 432-837-3103

Buffalo Rose Saloon—2010 E Hwy 90. Just outside the city limits. Full bar, no membership required. 432-837-9700.

Crystal Bar—401 E. Holland. The mural outside belies the spartan, clean interior. This is probably the best place to meet a real cowboy or cowgirl. Play dominoes, or chat. 432-837-2819.

Reata Restaurant—203 Fifth Street. Full bar with a strong selection of tequila. Open lunch and dinner, 6 days. Membership required ($5). 432-837-9232.

Where To Go—Art Galleries

Kiowa Gallery—"Art of the Big Bend". 105 E. Holland. More local artists' work is displayed here than you can imagine. Owner Keri Artzt started Gallery Night. Large mural outside. All mediums, wide price range. Framing. Strong on jewelry. Unusual Day of the Dead work. www.kiowagallery.com. 432-837-3067.

Bell Gallery—410 N 5th Street. Contemporary West Texas Art.; Featuring work by Charles Bell, Ling Dong, Carlos Campana Karl Glocke and ranges from handmade paper bowls to mixed media pieces to representational landscapes. Wednesday–Saturday 10–6 or by appointment. 432-837-5999.

Catchlight Art Gallery—117 W. Holland. Open daily 10–6, except Tuesday. This new gallery currently shows work by over a dozen local artists. The media includes watercolor, oil painting, acrylic painting, jewelry, stained glass, ceramics, photography, fiber arts and mixed media. Look for Martha Scott's angles and crosses made from found items. www.catchlightgallery.com. 432-837-9422.

Avram Dumitrescu—Irish-born artist and illustrator Avram Dumustrescu's bold paintings of west Texas animals, landscapes, vehicles and architecture is moving. For location, check www.onlineavram.com. 432-837-9956.

Mi Tesoro—109 W. Holland. Tucked away inside Ivey's Emporium, this elegant little shop offers a slice of "Old Mexico". Mi Tesoro means "My Treasure" and offers originals in contemporary and vintage sterling silver jewelry, quality Mexican art work, and other fine arts and crafts. Artisans David and Susana Sandoval-Busey also design and create custom gold and silver jewelry originals. www.mitesorojewels.com. 432-837-1882.

Spirit of the West Gallery—At Apache Trading Post, 2701 W. Hwy 90. Permanent exhibitions by award-winning fine art photographer

Diane Lacey of working cowboys on her family ranch. Recently added has been Big Bend landscapes by Spiral Art Photography, Dan Gauthier. Also oils and watercolor paintings by a variety of local artists. 432-837-5506.

Quetzal International Folk Art Gallery—302 W. Holland. Pictures, weavings and so much more, much in startling bright colors. A potpourri of Central American folk art and items from further afield. Baskets, wood work, glassware and ceramics. Strong on Talavera ceramics, and Oaxacan woodcarvings. 432-837-1051.

Gallery on the Square—Old Town Square, 106 W. Sul Ross Avenue. Work by Big Bend Arts Council members. Over a dozen local artists display their work in a variety of media. Enter through the adjacent office during normal working hours. www.bigbendartscouncil.com. 432-837-5017.

Tom Curry Gallery—106 W. Murphy Street. Located in the old Alpine Studio on up-and-coming Murphy Street, the space serves as a studio for Tom Curry and gallery for himself and other artists. Tom, an award-winning graphic artist, cartoonist and illustrator of children's books, now applies himself to fine art representations of regional scenes. Exhibitions run for about two months. To visit, 432-940-9861 or 432-386-7473

Off the Wheel Pottery—Pauline Hernandez has worked for many years creating highly decorated earthenware household items in colors inherited from her previous watercolor paintings and reflecting the border influence. For an appointment, call 432-837-3929.

Bread & Breakfast Gallery—113 W. Holland. A changing display of paintings by local artists is easily viewed in this central coffee shop and bakery. Open Monday–Saturday, 7:30–11, 11:30–2:00, Sunday 8–12. 432-837-9424.

Francois Fine Arts Gallery—at Sul Ross State University. Periodic displays by students and invited artists. Adjacent to the Museum of the Big Bend. 432-837-8218.

Where To Go — Shopping

The last few years have seen an increase in the quantity and quality of stores, galleries and boutiques in Alpine.

Quetzal—302 W. Holland Ave. International Folk Art Gallery, especially Central/South America. 432-837-1051.

Ivey's Emporium—109 W. Holland. Packed with merchandise from Native American jewelry to Hispanic Art & Devotion. Art, cards, candles, and foodstuffs. www.GhostTownTexas.com. 432-837-7474.

Big Bend Saddlery—2701 US 90 E. Ropes, chaps, saddles, and a lot more. Cow hides, long johns for kids, books, and palm leaf hats. Workshop on site, aroma of leather. 432-837-5551.

Front Street Books—121 E. Holland Ave (US 90 E.). Well-stocked, independent bookstore with remarkably well-informed, good-natured staff. Strong on Big Bend literature. Large used book section in separate premises across the street. Frequent book signings and talks. Gallery in back. Branch in Marathon. Open daily. Phone: 432-837-3360. www.fsbooks.com.

Apache Trading Post—US 90 W., outside town. All sorts of gift items, including Native American and Mexican. Best selection of maps. Books, clothing, and cards. Immediately adjacent, Jackassic Park is a "must" for kids. Spirit of the West gallery portrays cowboy life. The Marfa Lights video is always ready to show. Open daily. 432-837-5506. www.apachetradingpost.com.

Ocotillo Enterprises—205 N. Fifth Street. Between Reata restaurant and Old Town Square. Fascinating collection of books, beads and rocks. An intriguing, specialist place. Bead exhibits by owner. 432-837-5353.

Blue Water Natural Foods Co.—45978 Hwy 118 S. A large store with bulk food, gourmet cheese, fresh produce, vitamins and more. Open daily 10–6. 432-386-2044. www.bluewaternf.com.

Alpine Antiques—114 N 5th. General line antiques and "Mission Oak" furniture. Modern and antique dolls. www.lonestardolls.com. Call for appointment: 432-837-1711 or 432-386-3537.

Johnson Feed & Western Wear—2600 E. US 90. Jeans, shirts, hats, belts and silver jewelry. 432-837-5792.

Bronco Betties—207 W. Holland, next to Holland Hotel. Ladies' apparel with a bohemian flair, jewelry and accessories. Closed Sunday and Monday. 432-386-6268.

Patti Hildreth Studio—210 W. Murphy Street. Private label cosmetic studio. Furniture, leather goods, candles. 432-837-3567.

La Junta—113 E. Holland. Buy, sell and trade. Men's' and Women's Clothing including vintage character items, also household goods. 432-837-5736.

Spriggs Boot & Saddle—608 W. Holland. Hats, boots, chaps, spurs, buckles and and other cowboy needs. Enough other stuff to warrant a visit. Boot repairs. Birkenstocks. 432-837-5000.

Digital Studio—115 N. 6th Street. Computer sales, service, and parts. Also, graphics design, scanning, and publishing. 432-837-1686. www.TheAlpineCompany.com.

Trans Pecos Guitars—311 E. Holland. Buys, sells and repairs guitars, banjos, mandolins, etc. Acoustic and elecronic. Parts and accessories available. 432-837-0101.

Cedar Rose—112 N. 6th Street. Flowers, floral design. Western belts and gourmet food items. 432-837-2100

One-Way Plant Nursery—308 W. Avenue E. Unusual native plants and cactii. Shade trees, fruit trees and ornamental trees. Contemporary plant containers. Postcards by the artistic owner. 432-837-1117

Morrison's True Value Nursery—302 N. 5th. Large, multi-purpose nursery located next to Baeza's Thriftway. Across the street from the main hardware store. 432-837-2061.

What to Do/Where to Go

Museum of the Big Bend at Sul Ross State University—A real treasure for visitors and local folks alike. Now housed in large premises, sufficient for its collection, the last rock structure on campus. Home to a wide collection of art, old and contemporary. The annual Trappings of Texas showcase, held in conjunction with Cowboy Poetry Gathering, features cowboy art and artifacts. Periodic exhibits by regional artists. Open daily, except Monday. www.sulross.edu 432-837-8143.

Walking Tour—Grab a pamphlet *Historic Walking & Windshield Tour* at the Chamber of Commerce and set out around the 44-point sightseeing tour. Depending on the season, the itinerary can be covered on foot since it extends only five blocks by four blocks, using sidewalks with reasonable shade. It includes a variety of buildings reflecting Alpine's history: the 1891 School House, County Courthouse, Jail, and the Masonic Lodge (1912).

After the Walking Tour, 25 more distant sights are described in the Windshield Tour. The first one, on the south side of the tracks, is Our Lady of the Peace Catholic Church. The last one is the campus of Sul Ross State University, home to the Museum of the Big Bend. Stop here and enjoy views across Alpine to Twin Peaks, the mountain immediately west of town.

Walk around City Park and Kokernot Field—Local rancher Herbert D. Kokernot was a baseball fan with no place to watch the game. So, in 1947 he bought his own minor league team (the Alpine Cowboys), and spent more than a million dollars to build Kokernot Field. The ballpark walls are made of native stone and wrought iron, featuring iron baseballs embedded in the gates and ticket window. The Alpine High School and Sul Ross teams now use the stadium.

Find the Desk (on top of Hancock Hill behind Sul Ross campus)— From now empty Morningside Dorm, start from the highest point in the parking lot and head up hill on a rough trail. You arrive at a rock cairn, then the trail flattens out. Soon you reach a second rock pile. Follow round to the right, and continue always trending right where there is a choice. Beyond the rock pile, the trail become less distinct but you are almost there. Follow slightly downhill till you come to a fence line.

Just before, on the left, you will note a bicycle sculpture on a small tree. Cross the broken down fence line, squeeze past some rocks, and you will find the desk. You are on the southeast corner of the hill, overlooking Pizza Hut, Best Western etc. on US 90. Ignore these urban intrusions, and look towards the northeast. Depending on the weather, temperature and your mood you might be tempted to write something in the notebook in the desk drawer, thereby adding to a Sul Ross tradition.

County Courthouse—Don't forget the County Courthouse down-town; the lobby is full of historic pictures. Look for the story about "Horizon City," an early scam to sell plots on top of Santiago Peak.

Health Club/Gym

A Cut Above Fitness Club—202 W. Holland, opposite Holland Hotel. Well- equipped, central, membership club. Walk-ins are wel-come. Open Monday–Thursday 8–6, Friday–5. Saturday and Sunday by appointment. 432-837-9905.

Health Services

White Crane Acupuncture Clinic—505 E. Sul Ross Avenue. Asian body work massage. Chinese herbal medicines, and tai chi. Monday–Friday by appointment. 432-837-3225.

Janna & Company—Body Works of the Big Bend. 903 W. Avenue E. Therapeutic massage and spa services. 432-837-5228

Purple Cactus Massage—209 E. Holland at the Granada. Massage by Mary Pollock who has 20 years experience in the field. $50 for one hour, $65 for 1 1/2 hours. By appointment. 432-837-7222.

Big Bend Yoga—Upstairs at the Granada Theatre. State of the art studio in a historic building. Yoga with Mary Pollock. Check www.bigbendyoga.biz or call 432-837-7222.

Golf Course

Alpine Country Club—9 hole course open to the public. Small greens. 6,600 yards using multiple tees. Fees: $16.25 weekdays, $21.65 on weekends. Cart $10 per 9 holes 432-837-2752.

Horseback Riding

Texas Horseback Adventures—1 to 3 day custom horseback trails on sturdy Quarter Horses on private rangeland near Alpine or in the Davis Mountains, with hearty campfire meals and luxurious linens in your cowboy bedrolls. All day with lunch $185. Also multi- day rides in the Davis Mountains and Big Bend Ranch State Park. P .O. Box 1645, Alpine, TX 79831. 866-575-1966. wwwtexashorsebackadventures.com

Swimming

Sul Ross State University—Men and women visitors may use Sul Ross University's indoor swimming pool, ($2), open year-round when the university is in session. Call 432-837-8226 for times.

The City Park—Outdoor swimming pool. Open during the summer, Tuesday–Sunday, 1–6. Admission 50¢. Adult swimmers 12–1. Women's aerobics 6 P.M. Tuesday–Thursday. 432-837-5130/3301.

Bike Rental/Repairs

Bikeman— 602 W. Holland. Does rentals 432-837-5050.

Murphy Street Raspa Company—Rentals $12/day. 432-837-5556.

Rock Shops

Antelope Lodge—To the west of town 432-837-2451 has an intriguing rock museum and gift shop.

Ocotillo Enterprises—Downtown, has a strong rock and gem collection, as well as books and gifts. 432-837-5353.

SRSU Range Animal Science Arena

Check out the cowboys of tomorrow practicing their roping skills prior to the National Intercollegiate Rodeo in October.

Summer Theater

Outdoor theater has been part of the Sul Ross experience since the inauguration of Kokernot Amphitheater in 1934. The season opens in July and runs through August, delighting locals and visitors alike.

Other theater events take place throughout the year, including performances in the Grenada theater. The Big Bend Players, Alpine's civic theater group, and SRSU Department of Fine Arts both perform plays for public viewing, advertised in the local papers.

Excursions

Woodward Ranch—16 miles south of Alpine on TX 118. One of the few ranches in the area to have switched to tourism. Source of red plume and pom pom agates, also precious opal. Buy at the ranch store or wander around (advice is given), pick your own and pay per lb. RV Park, also primitive camping two miles from headquarters at oak-lined creek.

Woodward Ranch	
Woodward Ranch HC 65, Box 40 Alpine, TX 79830	Phone: 432-364-2271 www.woodwardranch.com

Chihuahuan Desert Nature Center & Botanical Garden—22 miles north of Alpine on TX 118. 507 acres of research facilities (arboretum, greenhouse, botanical garden) open to the public, also 3 hiking trails. Gift shop and headquarters. Open Monday–Saturday.

Chihuahuan Desert Nature Center	
Chihuahuan Desert Nature Center & Botanical Garden Box 905 Fort Davis, TX 79734	Phone: 432-364-2499 www.cdri.org

Alpine Calendar Of Selected Events

January	Big Bend Livestock Show.
February	Cowboy Poetry Gathering.
	Trappings of Texas.
April	Gem and Mineral Show.
May	Cinco de Mayo.
June	Fiesta del Sol,
	Texas Mountain Music Festival.
July/August	Way Out West Bookfest,
	Theater of the Big Bend,
	Big Bend Ranch rodeo.
September	Hot Air Balloon Bash.
October	NIRA 61st Rodeo, Sul Ross State Univ.
November	Alpine Gallery Night/Art Walk.
December	Mountain Country Christmas Crafts,
	Christmas Tour of Historic Homes.

Balmorhea
(The Oasis of West Texas)
Elevation: 3,030 feet   Population: 527 (incl. Toyahvale)

Fifty miles west of Fort Stockton, one mile off I-10, Balmorhea (pop. 800) enjoys a sleepy, rustic existence unknown to most of the travelers on the interstate. Named after three early settlers, Balcom, Morrow, and Rhea, the town (pronounced Bal-mo-RAY) owes its existence to nearby San Solomon Springs, four miles to the west.

The treelined main street (TX 17) features to one side a fast flowing stream. Three motels and two restaurants provide services to visitors, some in transit to Fort Davis, the majority heading to Balmorhea State Park. A small number of savvy visitors fish or birdwatch at Balmorhea Lake, one mile to the southeast.

San Solomon Spring pumps 17 million gallons of water daily into the swimming pool, which is the main attraction of the park. What better way to end the 550-mile drive from Houston than to jump into the clear, cool (72–76°F) waters of the pool, then settle into one of the red-tile roofed cottages in the park after a meal at nearby Cueva de Oso restaurant? The following morning a drive over the Wild Rose Pass, one of the prettiest scenic drives in West Texas, will bring you to Fort Davis for the start of your Davis Mountains/Big Bend vacation.

Access/Orientation/Information

Van Horn lies 79 miles to the west on I-10, and Fort Stockton 51 miles to the east. TX 17 intersects I-10 (Exit 212) at Balmorhea, connecting Pecos (38 miles to the north) with Fort Davis (36 miles south). The route over the Wild Rose Pass to Fort Davis is one of the prettiest drives in the whole region.

Public Transportation— Greyhound makes stops on request on the El Paso/San Antonio route. For information call 800-231-2222. The nearest airport is Midland (MAF), 120 miles away.

Where To Stay—Cottages

San Solomon Courts—Toyahvale. Balmorhea State Park offers (unusual for a state park) 18 Spanish-style cottages with a flowing stream right in front and the swimming pool a short stroll away. All have central heat and air-conditioning, TV, and linens. Ten units have kitchenettes, but bring your own utensils. No pets. The cottages with kitchenettes have two double beds, those without, three double beds. Rates (double occupancy) are: Two double beds within kitchenette $80; Two double beds without kitchenette $60. Three double beds without kitchenette $75 For each additional person over 12, add $7. Maximum number permitted per unit is eight persons. For more information call 432.375-2370. For reservations call Central Reservations 512 389-8900 or book via www.reserveamerica.com.

Balmorhea State Park—Reservations	
Balmorhea State Park—Reservations P. O. Box 15 Toyahvale, TX 79786	Phone: 512-389-8900 www.reserveamerica.com

Where To Stay—Motels

El Oso Flojo—208 San Angelo Street, going west on Hwy 17. A recent addition to Balmorhea's room supply, run by the energetic Madrid family who own La Cueva de Oso. 20 rooms, individually themed, with king or double beds, around a courtyard.

Rates (guideline) from $75/night.

El Oso Flojo	
El Oso Flojo 208 San Angelo Balmorhea, TX 79718	Phone: 432 375-0502/2273 www.elosoflojolodge.com

The Eleven Inn—504 S. Main Street. 11 rooms. Old fashioned, but renovated. Upgraded with new room decor and flat panel TV. Some rooms with fridge and microwave. Room with one full-size bed $50.85, two full beds $56.50, two queen beds $67.80—prices include tax. 432-375-2263.

Cactus Motel—102 E. North Main. Downtown, on the plaza. Two-story structure undergoing complete renovation. King bedrooms ($61.85 incl. tax) and rooms with two double beds ($79.10). Optional breakfast $4.50.432.375.0652.

Where To Stay—Bed & Breakfast

Laird Ranch Bed & Breakfast—8610 Hwy 17. Beautifully restored ranch headquarters, built originally in 1952. Five modernized rooms with queen beds. Extras such as hot hors d'oeuvres and wine, a jogging trail, and horseshoe pitching set this B&B apart. The "Texas Hearty" breakfast sounds like something to look forward to. Hosts John and Beth Laird also provide RV hookups ($20), and invite those guests to share the hors d'oeuvres and breakfast. Quiet Night Special, and Quiet Weekend Specials $99–$239 for two, plus tax. No pets.

Laird Ranch Bed & Breakfast	
Laird Ranch Bed & Breakfast P. O. Box 236 Balmorhea, TX 79718	Phone: 432-375-0158 www.lairdranch.com

Where To Stay—RV Park/Camping

State Park, Toyahvale—34 sites, some full hookups, others are tent camping only. First come, first served. From $11 for tent camping, $14 for hookup with water/electricity, and $17 with water/electricity and Cable TV. Plus $7/person entrance fee. For more information call 432-375-2370.

Lake Balmorhea (Balmorhea Fishing Resort)—One mile from Balmorhea. For fishermen and birders. Unfenced, primitive ambiance. RV hookups $16 plus $4 per person. Tent camping $4 per person, includes the tent. Fishing licenses are on sale at the State Park. 432-375-1010.

Saddleback Mountain RV Park & Circle Bar—Exit 212 on I-10. 25 pull-through sites, with TV, $20 per night. Bar/Games Room adjacent. Next to 24-hour Fina Station. For more information call 432-375-2418.

Shady Oasis RV Park—Downtown next to Balmorhea Imports store. Operated by Cactus Motel. Phone: 432-375-0652.

Where to Eat

Cueva de Oso—Successful, family-run restaurant, previously The Bear's Den, one block south of Main Street on El Paso. Four small gaily-decorated rooms. Long menu, low prices. Mexican food, burgers, and sandwiches. Special plate dishes named for the family range from Joelito's ("Bubba"—a taco and two flautas) to the most popular Joel's ("Un poquito de todo"). Open daily, except Wednesday 11–2, 5–9, Saturday & Sunday 11–9.

Cueva de Oso	
Cueva de Oso 209 N. El Paso Balmorhea, TX 79718	Phone: 432-375-2273

Rodriguez Café—In Saragosa, 8 miles north on Hwy 17. Open 6–10 daily. Popular and new. The café is inside a small grocery store. Menudo is served on Sundays. 432-375-0153.

Snacks

Balmorhea Grocery—432-375-2425. Located downtown, Sells burritos ($2.17). Their specialty is the Green Burrito (brisket, onions, green chiles), which is well known even in Fort Davis.

Carrasco's Grocery—On the east side of town. 432-375-0259

I-10 Travelstop & Restaurant — At mile marker 212 on I-10. The convenience store is open 24 hours for snacks, groceries, and gas.

Shopping

Balmorhea Imports—Downtown, 105 North Main Street. Open Friday–Sunday, 10A.M.–5P.M. and weekdays during the summer. Handmade Tarahumara furniture, baskets, pottery, old saddles, drums, and lots of decorative items. All bought on the spot and imported directly. Phone: 432-375-2676.

Toyahvale Desert Oasis Scuba and Souvenir Shop— adjacent to the State Park. Outfitters, instructors in snorkeling scuba diving and swimming. Souvenirs and books. 432-375-2572. Personable and helpful folk. Excellent web page. www.toyahvale.com. The 115-year old post office next door. is still functioning.

What To Do/Where To Go

Balmorhea State Park—Four miles west on Hwy 17. Open year round. A 3.5 million gallon open-air pool. See page 53.

Balmorhea Lake (Balmorhea Fishing Resort)—Two miles southeast of Balmorhea is an unfenced, 600-acre reservoir stocked with catfish and bass. This is a popular place for fishermen and birders, since the nearest lake is a long way off. The untended look of the shoreline, with cattle standing in the water and a some old trailers parked nearby, gives the place a more primitive appearance than the State Park. Services (rest rooms/groceries) are strictly limited.

The store by the lake sells permits for RV and tent camping (see above, under Where to Stay). For a fishing license, apply to the State Park. License fees, for Texas residents, range from $28 per year September–September or daily /weekly rates. The lake is kept well stocked and good catches can be obtained from the shore as well as from a boat. The lake is well known to birders. Around 146 different species have been observed at the Wetlands Project and at Balmorhea Lake. The Balmorhea State Park office carries a bird checklist. 432-375-1010.

Fort Davis
Elevation: 5,050 feet   Population: 1,252

History

At an altitude of 5,050 feet, which makes it the highest town in Texas, and located at the base of the Davis Mountains, which rise to 8,382 feet, the unincorporated township of Fort Davis has long enjoyed the reputation as the best known resort in the region. Years before the arrival of air-conditioning, wealthy residents of the Gulf Coast sought out Fort Davis to spend their summer. Some of their homes can still be seen on Court Avenue.

The earliest European visitors to the region were Spanish explorers of whom the first was Cabeza de Vaca. His epic, 8-year, 6,000-mile odyssey (1527–35) from the Gulf of Mexico to present-day Sinaloa, Mexico took him through the Big Bend region, although his exact route remains somewhat vague. The first precise account of exploration to the Davis Mountains area comes from Antonio de Espejo who journeyed through Limpia Canyon in 1583.

One hundred and fifty years ago, the military fort from which today's town gets its name was established (1854). Four years earlier, Henry Stillman had contracted to carry mail from San Antonio to El Paso. The route, which became known as the Overland Trail, cut through Apache territory and across the Comanche Trail. Fort Davis, named after Jefferson Davis, Secretary of War in the Pierce administration, was one of a string of forts set up to protect the mail and westbound travelers. In those days, the mountains were called the Apache Mountains.

Fort Davis saw some early military action, but was abandoned during the Civil War and left to the Apaches who destroyed many of the original buildings. Reestablished after the war, it was garrisoned by black troops, nicknamed buffalo soldiers, and together with the rough-and-tumble adjacent community known as Chihuahua, became known as the most important town in the Trans-Pecos country. By 1891, having outlived its usefulness, the fort was abandoned for the second and last time.

Meanwhile, with peaceful conditions prevailing, the township grew and spread. The merchants began to prosper as they catered to the increasing number of ranchers attracted to the fertile grasslands and

169

water supply in Limpia Creek. At the time of the dispute involving the creation of Presidio and Jeff Davis Counties, Fort Davis Township had an estimated population of 1,200, about the same as today.

Presidio County, a vast area including present-day Brewster and Jeff Davis Counties, was the first county in the area to be organized (1876). Vested interests then began to try to influence the choice of county seat. Initially Fort Davis gained that recognition, but later Marfa, helped by its access to the railroad, obtained the title after a disputed election. The residents of Fort Davis and the surrounding area then voted to carve out a new county for themselves, named Jeff Davis County, which they did in 1885 and named Fort Davis the county seat.

In the first half of the twentieth century the ranching industry prospered, aided by high beef prices during the world wars and favorable climatic conditions. In the fifties and sixties however, due largely to the drought condition during the earlier decade, the cattle raising industry fell into a decline that has not been reversed. Slowly a new influence, tourism, began to make itself felt. Visitors from the cities of east Texas, attracted to the wide-open spaces and the high desert climate, began to discover the region. Hunting opportunities appealed to some, and the

Officers' Quarters

reputation of nearby Davis Mountains State Park, Prude Ranch, and the McDonald Observatory attracted family groups.

Meanwhile, a steady increase in the number of retirees attracted to the area by the healthy climate, of artists deriving stimulus from the magnificent landscape, and of persons bringing new business ideas has changed the nature of the community. Fort Davis still acts as source for supplies and as a place of worship for town residents and ranchers, but increasingly it is the visitors who are being catered to. New bed & breakfasts, eating places, a riding stables and galleries are providing additional appeal to this long-established tourist town. Fort Davis was recognized in 2008 as one of a Dozen Distinctive Destinations by the National Trust for Historic Preservation and in 2009 as an Official Best Small Town Texas.

Access/Orientation/Information

TX 118 runs SE/NW from Alpine to Kent on I-10 and intersects in Fort Davis with TX 17 that runs NE/SW from Balmorhea on I-10 to Marfa. The most scenic approach to the whole region is Hwy 17 from Balmorhea over the Wild Rose Pass to Fort Davis (39 miles). A second scenic route, from those coming from the north or west, is from Kent on I-10 over the Davis Mountains via McDonald Observatory to Fort Davis (51 miles). These two highways join to form the main street through Fort Davis. Gravel roads lead off on either side. In downtown Fort Davis, in the vicinity of the Court House and the Limpia Hotel, the speed limit is 25 m.p.h. Fort Davis National Historic Site is one mile north of downtown.

For more information contact the Fort Davis Chamber of Commerce, located on Memorial Square, next to the library. The office is open daily except on weekends.

Fort Davis Chamber of Commerce	
Chamber of Commerce P. O. Box 378 Fort Davis, TX 79734	Phone: 800-524-3015 or 432-426-3015 www.fortdavis.com Email: info@ftdavis.com

Mileage to: Midland 160 miles, San Antonio 346 miles, Houston 528 miles, Dallas 452 miles, and El Paso 198 miles via Valentine and 210 miles via Kent.

Public Transportation

The nearest train and bus service is in Alpine. The nearest com-mer-cial airport is at Midland (165 miles), otherwise El Paso (198 miles); the closest private airports are Marfa (20 miles) or Alpine (25 miles).

Local Publications

The *Jeff Davis County Mountain Dispatch* is Fort Davis' weekly paper and is published on Thursday. The Chamber of Commerce has numerous travel pamphlets about Fort Davis and members' businesses as well as the regional *Big Bend & Texas Mountains* travel guide.

Where To Stay

There's lots of comfortable accommodation although the nomencla-ture is sometimes misleading: Three hotels (including Indian Lodge, 4 miles distant), two inns (by name at least), two motels, four B & B's, two guest ranches, five campground/RV parks and many guest houses/cabin/cottages in or near Fort Davis. Prices quoted below are generally without tax. The room tax is 13%.

Hotels

Hotel Limpia—On Old Town Square. Built in 1912 from local limestone, named after nearby Limpia Creek and carefully restored by the current owners Lanna and Joe Duncan, this landmark hotel domi-nates downtown. There are 43 rooms and suites in three historic buildings including three restored guesthouses and a cottage (for details of these, see Cottages/Guesthouses below. The main hotel building reflects an aura of gracious living in the decor and furnishings, and history in the artifacts and pictures. Small touches (matching leather bags in the lobby, a local stone holding down the pages of the visitors' book) show the careful attention to detail of the owners. A sunny, plant-filled veran-da with rocking chairs and the open fireplace in the parlor invite you to sit down in comfort and quiet. New swimming pool in the garden setting. Prices from $89 to $195. Rollaway $10. Pets, in specified rooms, $20. AARP and Govt. rates apply Sunday–Thursday.

Hotel Limpia	
Hotel Limpia P. O. Box 1341 Fort Davis, TX 79734	Phone: 800-662-5517 432-426-3237 www.hotellimpia.com Email: frontdesk@hotellimpia.com

Harvard Hotel—109 State Street. Downtown hotel with eight capacious and well-appointed rooms/suites, furnished with refrigerators, microwaves and other amenities. Suite with king-bed $95; Suite, king bed, with balcony overlooking State Street $125; Suite with two full beds $115. Elevator. Wireless internet. Part of the Sproul Ranch consortium. Jeep Tours (see below).

Harvard Hotel	
Harvard Hotel P .O. Box 833 Fort Davis, TX 79734	Phone: 432-426-2500 fax: 432-426-2501 www.sproulranch.com

Indian Lodge—Hotel within the Davis Mountains State Park, four miles north of town. Owned and operated by Texas Parks & Wildlife Department. Lovely location at 5,200 feet. Pueblo-style adobe lodge built (the old part) on a mountainside by the Civilian Conservation Corps in 1933. 39 rooms and suites. Rates for two persons range from for a standard room with two double beds ($90) to the executive suite with two double beds and a sitting room in the old section ($135). $10 per extra person on rollaway (standard rooms only). Pleasant public rooms. On site Black Bear Restaurant open each day. See page 65 for details Pool. Email: Indian.Lodge@tpwd.state.tx.us. 432-426-3254 (24-hours).

Indian Lodge	
Indian Lodge P. O. Box 833 Fort Davis, TX 79734	Phone: 432-426-3254 Reservations: 512-389-8900 www.tpwd.state.tx.us/park/indian

Where to Stay—Inns

Old Texas Inn—Downtown. Closed at time of writing.

Butterfield Inn—Main at 7th Street. Four brightly painted cottages around a grassy courtyard, each with cathedral ceiling, queen-size beds, cable TV, Jacuzzi and fireplace (wood provided). Hospitality Room with coffee maker, microwave and icebox. Rates from $80 for one queen-size bed to $225 for three bedrooms with kitchen sleeping up to 8. Recently remodeled. 432-426-3252. Web: www.butterfieldinn.com.

Where to Stay—Motels

Stone Village Tourist Camp—Newly renovated 1935-era tourist court in central location. 14 motel rooms, prices from $59–$89 depending on the season. 7 innovative camp rooms ($29) which comprise two twin beds, ceiling fan and wash basin, with shared shower and rest rooms, male and female, separate. Wi-Fi. 432-426-3941. www.stonevillagetouristcamp.com.

Fort Davis Motor Inn—Just outside of town on TX 17 north. The adobe-style 48-room unit built in 1994 offers western decor in a rural setting just below the Scobee Mountains. Smoking and non-smoking rooms, also handicap accessibility. Coffee is available in the lobby from 7:00 A.M. Lobby closes at 10:00 P.M. Prices from $59.95 for two persons, queen bed, to $69.95 for king bed, plus tax. 10% off for AAA, AARP—doubles only. 800-803-2847 / 432-426-2112.

Where to Stay — Guest Ranch

Prude Ranch—Five miles north of town. See page 58 for description. 800-458-6232.

Sproul Ranch—About 8 miles north. A working cattle ranch of 25,000 acres since 1886, now offering varied luxury facilities in a peaceful, beautiful setting. These include a 15-acre lagoon for fishing and water skiing with a two-story floating dock , a trap and skeet range and a 1,000 square foot fitness room. Seasonal hunting, and facilities at the Harvard Lodge and Jaynes Pavilion for groups. Jeep Tours available (see page 91). Accommodation ("The finest western accommodation in the county" claims owner Tony Timmons) is provided in six suite-style hotel rooms ($125 for two) with king-size beds or queen and bunk beds. TV, refrigerator, microwave and coffee maker. Wireless internet. The

Ranch also offers The Cabin ($200 for four), with the same amenities. $10 for each extra person in rooms or cabin.

Sproul Ranch	
Sproul Ranch Fort Davis, TX 79734	Phone: 432-426-3151 www.sproulranch.com

Where to Stay — Bed & Breakfast

The Veranda Historic Inn — Court Avenue. You can sense you are somewhere special when you enter this historic building that opened in 1883 as the Lempert Hotel. High ceilings, long corridors, and twenty-inch thick adobe walls tell of a distant, non-air conditioned era. Outside there are courtyards and porches giving shady seating and views of the spacious gardens. Attention has been given to filling the spotless rooms with period furniture. 14 rooms and suites with private bath, including two properties adjacent to the main house—the Garden Cottage and the Carriage House. Rates: from $95–$125 for two persons. Substantial and imaginative breakfasts are taken around a large table. No pets. Close to Courthouse.

The Veranda Historic Inn	
The Veranda Historic Inn 210 Court Ave., Box 1238 Fort Davis, TX 79734	Phone: 888-383-2847 432-426-2233 www.TheVeranda.com

Wayside Inn—Near to Museum and close to Fort Davis National Historic Site. There are seven rooms in this, the oldest B&B in Fort Davis, known as "The family place." The Ward family set the tone of down-home friendliness in this unpretentious house that enjoys good views over the town. Families are welcome. The furnishings are early attica, with personal belongings and other family memorabilia on display. The full and healthy breakfast is buffet-style. All rooms with private bath and TV. Rates are $65–$95, with breakfast. 10 % discount for seniors, military, home school families and ministry members. The whole house can be rented for family reunions and weddings. Welcome treats await guests when they check into their rooms.

Wayside Inn	
Wayside Inn 400 West Fourth St. P. O. Box 2088 Fort Davis, TX 79734	Phone: 432-426-3535 Fax: 432-426-3574

Old Schoolhouse Bed & Breakfast—Steve and Carla Kennedy came from Austin in 1999 to open a new Bed & Breakfast. The handsome adobe building stands in a one-acre pecan grove and offers three tastefully renovated rooms which, as befits a former schoolhouse, go by the names of: Reading Room, 'Riting Room, and 'Rithmatic Room. Also The Common Room, for sitting and talking. The largest has a private bath, the other two share a bath. Large shady deck. Very friendly dog. Walking distance from downtown. No pets. Guests can help themselves to soft drinks in the fridge in the Common Room. Rates (for two) from $93 (shared bath)–$101(private bath). The Kennedys also run Hope's Ranch (see below).

Old Schoolhouse Bed & Breakfast	
Old Schoolhouse Bed & Breakfast P. O. Box 1221 Fort Davis, TX 79734	Phone: 432-426-2050 Fax: 432-426-2509 www.schoolhousebnb.com

Davis Mountains Bed & Breakfast—New. Half a mile west of town on the Marfa highway, this new B & B offers 7 suites and rooms, from $89 for two including a full breakfast. Elegant décor in an Old World style inside, 6 acres of grounds and shade trees outside with good mountain views. Accommodations, named after local mountains, range from Guide Peak room with queen bed and bath adjacent ($94 for two) to Sleeping Lion master suite with king bed and en suite bath with Jacuzzi ($139 for two) to the 800 foot two-bedroom Fisher Hill suite ($169 for two). Art workshops and getaway packages. There is also a private working artist's studio 8 miles away. Enthusiastic hosts Nancy and Bill Davis, who is an artist, are ever-attentive. 43417 Hwy 17 South, Fort Davis, TX 79734. http://web.mac.com/davismtninn/. 432-426-3939.

Where to Stay—Cottages/Cabins/Guest Houses (In Town)

The Awakening Place—103 E. Cavalry Road. Central yet secluded, a place for reflection. 2-bedroom (queen; two extra large twins), 1 bath, fully equipped kitchen. Rustic feel, pine walls. Reading and CD library. $110 for two, $150 for four. 432-426-3789.

Hotel Limpia Properties—The following five accomodations are owned and operated by the Hotel. www.hotellimpia.com 800-662-5517, 432-426-3237.

> **The Mulhearn House**—Court Avenue. Three suites, two with bedroom and sitting area, one without sitting room.$145–$159.

> **The Dr. Jones House**—Three deluxe suites, each with different options: fireplace, jacuzzi, screened porch, upstairs/downstairs. $165–$175.

> **The Cottage**—Two-bedroom, one bath, with kitchen, for up to four guests. $180.

> **The Trueheart House**—1896 adobe house. Three suites, two with sitting rooms and one without. $169–$175.

> **The Carriage House**—Also an historic adobe, but smaller. Two suites with sitting rooms $169–$275.

The Historic Veranda's Properties—The following accomodations are owned and operated by The Historic Veranda. 210 Court Avenue. www.theveranda.com. 888-383-2847. 432-426-2233.

> **The Garden Cottage**—One bedroom. $95.

> **The Carriage House**—Two bedrooms. $125.

Wildflower Cottages—Two night minimum. 432-426-1234. Pets accepted. Higher rates during Spring Break. All properties are within a two-block distance of each other. www.wildflowercottages.net.

> **Webster House**—105-year old "Territorial Victorian" house next to High School. Four bedroom, two bathrooms, kitchen, TV etc.. $190 for two to $375 for seven guests.

> **Hummingbird Cottage**—A private adobe for two. One bedroom with kitchen Sleeps two. $95.

> **Wildflower Cottage**—adjacent to Webster House. Three bedroom,

two bathroom. Fully equipped with kitchen and TV. $150 for two–$275 for six.

"Mrs Mims House"—named after a beloved Fort Davis teacher. Master bedroom with queen bed, two twin beds in the living room. $135 (1–2 persons)–$159 (up to four).

Casa Hermosa Duplex—Two luxury suites. One with two bedrooms ($145 and up, depending on number of guests) and the second with one king-bed and kitchenette $120.

Blue Agave Bungalow—Two bedroom stucco house with two full bathrooms. $120 (1-2 persons), $250 (3-4 persons).

Hope's Ranch—1100 Cemetery Road. Pueblo-style adobe, set in 40 acres, two miles from downtown. Named for Hope Wilson, daughter of west Texas pioneers. Three bedrooms, two and a half baths, generous living room with fireplace. $195 for four persons, $25 for each extra guest. Reduced rates for longer stays ($60 cleaning charge per visit). 432-426-2050. www.schoolhousebnb.com.

Mary's Post Office—102 N. Davis Street. Built in 1908 and served as Post Office until 1922. A unique getaway for couples. Queen-bed with claw foot tub and kitchen. Non-smoking. No pets. Cute place! Coffee maker and refrigerator. Two-night minimum. Available April–September. $95, plus tax. 432-426-3097. www.rmsproulranch.com.

Overland Trail Campground Cabins—In town center. Small (2-3 persons) and large (up to 9), equipped with microwave, refrigerator and TV. Wireless internet. Laundry on site. From $70 (small cabin, one person) to $155 (nine guests). Discount for on-line booking.

Casa Mama Tea—Three-bedroom, one-bath adobe cottage at Dakota and Commerce streets. The low price, $25 per person, comes with a requirement to tidy up afterwards. www.casamamatea.com. 281-412-5105.

Where to Stay—Cottages/Cabins/Guest Houses (Out of Town)

Double M Ranch—10 miles north on Hwy 118 on 1,500 acres. Modern Getaway Suite. King-size bed, TV, well-equipped kitchen. Option for tours. Two-night minimum. $100/night. $25 for one extra person. 432-426-2473. www.mmguestranch.com.

La Cabana Escondida—TX 118 north two miles from downtown, then one mile across Limpia Creek. Log cabin-type, queen-size bed with sofa/futon. Fully equipped kitchen. Very secluded, excellent for star gazing and wildlife watching. Two-night minimum. $125 for four persons. 432-426-3097. www.rmsproulranch.com.

Crow's Nest—TX 166, 18 miles west of Fort Davis. Three log cabins, each with queen- and full-size beds. Kitchenette. Secluded rural location. Lots of hiking trails. From $65. 432-426-3300.

Where to Stay — RV Parks

Overland Trail Campground — Could not be more central, 100 yards from Limpia Hotel. 27 sites, nine rustic cabins and tent camping. $25 for full hookup, $10 for dry camping. Cabins rent for $85. Laundromat and showers/bath. Strict management. Discount for on-line booking.

Overland Trail Campground	
Overland Trail Campground P. O. Box 788 Fort Davis, TX 79734	Phone: 888-478-5267 432-426-2250 www.texascamping.com

Fort Davis Motor Inn—Fourteen full hookups next to the inn, two miles north of town beneath Scobee Mountain. $18.50/night. 800-803-2847. 432-426-2112.

Prude Ranch—Five miles north of town on TX 118. RV hookups, $18.50. 800-458-6232.

Davis Mountains State Park—Four miles north on TX 118. 33 tent camping sites with water ($10) and 61 RV hookups ($15-$20). Plus $4 entry fee per person. 432-426-3337.

Crow's Nest RV Park—18 miles west of Ft. Davis on TX 166. Wonderful views and access to hiking trails. 20 sites. $25–$30 full hookup. $15.00 for a tent with up to three persons. 432-426-3300. www.crowsnestranch.com.

Where To Drink

To buy beer or wine, try Stone Village grocery store or Porter's Thriftway.

The Sutler's Club—A bar above the dining room of the Hotel Limpia, is the only place to drink an alcoholic beverage in this county. To comply with the law you have to join the Sutler's Club, paying a temporary membership fee of $3, which is valid for up to three days and covers four persons. Guests at the Limpia Hotel don't have to pay.

Where To Eat

Limpia Hotel Dining Room—On Main Street. Dinner 5:00–9:00 Tuesday–Saturday, and lunch 11:30–2:00 on Sunday. You pass rocking chairs on the porch and enter via a gift shop to find a cozy dining area with stairs leading to the upstairs bar. Burgundy marinated meat loaf ($14) is the most popular entrée, and meatloaf, spinach lasagna roll-up, fried chicken livers and a garden plate show variety. You help yourself from a bowl of salad and to the vegetables brought to the table. Reservations 432-426-3241.

Cueva de Leon—Easily visible on the west side of Main Street, this Mexican restaurant has been a favorite with locals and visitors for 30 years. The Cueva ($9.79) combination plate special ("a little bit of everything") is popular, also the buffet ($7.00 at noon, $8.75 Saturday night) and chiles rellenos ($2.25 each). Open Monday–Saturday 11:30–3:00, 5–9. Sunday 11:30–3:00, when Sunday buffet is served ($8.99). 432-426-380.

Drugstore at Old Texas Inn—Closed at time of writing.

Murphy's—Across from the Courthouse, the new owners are determined reclaim its former reputation. An olive-oil based crust adds to the appeal of the pizzas, and the salads (5) are big; pasta (including vegetarian) and subs/sandwiches round out the menu. Prices have come down. "Simply good food" was the original slogan, hopefully Murphy's will earn this claim again. Open 6 days, 11–8. 432-426-2020.

Chuck Wagon BBQ—1300 N. State Street. Opposite the entrance to the fort. A comprehensive menu specializing in barbecue brisket, ribs, sausage and chicken smoked on the premises and claiming to be the best in the area. Burgers and sandwiches Open 7 A.M.–9 P.M. every day 432-426-2900.

Nell's Coffee Shop—Next to the Book Feller used books. N. State Street. Sandwiches, soups, salads. The soups are made from scratch, and the tomato basil soup is popular. Five sandwiches ($4.49), of which Turkey and Monterrey Jack with Nell's cranberry cream sauce, and the Jerry Special are favorites. Coffee from Big Bend Roasters. Ice Cream.

Open 10 A.M.–4 P.M. daily. 432-426-3722.

Lupita's Place—Outdoor seating under canvas for burritos, gorditas and burgers. Most popular is the Texas tornado sandwich (brisket, avocado, lettuce and cheese) at $4. Horchata (rice water) is $3, lemonade $2. Open Thursday–Tuesday 11:30–9:00.

Mary Lou's Place—Handily situated on Hwy 118 south of town. The fare is Mexican/American. The most popular dish is green enchiladas ($5.75) as well as the buffets ($6.50), Tuesday–Friday, with chicken fried steak and catfish on Friday. Open 6:30–10:30, 11:30–1:30, Monday–Friday. 432-426-9901.

Caboose—Ice Cream Parlor. Opposite fort entrance. 24 flavors of Blue Bell ice cream. Train memorabilia and t-shirts. Open 12–9, 7 days. 432-426-2742.

Poco Mexico—TX 17 north, just outside of town. Rustic restaurant, open for 25 years. Lunch 11:30–2:00 every day except Thursday, April–October. Gets high praise for their green enchiladas ($6.00) and tamales. 432-249-0536.

Sunrise Bakery—411 N. State Street. Breakfast burritos, ($3.25), donuts ($.65), lunch specials such as Red Enchiladas ($6.75). Open Tuesday–Sunday. 7–1. 432-426-3555

Heavenly Skies—603A Main Street (N. State St.). Deli sandwiches on special La Baccia bread, unusual side dishes, stoups (stew/soup hybrid), desserts and ice cream. Retailers of teas and tea products, also binoculars, telescopes (buy or rent) and hummingbird feeders. Bike rentals. Open 11:30–5:30 Monday–Friday, till 3:30 P.M. on Thursday. 432-426-2007.

What To Do/Where To Go

Fort Davis National Historic Site—One mile north of downtown on TX 118/17. Open daily except Christmas. Established 1854, the site includes officers' quarters, barracks, a museum and Visitor Center. See page 65 for further description.

Davis Mountains State Park—Four miles north of Fort Davis on TX 118. Measuring only 2,700 acres, it contains Indian Lodge, biking and hiking trails (including a 4-mile trail to Fort Davis National Historic Site, described above), Skyline Drive driving route, bird viewing areas, a large campground, and Interpretive Center. There are regular events during summer. See page 60 for further description.

Overland Trail Museum—Look for the sign on Main Street and go two blocks west to where you cross part of the old Overland Trail. The building was originally the home of local barber and Justice of the Peace Nick Mersfelder, who is described inside. Four separate rooms display everything from arrowheads, saddles, and a barbed-wire display to a pair of zippered boots. The truly amazing story of Diedrich Dutchover, shanghaied in Antwerp, Belgium and buried in Fort Davis, is told. Open Tuesday, Friday, Saturday 1–5 P.M. $2 for adults, $1 for children. For special openings for groups: call 432-426-3213/2011

Rattlers & Reptiles — Opposite entrance to National Historic Site. Buzz Ross, the owner, regards his museum as an educational center. He is particularly gratified when children feel at ease handling some of his pets, and when adults break through their snake phobia. There are 35 different exhibits of more than 100 animals, including 70 snakes. By providing information on snakes' habits and bringing us closer to them, Buzz helps to reveal the beauty of these misunderstood creatures. Open 7 days, from 10 until dark. Entrance $4 adults, $1 children (10 and under), family $12.

The Fort Davis Library—Previously located in the old jail, the library now has much more spacious quarters in the Union Mercantile Building on Old Town Square. For older documents on genealogy and other records, visitors will need to go to the Court House, but for a strong collection of southwest historical books, the library is the place to visit. Open Monday–Friday, 10–6. 432-426-3802.

Jeep Tours—Wildlife & Scenery tour, 2.5 hours. To Cook Mountain and Frasier Creek, north of Fort Davis on private ranch land. Adult $55 Child under 12, $45.

Ranch Fishing Tour—5 hours. We drive through magnificent scenery and visit a mountain top pond to try our hand at catching crappie, bass or catfish. Catch and release. Adult $125 Child under 12 $115. 432-426-2500. www.sproulranch.com

High Desert Yoga—At Front Street and Hwy 17 south. Classes Tuesday/Thursday 9:30–11:00, Wednesday/Friday 11:00–12:30. Beginners and Intermediate Classes in Hatha yoga with emphasis on body alignment, strength, flexibility and balance. Visitors welcome. $10. Call Maggie 432-426-2497 or email: highdesertyoga@hotmail.com.

Other

Pioneer Cemetery—Look for a small sign on the right side of TX 118 heading for Alpine, opposite Mary Lou's restaurant. Park and follow a narrow, fenced path that will take you to an unkempt pasture, which is the unhallowed graveyard of early settlers and others from that era. Among those buried in the scattered graves are Diedrich Dutchover, whose story is told in the Overland Museum, also the Frier Brothers who were shot as horse thieves by a posse of Texas Rangers. There are many others lying here whose names were forgotten when their wooden cross disintegrated or the grave became overgrown with weeds. There is a strong sense of history in this untended graveyard beneath Dolores Mountain.

Galleries

Wild Ridge Photography Gallery—400 N. State Street. Black and white fine art photography of desert and mountain landscapes, artfully enhanced in development. Call Charles Wildridge, 210-414-4284 for appointment.

Shopping

Javelinas & Hollyhocks—Main Street, opposite Limpia Hotel. A nature store with museum-quality gifts. Attractively decorated with well-informed staff to match. I noticed natural bath products, a body-cooling neck wrap, toys and marbles, and a wide selection of books including children's books. Open every day 9–6. 432-426-2236.

Along the Trail Antiques Gifts & Gardens—205 N. State Street. Retail antiques, gifts and garden store with hanging plants, large selection of cactus, also other plants, hummingbird feeders and garden art. Open 9–5, 6 days (closed Tuesday). 432-426-2041.

Hotel Limpia Gifts—Three well-filled rooms packed with gift items, inluding ladies clothing. Candles, potpourri, soaps, housewares, ornamental and decorative gifts, plus a strong section on Texas and Southwestern books. Look for the Limpia cookbook. 432-426-3241.

1800's Working Broom Shop—401 N. State Street. Mr. Cox painstakingly crafts brooms ($15-$47) and walking sticks ($15-$125) from yucca and cholla wood using a 19th century spindle Embellished sticks, cake testers ($7) and staffs from sotol plants. Open Friday–Monday 9–4. "Mostly closed on Sundays." 432-426-3297.

Stone Village Market, Whole Foods & Deli—State Street next to Stone Village Tourist Camp. Open 7 days, 7 A.M.–7 P.M. Attrac-tively laid out and well stocked. Strong on deli meats, coffee, beer and wine. organic produce. Sandwiches "if we have it in the store, you can have it on your sandwich." 432-426-2226

Davis Mountains Nut Co.—610 N. State Street. Choice Texas pecans, flavored on-site. Packed in small sample bags ($6) or in fancy tins (up to $42). Most popular is the combination box of all six flavors ($22 or $38). Order on-line at www.allpecan.com. Free samples. Monday–Saturday 9–5, Sunday 1–5. 432-426-2101.

Old Fort Country—1250 N. State Street. Next to Caboose. Antiques, western art, and USGS maps, old and new. Homemade fudge. Of special interest in this well-stocked store are Frederick Rem-ington memorabilia and movies filmed locally (like *Giant*) There are even some museum items like artifacts from the old fort and, owing to a family connection, a Wally Moon exhibit. Local wines. lst Saturday flea market is here. Open 12–9, 7 days. 432-426-2742.

Blue Agate Rocks and Gifts — 603A N. State Street. Rocks of the Chihuahuan Desert, especially blue agate from Balmorhea. Also local metal work items. Monday–Saturday, 9:30–5. 432-426-3519.

Excursions/Side Trips

Scenic Loop including McDonald Observatory and Bloys Camp—Varied terrain, great views, stopping points of interest, this must-do 78-mile circle trip starts at the Courthouse. For a more de-tailed description, see page 128.

Bloys Camp—The first meeting at the camp, founded in 1890 at Skillman Grove by the Reverend Bloys, had 47 participants who ate meals cooked in Dutch ovens and slept in bedrolls. Twenty years later 575 campers attended. One hundred years later 400 cabins are filled during the one-week camp meeting each August. The Spartan, non-denominational event is a highlight of the summer for those ranching families and others who hold closely to the moral and cultural ties of the region. Several thousand attend and participate socially and spir-itually, enjoying cowboy fare from a campfire and relishing the traditions of the place. Located 17 miles west of Fort Davis. For those want-ing more information on how to attend, call 432-426-3375.

Hiking Trails

Fort Davis National Historic Site to Davis Mountains State Park, or vice versa—This four-mile trail requires a medium amount of effort to cope with some elevation gain and a sometime rocky path. It also requires a plan for the return trip, unless you are going to turn round, at the end or part way, and retrace your steps. The reward for the effort is a pleasant, varied trail with some fine views and a good sep-aration from highway noise. See page 63 for more details.

Davis Mountains State Park—Primitive Area trails, four miles round trip. Check at Park entrance for map and details. See page 60 for more details on the Davis Mountains State Park.

Chihuahuan Desert Nature Center & Botanial Garden—Four miles south on TX 118. Cactus and succulent greenhouse. Botanical gardens. Self-guided tour to the botanical gardens and 1-2 hour dura-tion hiking trails into Modesta Canyon and to Clayton's Overlook. Open year-round, 6 days, 9–5. See page 55.

Horseback Riding

Fort Davis Stables—Located at the intersection of TX 17 and TX 118 just north of town. A great variety of rides from one hour ($30), half day with lunch ($90) to multi-day with attentive per-sonnel on well cared-for mounts. These folk also lay on a cattle drive in October and offer horseback hunts (for example for aou-dad sheep), Much of this is on 10,000 acres of leased land. 800-770-1911. 432-426-9075. www.fortdavisstables.com.

Prude Ranch—five miles north of town on Texas 118 also offers horse rides. Famous for its horse riding reputation and affording glorious riding country. 65 well trained, gentle horses to choose from. The price is $30/hour, $50 for two hours. The trail takes you around the ranch property and, time permitting, into the canyon. Be sure to call in advance since the Prude Ranch stables are often busy with groups. Pen rides for little cowpokes under six–free. 800-458-6232. 432-426-3201. www.prude-ranch.com.

Texas Horseback Adventures—One to multi-day rides on Quar-ter Horses through private rangeland with hearty campfire meals and a high degree of comfort. See additional information in the Alpine section. www.texashorsebackadventures.com.

Davis Mountains Therapeutic Riding Center—Principally for those with physical and developmental disabilities. Certified instructors use horses carefully selected for their therapeutic qualities. La Fondarosa non-profit DMTRC also offers riding instruction to persons without an identified disability. 432-426-2303. www.narha.org.

Fort Davis Calendar Of Selected Events

February	Texas Mountain Writers' Retreat
March	Overland Trail Museum reopens
April	Desert Plant Sale at Chihuahuan Desert Research Institute
	Hammerfest Bike Race
May	Texas Star Party at Prude Ranch,
	Memorial Weekend dance
June	Sports Medicine Clinic at Prude Ranch,
	Missoula, Montana Childrens Theater
July 4th	Coolest July 4th in Texas.
August	Bloys Camp Meeting,
	Hummingbird Roundup.
September	Cyclefest and Race,
	Fort Davis NHS Preservation and Restoration Festival,
	Davis Mountains Brigade Black Powder Shoot
November	Arts & Crafts Fair in Parish Hall
December	Christmas at Fort Davis National Historic Site, Private Home Visit and Art Display,
	Frontier Christmas Celebration.

Fort Stockton
Elevation: 3,052 feet   Population: 8,643

History

Fort Stockton sits to the south of the Permian Basin oil and gas fields and is best known as a busy pit stop on I-10 between San Antonio and El Paso. It is the largest town in the region and county seat of Pecos County, the second largest county in Texas. But it is also known as a gateway to the Big Bend and has one or two surprises for visitors who take the time to get to know the town.

The town came into being due to the abundant supply of water from nine springs that flowed at a nearby site. Comanche Indians, Spanish explorers, and the U.S. Army all availed themselves of the plentiful supply. The first Spanish explorer to reach the area was Dominguez de Mendoza who passed through in 1684. In 1840, Anglo settlers founded a community, which they named St. Gall, patron saint of the Irish trader Gallagher who headed the group.

A frontier post, Camp Stockton was established near the springs in 1858 by the U.S. Army to protect the westbound travelers on the Government Road from San Antonio to El Paso. The camp was named after Commodore Stockton, an American naval hero of the Mexican War. The army abandoned the camp in 1861 and by the end of the Civil War little remained of the original buildings.

In 1867, the 9th U.S. Cavalry reestablished Fort Stockton at its present location. Its 960 acres were leased from civilian landowners. Black enlisted troops, called "buffalo soldiers" by the Indians, were garrisoned there and patrolled the region. In 1880, the residents of the community voted to change the town's name to Fort Stockton. By 1886 the fort's purpose had been achieved and it closed for good.

With peaceful conditions prevailing, ranching and irrigated farming began to flourish. The first train of the Kansas City–Mexico & Orient Railroad arrived in 1912 linking the cities of east Texas to the Pacific coast of Mexico via the shortest route. This railroad venture never really prospered, but by the 1920s a new discovery, oil and gas, was being extracted in large quantities in Pecos County, and Fort Stockton became the service center.

The early 1950s brought a seven-year drought to the region. That, combined with the increased use of irrigation, caused the drying up of the Comanche Springs. Today the spring still flows slightly during wet periods and irrigation of cotton and alfalfa land near to Fort Stockton continues. But the spring, which used to produce 65 million gallons of water daily, is no more.

The fluctuating fortunes of the energy business have been felt in communities through west Texas for the past two decades. But, by continuing farmland irrigation, increasing pecan production, and energetically expanding its services, especially in the field of tourism, Fort Stockton has managed to keep its strength.

A Main Street program was put in place, the historic fort and nearby Annie Riggs museum were spruced up, and a Fort Stockton Historic Tour was identified and signposted. Step beyond the main commercial drag, Dickinson Boulevard and you will find local history carefully recreated and proudly displayed.

Access/Orientation/Information

Interstate 10 bypasses Fort Stockton immediately to the north. Dickinson Blvd. is the main commercial street, running east west. Roads lead off Dickinson south to Marathon (58 miles), southeast to Sanderson (65 miles), north to Monahans (51 miles), and northwest to Pecos (54 miles). Midland/Odessa is 95 miles northeast.

Annie Riggs Museum

Information is available from the Chamber of Commerce Depot Visitor Center in the old railroad depot at 1000 Railroad Avenue, which has brochures galore.

Fort Stockton Chamber of Commerce	
Fort Stockton Visitor Center 1000 Railroad Ave. Fort Stockton, TX 79735	Phone: 800-336-2166 432-336-2264 www.tourtexas.com/fortstockton

Public Transportation

Bus—Two buses daily serve Fort Stockton on the El Paso/San Antonio route, stopping at the dismal bus station at 800 North Williams Street. 432-336-5151. For Greyhound fares call 800-231-2222. All-American bus line serves the north–south route from Midland to Presidio twice daily. 432-682-2761.

Air—The nearest commercial air service is out of Midland Airport (MAF).

Inner City Transportation—TRAX 432-336-8057.

Hospital

Pecos County Memorial Hospital—432-336-2004.

Where To Stay—Top End

Atrium—1305 N. Hwy 285. 84 suites surrounding a pool. Spa. sauna. lounge. 432-336-6666.

Best Western/Swiss Clock Inn—3201 W. Dickinson. 112 rooms. Free full breakfast. Restaurant. 800 528-1234, 432-336-8521.

Comfort Suites—3101 W. Dickinson. 432-336-3224.

Days Inn—1408 N. Hwy 285. 50 rooms. Pool. Free continental breakfast. 800-DAYS-INN. 432-336-7500

Hampton Inn — 2271 W. I-10. 59 rooms. Pool. Full breakfast. 800-HAMPTON. 432-336.9602.

Holiday Inn Express—2915 W. Dickinson. 73 rooms. Pool, breakfast. 888-465-4329, 432-336-3421.

La Quinta—1537 N. Hwy 285. 90 large rooms. Pool. 800-642-4239. 432-336-9781.

Quality Inn—1308 N. Hwy. 285. 44 rooms. Pool. 432-336-5955.

Sleep Inn—3401 W. Dickinson. 49 rooms. Indoor pool, Jacuzzi, fitness center. 432-336-8338

Where to Stay—Medium Range

Comanche Motel—1301 E. Dickinson. 22 rooms. 800-530-3793, 432-336-5824.

Rodeway Inn— 800 E. Dickinson. 84 rooms. 800-553-2666, 432-366-9711.

Motel 6—3001 W. Dickinson. 106 rooms. 800-466-8356, 432-336-9737.

Super 8—3200 W. Dickinson. 432-336-8531.

Texan Inn—1801 W. Dickinson. 50 rooms. 432-336-7300.

Town & Country Motel—1505 W. Dickinson. 16 rooms. 432-336-0600.

Where To Stay—Economy

Budget Inn—801 E. Dickinson. 29 rooms. 432-336-3311.

Executive Inn—901 E. Dickinson. 28 rooms. 432-336-2251.

Deluxe Motel—500 E. Dickinson. 22 rooms. 432-336-2231.

Gateway Lodge—501 E. Dickinson. 22 rooms, kitchenettes available. 432-336-1568.

Where To Stay—Bed & Breakfast

Tunas Creek Bed & Breakfast—28 miles east on I-10. All rooms include microwave, refrigerator and coffee maker. Breakfast included. Hiking and biking trails, skeet shooting. 432-395-2271.

Where To Stay—RV Campgrounds

Of the seven campgrounds in or near Fort Stockton, two stand out:

Fort Stockton RV Park—Exit 264 off I-10. Home of the Road-runner Café. Pool Hot tub. Cabins. 432-395-2494.

KOA Campground—4 miles east of town on I-10. Stands back from the interstate and has all the amenities including cabins and a pool. 432-395-2494.

RV Campgrounds—Other

Parkview RV Park—In town on TX 285. near Rooney Park. 100 sites. Pool. 432-336-7733.

A & M Park—1000 N. Gatlin. 26 sites 432-336-6401.

Comanche Mobile Park—1301 E. Dickinson. 7 sites. 432-336-5864.

Comanche Land RV Park—Exit 257 off I-10. 58 sites. 432-336-6403

I-10 RV Park—Exit 259 off I-10. 30 sites. 432-336-3486.

J & L Mobile Home & RV Park—FM 1053 and 46th Lane. 432-365-0695.

Where To Eat

There are 30 eating places in town, mainly Mexican, but also including two steakhouses, a BBQ place, IHOP, and all the usual chain restaurants/cafes.

Where to Eat—Mexican

Most restaurants carry Mexican dishes, but restaurants offering principally Mexican dishes are Bienvenidos, Pacheco's, La Rosita, and Burrito Inn. Noted are:

Mi Casita—405 E. Dickinson, 432-336-5368, "always packed for lunch", open Tuesday–Friday, 11–2, 5–9 P.M.

Acosta Tortilla Factory—208 W. 8th. 432-336-6949. Good for takeaway burritos, Monday–Sunday.

Where to Eat—BBQ

Rix Pit Barbecue—1712 Front Street. Inside a discount warehouse. A BBQ expert reported favorably on the brisket, ribs and sausage with choice of sweet or tangy sauce. Monday–Friday, 11–8. 432-336-7636.

Where to Eat—Steakhouse

K-Bob's Steakhouse—2800 W. Dickinson. Monday–Saturday 11–2, 5–9 (Saturday til 10 P.M.). 432-336-6233.

Where to Eat—General—American

Desert Pines Cafe at Golf Course—Herb crusted salmon ($14) combine with burgers and standard fare. Beer available. Nice setting, limited décor. Tuesday–Sunday 11–2, 4:30–8:00 P.M. 432-336-8433

Where to Eat—Other

Happy Daze @ Bulldog Corner—101 S. Main. Fifties decor (Elvis on the wall) in an exuberant diner and soda fountain. 10–8. Closed Sunday. Burgers, sundaes, etc. 432-336-3233.

Comanche Springs Truck Stop—24-hour. 2501 W. I-10. Their "big, old burger" turns out to be a mighty burger on a 10" bun, known as "Big Chief Sitting Bull," $18.95, or if you eat it with all the accompaniments, it's *free!* 432-336-9713.

What To Do/Where To Go

Fort Stockton Historic Tour (1–1.5 hours)—Self-guided. Get a map from the Chamber of Commerce Depot Visitor Center, then follow the signs. There are 17 points of interest on the tour, in particular the fort, the museum, and the old cemetery.

Points of Interest Along The Route

1. Depot Visitor Center.

2. Paisano Pete—11 foot tall, 22 foot long roadrunner, Pete is Fort Stockton's mascot.

3. The Old Riggs Hotel—Now the Annie Riggs Museum. $3 entrance fee. Open daily. 14 rooms, packed with history, around a courtyard that is open in summer for concerts.

4. Old Mission Church—Built in 1875, the walls are 4-feet thick.

5. Early Jail—Built 1884. Currently occupied by the sheriff, as his home!

6. Zero Stone Park—The survey stone, from which the survey of all trans-Pecos was started, is set into the ground among pecan trees.

7. First School—Built 1883.

8. Oldest House—From 1859. Gunslinger Barney Riggs, unarmed, was shot outside this house by his son-in-law.

9. Gray Mule Saloon—Built by A. J. Royal. While still sheriff, Royal was also shot—at his desk in the courthouse. The desk is now in the Annie Riggs Museum. Royal is buried in the Old Cemetery near Barnie Riggs.

10. Young's Store—Opened in 1876 as a sutler's store.

11. Koehler's Store—Acted as bank and saloon. Koehler is another occupant of the pioneer cemetery.

12. Comanche Spring Pavilion and Swimming Pool—Built in 1938 over Big Chief Spring. Site of today's annual water carnival.

13. Rollins–Sibley House—Built partly on the site of the old fort hospital.

14. St. Stephen's Episcopal Church—An early Protestant Church, finely proportioned.

15. Historic Fort Stockton—Rebuilt on this site following the Civil War. See text.

16. Fifth Street House—Ordered from the Montgomery Ward catalog in the late 1920s, cost $1,200.

17. Old Fort Cemetery—Used from 1859–1912. Most of the military dead were subsequently moved to San Antonio. The headstone of A. J. Royal's gravesite simply states, "assassinated." This was because straws were drawn before he was killed and to this day no one has revealed the identity of the killer.

Annie Riggs Memorial Museum—301 S. Main. 432-336-2167. Open Monday–Saturday 9–5, Summer hours (June-August) until 6:00 P.M. Admission $3.00, seniors $2.50, children under 12 $2.00, under 6 free.

A beautiful example of the Territorial style of architecture including adobe walls, a courtyard, and a veranda—the building was constructed in 1900 as a hotel. Later Annie Riggs, widow of the slain Barney Riggs, bought the hotel and ran it strictly, enforcing rules posted on the dining room walls, until her death in 1931.

For an entrance fee of only $3, visitors can see a well-restored historic building with 14 rooms, each with a different focus, packed with a huge collection of memorabilia. Most of the rooms you can walk into, others you observe from behind a rope. Among the many varied items on display are: a butter churn and fluting iron, information about "Frank-and-a-half," and the remains of a 22,000-year old mastodon.

You can step inside a typical hotel room from the early 1900s where you might find another guest booked into the same bed! The bed itself would be of cast iron, from Sears, costing $6.75. Rooms are dedicated to pioneers, cowboys, archeology, and to Judge Butz, among others. Old recorded tunes are played in the parlor and newer live tunes are played or sung in the courtyard during the summer months, "Summer Off The Patio."

Annie Riggs Memorial Museum	
Annie Riggs Memorial Museum 301 South Main Fort Stockton, TX 79735	Phone: 432-336-2167

Historic Fort Stockton—300 East Third Street. 432-336-2400. Open Monday–Saturday, 9–5, June–August 9–6. Admission $3, seniors $2.50, children 6–12 $2.

The fort was moved to its present site when it was rebuilt in 1867. Subsequent to its abandonment in 1886, the 35 buildings on the 960 acres fell into disrepair. Of the original buildings, only four remain, thanks to the restoration work of the Fort Stockton Historical Society that manages the property.

The first stop should be at Barracks #1, which is the fort museum. Here you pay the entrance fee and can watch a 15-minute video. You can then proceed to the three remaining Officers' Quarters, followed by the Guardhouse containing the jailer's quarters and confinement cells.

Historic Fort Stockton	
Historic Fort Stockton 300 East Third Street Fort Stockton, TX 79735	Phone: 432-336-2400

Comanche Springs Pool—200 Spring Drive. Open June–August, 1–9 P.M. Closed Monday. $1 entrance fee. 432-336-2751.

Desert Pines Municipal Golf Course—An excellent, all round, 18 hole course. The home course of PGA contender Blaine McCallister. The weather conditions are often windy. Practice range. 432-336-2050.

Entertainment

Stockton's Entertainment —bowling, miniature golf, movie theater, sport bar, arcade. Behind IHOP on I-10. 432-336.2101.

The Neon Palm—Las Vegas-style games. 1407 N. Front Street. 432-336-3840.

Stixx—Billiards and sports bar. 1216 Hwy. 285. 432-336-6898.

Shopping

Gray Mule Saloon—Across from the Annie Riggs Museum. Gift shop and small gallery with work by local artists. Extended hours, including Sundays, during summer. 432-336-8052.

Mesquite Tree—1101 W. Dickinson. Gift items, including kitchen utensils, baby stuff and books. 432-336-6781.

Nolen's Pharmacy—700 W. Dickinson. Gift shop filled with cards, decorated items and local treasures. 432-336-2201.

Fort Stockton Calendar Of Selected Events

January	Pecos County Livestock Show, Sheepdog Trials.
April	Big Bend Open Road Race. Fort Stockton to Sanderson and back to Fort Stockton.
May	Cinco de Mayo.
June	A Night on the Town.
June–August	"Summer Off The Patio." Concerts every other Thursday at Riggs Museum. Alternate weeks' concerts in Zero Stone Park.
July	4th of July celebration in Rooney Park.
	Water Carnival celebrating Comanche Springs. This annual event started in 1936.
August	HarvestFest–Fun-filled family event held in Rooney Park.
September	Frontier Days at Historic Fort Stockton.
October	Roadrunner Open Road Race from Fort Stockton to Marathon and back.
November	Arts and Crafts Show.
December	Christmas Parade and festivities at Old Fort Stockton including breakfast with Santa.

Lajitas On The Rio Grande
Elevation: 2,440 feet   Population: 95

History

The age-old crossing of the Rio Grande in South Brewster County was called Lajitas (flagstones) by the Spanish because of the flat, limestone rocks that formed the riverbed and allowed easy passage for horses and carts. The river also broadens at this point, and divides into two channels, making the passage even easier.

In the nineteenth century, this ford was known both as San Carlos Crossing and Comanche Crossing. San Carlos was the pre-Revolutionary name for the small town at the end of a bumpy road 18 miles south of here. The Comanche who passed through here on their annual raids into Mexico seeking livestock and hostages had also used the crossing in earlier years.

By the late 1800s the area was relatively peaceful. Anglo ranchers, farmers, and mining prospectors established themselves along the Rio Grande. At the turn of the century, H. W. McGuirk bought land at present-day Lajitas, farmed cotton, opened a store and saloon, and built the original church.

Around 1916, the Mexican Revolution started to spill over into U.S. territory. Because of Mexican raids into Columbus, New Mexico and Glenn Springs, Texas in that year, U.S. troops were stationed along the border. A cavalry post was established at Lajitas, and the community prospered.

After the soldiers left, Lajitas settled back into being a trading community of both legal and illegal goods, which crossed in both directions. Lajitas Trading Post became the place to meet and drink as well as a source of provisions. This situation lasted about 50 years.

In the late 70s, a Houston realtor, Walter Mischer, began buying land around Lajitas. In 1976 he started construction of a resort, intended to be the "Palm Springs of West Texas." While some buildings, including the church and the cavalry post, were accurately restored, the main structure had a false front facade complete with boardwalk to give a Wild West image suitable for a movie backdrop.

With a golf course, swimming pool, tennis courts, RV Park, saloon, and restaurant, as well as over 90 rooms, Lajitas was the only full-service resort for a very long distance. But somehow, despite fly-ins by celebrities, golf tournaments, and special events designed to fill the resort's beds, Lajitas never reached the exclusive level of Palm Springs. Tour buses and Elderhostel groups accounted for much of its business.

In 2000, Austin businessman Steve Smith bought the property and started with vigor to expand and upgrade the resort, intent on lifting it to a new level of sophistication. Initial plans to refurbish all accommodations, improve the café menu, add a first class restaurant, transform the golf course to championship level, move and expand the RV Park, and relocate and extend the runway were all underway shortly after the purchase. The vision for Lajitas did not stop there. Phase II included the construction of a health spa, the building of housing to lease or sell, the addition of a second golf course, as well as expanding the central hotel and shopping complex along the boardwalk.

The anticipated visitors did not arrive and, after having spent $100 million, Smith's company went into bankruptcy in 2007. The property was purchased for $13.5 million by Dallas businessman Kelcy L.Warren who signed a long-term lease with a management company,

Lajitas Resort

to run the property. The new company took immediate steps to promote a more affordable, less exclusive Lajitas and greatly reduced prices for rooms, meals and other services. This move was gaining some headway when the floods of September 2008 swept down the Rio Grande and destroyed the golf course. At huge expense, part of the old course was raised above the flood plain by 25 feet, and a new section carved out of the desert at higher elevation.

Information

The Brewster County Tourism Council handles marketing for the region. Box 335, Terlingua, TX 79852. www.visitbigbend.com.

The Big Bend Chamber of Commerce represents Lajitas and four other communities in South Brewster County. www.bigbendchamberof commerce.com.

Lajitas Resort	
Lajitas Resort HC 70, Box 400 Terlingua, TX 79852	Phone: 877-525-4827 432--424-5000 www.lajitas.com

Where To Stay—Hotel/Motel

There are 103 rooms/suites at the Resort.

Badlands Rooms—Located above the Boardwalk, these 15 rooms are a reminder of saloon days gone by. $149.

La Cuesta Rooms—Hacienda-style decor plus accomodations make these 12 rooms comfortable and quiet. From $159.

Cavalry Post Rooms—26 individually decorated rooms, featuring Cow-boy Chic, Victorian, and Hacienda themes. Doubles starting at $169.

Officers' Quarters Rooms—Adobe-built rooms with patio, over-looking the golf course, with king size or two queen size beds. Double rooms from $179.

Boardwalk Suites and Condos—Directly across from the original boardwalk, these brand new rooms are plushly decorated, with jacuzzi and fireplace. 14 rooms with king beds, 4 with queen beds, Suites $431.

Condos $680. Note: Rates will vary with hotel occupancy. Rates over Christmas are higher. Additional cottage accommodation ("Casitas") is also available. Special rates on specific days (e.g., July 4, Father's Day) will be announced during the year.

RV Park

At the Maverick Ranch— Adjacent to the resort. $29/night for full hook up. 432-424-5000. 60 pull-through sites; the fee includes use of the pool, exercise room, laundromat and deluxe showers.

Where To Eat

Candelilla Café—Southwestern decor and comfortable seating, with fine views across the golf course. Open for breakfast, lunch and dinner. Breakfast: 7:00–11:00; Lunch: 11:00–2:00; Dinner: 5:00–10:00.

Chef Blas Gonzales cooks with 20 years of experience and uses his family heritage (including a 100-year old Mole recipe from his grandmother) as well as green chilies to add flavor to his Mexican dishes. Prices go from the five napkin burger ($7.95) to Poblano Tacos ($8.95) to 19 different entrees ($9.50–$24.00). 432-424-5030.

Where to Drink

Thirsty Goat Saloon—Full bar. Open 4–12, Monday–Friday; 12–12, Saturday–Sunday. Live music weekly in the summer, more frequently during the winter months.

Shopping On The Boardwalk

Christina's World—Fine jewelry, local and global folk art, collectible pottery. 432-424-3250.

Red Rock Outfitters—Outdoor apparel, gear, sunglasses, shoes. Booking office for local tours, either river trips run by Far Flung Outdoor Center or other trips, operated by Lajitas Resort, described under Tours below. 432-424-5170.

What To Do

Swimming—Kidney-shaped pool in the La Cuesta courtyard with beautiful flowering vines and useful shade areas. There is a second pool at the Maverick Ranch RV Park, good for lap swimming.

Golf—Black Jack's Crossing at Lajitas is the name of the new 18-hole course. The course architects have literally moved mountains to create a unique desert golf course, adjacent to the Rio Grande, with the mountains of Mexico as a backdrop. This course will be the corner stone of the new Lajitas. Fees and a full description of the facilities unavailable at time of writing.

Museum—The Longhorn Museum of over 800 mounted horns is housed is the former Lajitas Trading Post. Known as the Yates Collection from the name of the ranching family in Iraan, Texas which amassed this inventory, the largest in the world. The story of the iconic Texas Longhorn, the breed which originated in Spain and arrived in Mexico in 1521, is contained in these hundreds of mounted horns, including some head mounts and full body mounts. There are no regular hours of opening. In view of the value of this unique collection, resort personnel open up the collection at guests' request. Enquire at the front desk.

Agave Spa—The Spa at Lajitas. Call 432-424-5146. The 1500 square foot spa contains two massage rooms, a wet room and facial room.Treatments include Body Bliss, Massage treatments and energy work, three types of massage (from $96 for 50 minutes); Skin Sensations with scrubs and muds; Happy Face treatments; to Fabulous Feet, soaking and soothing of the soles ($25 for 30 minutes).

Lajitas Resort Art Workshops—(by appointment). A wide range of learning workshops such as Learn about Milagros and try your hand at making one, Flora and fauna charcoal rubbings, and Paper clay beads and jewelry making. For more information, call the front desk 432-424-5000.

Equestrian Activities—Rides by the hour, following a route which goes up Comanche Creek and around Mesa de Anguila with views of Mexico in the background. $45/person. Also, half-day, Sunset and Sunrise Trail Rides and Buena Suerte overnight (3 ½ hour ride) which includes a campfire dinner cooked on an open fire. Cots, sleeping bags and sleep mats are provided. Minimum four persons. $275/person.

Cowboy Action Shoot & Five Stand Skeet Shoot—Using live ammunition, minimum age requirement is 16 years, and there are clothing requirements. $80 per person.

Hunting at Palo Amarillo—(September–February, during Hunting Season). 34 miles from Lajitas on 640 acres of natural beauty within the Big Bend Ranch State Park. Morning or Afternoon Dove or Quail Hunt including transportation, guide, gun rental, beverages and breakfast or dinner: $275. Full day $500.

Tours

Guided ATV Tours—Visit 26,000 acres with 32 historic sites within minutes of the resort. Daily trips: 2-hours (Driver $135, Rider $70); 4-hours (Driver $270. Rider $70). Half-day: Driver $300, Rider $75). Lunch is included. 424-371-2489.

Bike Tours—(operated by Desert Sports).
Lajitas Short Ride—A 2-hour ride with a choice of routes.
Short ride without bike rental $90.
Short ride with bike rental $120.

Lajitas Long Ride—(Seasonal). A 4-6 hour ride which could appeal to an advanced beginner or an expert, with the route customized by Desert Sports to suit your needs.
Without bike Rental $108.
With bike Rental $138.

Big Bend National Park—All day ride. 8:30–4:30, lunch included. Route planned in advance to meet your needs. $180 (without bike rental), $210 (with rental).

Bike Rental for the Day—$36 per day. Drop Off and Pick Up fee, $50.

Fossil Tours—Take an hour of your time to see something from a time when water was all you saw in a now seemingly waterless desert. Check out the stomach contents of a mosasaur and the fossil of a 30' duckbill dinosaur. Your guide at the Mosasaur Museum (6 miles distant) will give you a museum tour, then will hike with you half a mile to a site where there is current digging for marine fossils. Two person minimum. $25 for up to 5 persons. 432-424-3447 / 432-371-2445.

Lajitas Stables — Now moved to 3 miles west on FM 170. Established in Lajitas in 1986, and now in Study Butte and Fort Davis, Lajitas Stables offers a traditional way to appreciate the majestic scenery. Horses can go where motor vehicles cannot, and with less exertion for the rider than on foot. Guided horseback rides range from hourly to daily, with horseback/rafting combinations and longer trips into Old Mexico also available. Linda Walker and her experienced staff can provide anything from a leisurely sunset trip on the back of a gently horse, to an energetic adventure ride of 4–5 days across the Rio Grande into Chihuahua State. For more information call 888-508-7667, or 432-424-3238, or visit their website at www.lajitasstables.com.

Barton Warnock Environmental Education Center—Located 1 mile east of the resort, the Center offers 2.5 acres of Desert Gardens and an interpretive display which covers the history, geology and natural wonders of the region. A must-see activity. See page 45. 432-424-3327.

Crossing into Mexico — Before May 2000, the crossing to Paso Lajitas, Chihuahua was the busiest of all four unofficial border crossings in the Big Bend area. A row-boat ferried visitors to and fro for $2 round trip. Since then, anyone crossing over to the Mexican side is required to re-enter the U.S. at Presidio or any other authorized port of entry. The population of Paso Lajitas, deprived of tourist income, has-plummeted.

Marathon

Altitude 4,040 feet   Population 458

Alfred Gage
1860–1927

The Early Days

"1882. He had invested all his money in a hundred head of cattle, which he realized were being sold at a bargain. There followed the severest winter the oldest inhabitant could remember. A blizzard raged for a whole week. When the roaring wind died down and the snow stopped falling, Alfred's herd of cattle, the pride of his life and his complete fortune, had totally vanished.

"For weeks he rode about forlornly searching for them, but was able to find only a few skeleton cows that had been too weak to stray far, but that were too hardy to die. As soon as it showed signs of spring, Alfred borrowed enough money to buy a covered wagon and some mules, and he set out to comb the plains for his lost possessions.

"All summer he traveled, covering hundreds of miles and inspecting every four-footed creature he saw. For days he would see no resemblance of the "//" (Lightning) brand he so eagerly sought, then he would find several cows in one herd, gather them together and move on. After working the entire summer, he had recovered fifty head, half of the original herd. He returned to Murphyville, which was now called Alpine, to find his family's fortunes in a perilous state.

"From this inauspicious start, Alfred Gage went on to become the dominant rancher of the area, his ranch extending to 384,000 acres. In 1926 he built the Gage Hotel which today is the preeminent hotel in the region."

From The Gage Family History

History

Marathon, the second largest town in Brewster County, enjoys a strategic location at the intersection of US 90 and US 385. It is the last stop for services for the majority of visitors to the Big Bend National Park.

Today's visitor, passing crumbling adobe houses and an antique car junk lot, might be excused from thinking the unincorporated township is on its last legs. Not so. Life is coming back to Marathon, but in a different way than before. Recent years have seen a wave of newcomers, mostly artists, retirees, and business entrepreneurs seeking to start tourism services. This modern transformation is breathing new life back into Marathon in a much different way than the raw energy of the early decades of the century when ranching boomed, six passenger trains stopped daily, and wagon loads of ore arrived from the Mexican border.

Cattle and the railroad arrived about the same time (1880s) and complemented each other. These two industries and mining, which started twenty years later, are the reason for Marathon's population growth, which peaked in the twenties and thirties at around 1,000 inhabitants. The actual date of the founding of Marathon was 1882 when Albion Shepard, a surveyor for the railroad with the responsibility for naming watering stops, called the place Marathon. He had previously been a sea captain, and the broad landscape of the Marathon basin, surrounded by mountains, reminded him of Marathon, Greece.

Marathon's initial prosperity was due to its location as a shipping point for the Brewster County cattle herds, as well as being the closest railroad loading point for the minerals (lead, zinc, silver, mercury, and fluorite) mined along the Mexican border. In the early days, wagon trains, some with up to 200 wagons each pulled by teams of 10 or more mules, would arrive with lead from the mine at Boquillas (Mexico). In addition, a rubber plant was set up in 1909 to process the local guayule plant. It operated on and off until 1926, when the supply of guayule was exhausted. The metal trade declined after World War II, but hung on until the sixties when the mine at La Linda, which produced fluorspar (for refrigerants) closed down. Cattle were all that remained, but the cattle industry had also suffered a long-term decline.

Following the introduction in 1878 of 100 Hereford cattle, and the arrival in the same year of Alfred Gage, Marathon's most prominent industry became cattle raising. The pastures were lush with waist-high grass, and the demand for beef in the big cities increased steadily. The best-known rancher was Alfred Gage, a banker from San Antonio, whose ranch extended to 600 sections (384,000 acres). From the high prices during World War I to the crippling drought of the fifties, cattle raising and the lifestyle that surrounded it dominated the life of Marathon and Brewster County in good times and bad for one hundred years.

By the time Marathon was established, the Indian threat, which elsewhere in the region had been the reason for the establishment of military forts, had largely evaporated. In 1879, the federal authorities leased some land locally and established a fort five miles south of Marathon near Peña Colorado Springs. But the Comanche raiding parties, which for years had cut like a knife through the territory, had now subsided and the fort saw little activity. Later, during the Mexican Revolution in 1915, Marathon became the center of military activity, but actual engagements occurred closer to the border.

There was plenty of activity in Marathon in those days without Indian raids or Mexican revolutionaries. Ranching flourished and the transshipment of minerals continued. Visitors and residents could visit the likes of Lemons' Elite Saloon or eat at the Greasy Spoon Cafe, play miniature golf, patronize the skating rink, or go to the movies. The economic prosperity fluctuated somewhat from year to year, but continued robustly until the last quarter of the century by which time the mines had largely closed down and the cattle industry was in serious decline. The population fell by 25%.

In the last few years of the twentieth century a new wave of immigrants and a new source of income had come to Marathon and the region. The

The Gage Hotel

immigrants were newcomers from elsewhere in Texas, from out-of-state or overseas. Some are artists who have picked on the remoteness and beauty of the region to stimulate their creativity. Some work two jobs in the service sector to make a living. The new source of income is the tourists heading for the Big Bend National Park whose annual visitation ranges from 350,000–400,000. The result is that Marathon has acquired a new look. Artists' galleries are replacing feed stores and tourist services are springing up to cater to visitors. Outside the dusty town, the land-scape itself remains much the same, if somewhat drier, as when Captain Shepard arrived: a wide vista of desert rangeland framed by mountains.

Access/Orientation/Information

US 90 runs east/west through Marathon and is intersected by US 385 connecting Fort Stockton on I-10 (58 miles), which heads south to the Big Bend National Park (69 miles to park headquarters).

The vast majority of visitors arrive by car directly from Texas cities to the east. Mileage from Dallas is 474, from Houston 550, from San Antonio (via I-10) is 368, and from Austin 393 miles.

The Marathon Chamber of Commerce has no office, but deals with mail and phone inquiries. Free publications are available at Front Street Books. The Chamber publishes two pamphlets: *Marathon, Texas, Where the Big Bend Begins;* and *Marathon, Texas, A Walking Tour.* For general information about Marathon, check www.marathontexas.net.

Marathon Chamber of Commerce	
Front Street Books P. O. Box 163 Marathon, TX 79842	Phone: 432-386-4516 www.marathontexas.net

Public Transportation

Fly/Drive—Midland Airport (146 miles) has about 30 flights a day in and out, including non-stops to Dallas and Houston. Service is by Southwest, American Airlines, and Continental Airlines.

Public Transportation—The nearest train and bus stations are in Alpine.

Car Rental—The nearest car rental agency is in Alpine (30 miles). 432-837-3463 or 800-894-3463.

Where To Stay—Hotel/Motel

Gage Hotel—Built in 1927 by rancher Alfred Gage, this hotel has become a destination objective and no article on the Big Bend area is complete without reference to this finely restored historical landmark, stuffed with antiques (Western, Indian, Mexican). A handsome new section, Los Portales (The Porches), was opened in 1993 doubling the number of rooms to 37. Here, as in the old building, careful attention has been paid to the decor: Mexican tiles in the bathrooms, hundred-year old covers for the beds, and numerous artifacts on the walls. Each room opens on a shaded courtyard with a pool immediately adjacent.

By 1920, Alfred Gage, a Vermont native who made a banking fortune in San Antonio, was making frequent trips to his 384,000-acre ranch near Marathon. To provide accommodation for himself and the purchasers of his cattle he decided a build a simple, but substantial, brick house. The original part of the hotel was designed by the regional architectural firm of Trost & Trost, known for other work in the area such as the El Paisano Hotel in Marfa and the Holland Hotel in Alpine.

Gage did not live long enough to make much use of his new home since he died the year after it was completed. In later years, attempts were made to turn the building into a museum and it was not until 1978, when Houstonian J.P. Bryan and his wife Mary Jon bought the property that thorough restoration was started.

What has been achieved is a museum-type recreation of a frontier hotel, with saddles, chaps, and ropes prominently on display in the lobby of the old section together with Native American fishnets, pottery, and baskets. Such is the careful attention given to the antiques and artifacts —many dating back two hundred years—that a complete list is available at the front desk specifying forty-three items in the old building as well as eight types of plants. Each bedroom has a different character, often highlighted by a fine old piece of furniture with a rich patina achieved by years of careful polishing.

The sixteen rooms in the historic building each have their own name. They rent from $90, with bath down the hall, to $142, with en suite bath. High season rates 10% more. The wood furniture, the natural fiber of the bedspreads, and the numerous artifacts all give a sense of history in a simple, stylish manner. There are no phones or TV's in the rooms. The only TVs are in the bar of the old part of the hotel and in the TV room. Hotel guests are offered a free Continental breakfast in the Reposa Room, 7–10 A.M. They may also enjoy the heated swimming pool, adjacent to Los Portales, and the Fitness Center which is directly across the railroad tracks

Los Portales, immediately next door to the historic building, provides 20 rooms and suites. All have a private bath, and some have open fireplaces. Rates are $183 without fireplace, $202 with, and $253 for the owner's suite. Prices are higher during weekends, and seasonally. A great deal of thought has been given these rooms regarding decor and comfort. The buildings are made out of adobe brick, the ceiling beams are ponderosa pine, and the sticks (latillas) between the beams are made of local sotol plants. The entrance doors are from hand carved mesquite wood and no two are alike. Outside in the courtyard the atmosphere is equally soothing. The shade trees cast shadows over the lawn and the water trickling from the fountain provides a musical backdrop.

The Wilson House and the Celaya House are available for families or larger groups. The Wilson House has a king size bed and a loft with twin beds, and rents for $350/night. The Celaya House has two bedrooms and one bath, and rents for $320/night. Both houses have a full kitchen. The Casa de Jardín ($320/night) features 1 king and 1 twin day bed. Rates are higher on weekends and seasonally.

The Gage Hotel has long been popular with folks in Midland/Odessa for weddings and other functions, and is regularly booked up well in advance for key periods such as Spring Break and Thanksgiving/Christmas. Make sure to book early.

Gage Hotel	
Gage Hotel US 90, Box 46 Marathon, TX 79842	Phone: 800-884-4243 or 432-386-4205 www.gagehotel.com

Marathon Motel—One half mile west of town, this upgraded establishment offers four renovated duplex cabins, each with two full-size beds, and two rooms with one full-size bed—a total of 10 rooms, plus 1 fully furnished apartment for up to 4 persons. Built in the 1940s, the motel was featured in the 1984 movie *Paris, Texas*. The cabins are set back from the highway on 10 acres, enjoying fine views of the desert and the Glass Mountains to the west, appealing to astronomers and birders.

The owner, Danny Self, greets guests with a broad smile, like a man who enjoys his work. Rates are $65 for one person, to $110 for up to 4 persons (plus tax). Recent improvements to the courtyard and landscaping have enhanced the property, which is popular for functions catered from the courtyard café. Until general cell phone reception arrives in Marathon, one reliable spot is on top of a rock, next to a wagon in the motel courtyard! There is wireless internet and even a broadcasting studio (local cable TV, channels 98 and 6, and radio). Look to see if the pleasant Courtyard Café has reopened.

Marathon Motel	
Marathon Motel US 90 West Marathon, TX 79842	Phone: 432-386-4241 www.marathonmotel.com

Marathon Motel

Where To Stay

Captain Shepard's Inn—This handsome two-story inn, opened in 1994, is located close to, and is managed by, the Gage Hotel. Captain Shepard who established the first post office in Marathon as well as giving the town its name built the building in 1890. As with the Gage Hotel, the furnishings here are historic, stylish, and appropriate. The downstairs common rooms (one with TV) exude an air of part western museum, part Texas Monthly fashion ads. The simple feel to the rooms seems totally appropriate given the landscape and climate outside. Original sash windows and long leaf yellow pine wood are complemented by careful, seamless restoration work.

Of the five guest rooms, the favorite is the upstairs room (#2) looking northwest to the Glass Mountains. Others book the room immediately below (#1), which originally was the kitchen of the private home, and which has a Jacuzzi. Bed configuration and size vary. Room rates (plus tax): $98, Room #1 with jacuzzi and king bed: $120.

Behind the main building is the Carriage House. This has been converted to form two bedrooms, with one bathroom, a sitting room with fireplace, and a kitchenette. Rates are $140 for up to four persons, and $10 for each additional adult, plus tax. For reservations: 866-386-4241, 432-386-4241, www.captainshepardsinn.com.

Eve's Garden—Avenue C and North 3rd. A straw bale Santa Fe-style dwelling featuring a kiva fireplace, banco seating, seven foot windows, and ponderosa ceiling with bedrooms adjacent. This extraordinary project impresses with its ecological message, convincingly articulated by hosts Kate Thayer and Clyde Curry through the organic garden, grape arbor and greenhouse. Constantly expanding, accommodations now provide for up to 20 persons in 7 rooms: The Garden Room, "classical vaults, arches and domes, with a feeling of old Mexico", $195 for two (king size bed); The Lotus Suite, two adjoining bedrooms (one queen bed, one full-size), stained glass windows, $195; The Orchard Room, spacious and color-filled, with two queen beds, $165 plus $25 for each additional adult. Also, The Boquillas and The Ocotillo rooms —all built with papercrete. A delicious, full breakfast is served. 432-386-4165. www.evesgarden.org.

Adobe Rose Inn— occupies a restored 100-year old adobe house just south of the railroad tracks. It offers guests 3 upstairs rooms with balcony access, an additional room that opens on to a spacious courtyard, and a detached room with two double beds. The rooms carry names like Ellen's Room which has a four-poster queen size bed ($135). Janet's, Henry's and Lolas's Rooms are all different in style and bed configuration. Rates from $12 for two persons. www.theadoberoseinn.com 888-452-3623, 432-386-4564.

Where To Stay—Cottage/House Rentals

Adobe Hacienda Lodges—Consists of four adobe cottages around town in addition to the old Monroe Payne House duplex. All have been recently restored with care and style. Each cottage features Talavera and Saltillo tile, cowskins, and Mexican fabrics. Each has a TV, refrigerator, washer and dryer, a comfortable porch, and a pleasant yard. Bed configuration varies in each unit. The quiet, friendly neighborhood still has the feel of a Mexican village. Rates from $98 per night for two persons, each additional person $10, children free. Weekly rate: $490. For more information and booking call 866-386-4241, 432-386-4241, www.chisosgallery.com.

Casa la Vista— A new property in the northwest corner of Marathon, set in 8 acres. Fine views towards the Glass Mountains, and also with a pond in the garden which attracts wildlife. Tasteful décor with a Mexican feel, featuring two bedrooms, one bath, and full kitchen. Also, a queen sleeper sofa, and a day bed. Sleeps up to 7. $275/night, with two-night minimum. 432-386-2222.

La Casita Grande—Spacious property with four bedrooms and two bathrooms. King or queen size beds. Large living room, with TV and fireplace. Also a library. Backyard with grill. From $250-$450/night. Two night minimum. Cleaning fee $75. www.lacasitagrande.com. 432-386-4439.

"The Animal House"—At corner of NW 5th and Avenue F. So called because the proceeds go to the local Humane Society. Two bedroom house surrounded by shade trees. $165/night, tax included, with two-night minimum. http://animalhouse.marathontexasrentals.com. 432-386-4435.

La Esmeralda—On the edge of town set on one acre. A 100-year old railroad house, with two bedrooms, one bath. Porch and back yard with firepit. $195/night with two night minimum. $60 cleaning fee. www.vrbo.com./145463. 858-395-3850, 858-755-8840.

Frankie's Hideaway—503 S. Lee Street. Two-bed, one bath. King bed plus two twin beds. Quiet. $195/night, two night minimum. $60 cleaning charge. $20 per person extra, if more than two persons. www.frankies-hideaway.com.

Where To Stay—Hostel

La Loma del Chivo—Hostel-style accommodation on the southwest corner of town. Six paper crete buildings, some still being completed, offer alternative rural accom-modation and the chance to meet out-of-the-ordinary travelers. Lounge on the two decks, eat bread baked in the Mexican oven. The largest hostel building sleeps 10, with toilet and shower. $15/night. Cross-country cyclists free. www.lalomadelchivo.net. 432-386-2116.

Where To Stay—RV Parks

Marathon Motel, RV Park—West U.S. 90. 22 sites. Renovated southwest-style bathrooms, kitchen, barbecue pit, courtyard with flower-ing native plants, and a fountain. $25/night, Tent camping $10/night for two persons. 432-386-4241.

Local Services

Propane—Now available in Marathon at Mustang Propane. 432-386-4422.

Wrecker Service—Sixto's Shell Service Station: 432-386-4551. Charges: $3.50/mile.

Marathon Health Clinic—Open all day Monday and Thursday. Efficient and friendly. 432-386-4316.

Where To Drink

White Buffalo Bar—At Café Cenizo in The Gage hotel. Western décor with a huge white buffalo head which dominates the bar, known for its margaritas. 432-386-4434.

Famous Burro—Well-stocked, full bar, favored by locals, right at the downtown cross roads. New and fun. Open Wednesday–Sunday, 5–midnight. 432-386-4100.

Oasis Bar—West side of town. Wine and beer. Pool table. Thurs-day–Sunday 6–midnight. 432-386-4521.

Where To Eat

Café Cenizo—Enter via a courtyard, where you can also eat, then turn left for the restaurant or go straight ahead for the White Buffalo Bar. The restful wood paneled restaurant comprises three rooms decorated western-style. The wait staff is youthful and proficient (perhaps students at Alpine's Sul Ross State University). A long and full menu comprises 9 starters, 9 entrees and 7 desserts The rich, comprehensive menu of chef Brandon Martin and his sous chefs, has a Southwestern orientation (bison) with Continental fusion (confit of duck). On a recent visit the writer tried an avocado soup, rack of lamb and dessert called Johnny Cakes a la Mode (Ginger ice Cream, caramelized apples). The wine list is extensive (Price range $60+). Open 6–9 P.M. Monday–Thursday, 6–10 P.M., Friday and Saturday. 432-386-4437, 432-386-4205.

The Famous Burro—A low key place to eat or drink (full bar) popular with locals as much as visitors. The well priced menu reflects country cooking with a short and varied selection (recently, New York strip steak, Southwest grilled chicken ($11.50), Cabbage rolls, and a Vegetarian Quiche plate ($10), using seasonal produce from their garden. Sit inside (observe the art work) or out. The atmosphere is bistro, the attentive staff pulling together under owner/manager Neil Chavigny's keen eye. A beer garden will open soon. Occasional live music by the incomparable Alpine Mountaineers and other local groups. Open for dinner, Wednesday–Saturday 6–9 P.M., bar Wednesday–Sunday 5–midnight, with light food on Sundays. www.famousburro.com. 432-386-4100.

Oasis Café—Open Monday–Thursday, 11:30–2:00 and 5:30–8:00. A colorful and clean cafe with a long choice of Mexican dishes and sandwiches. The popular Enchilada Plate costs $6.65, Ruben's burger $7.55 and Deluxe Nachos $5.95. The Oasis Bar is adjacent. 432-386-4521

Shirley's Burnt Biscuit—Next to the post office. Although Shirley has now retired, her successor has kept her name and formula, and has expanded the premises and the menu, specifically with hot food. Visitors can choose from kolaches ($3.99), croissant with sausage, egg and cheese, biscuits and gravy, sausage biscuits (best sellers) and burritos. There is a working coffee roaster, espresso machine and expanded seating. All of this is in addition to Shirley's menu of fried pies, sweet rolls, donuts, cookies and bread. The bakery opens six days a week 5:30 –1:00 P.M. (from 7 A.M. on Saturday) 432-386-9020, 432-386-4008.

El Peppercorn Café— (Old Marathon Coffee Shop). Just west of The Gage. Internet Café on Hwy 90 West. This new place has been getting good reviews from local patrons. Traditional Mexican cuisine: breakfast migas ($7.25) and fish tacos ($8.95) with European influence (White Bean and Hummus plate). Quality coffee, espresso and the like. Thursday–Sunday 7–2 P.M., on Monday til 12 noon. Sit inside or out. Wi-Fi. 432-386-4151. www.chloepeppercorn.com.

Johnnie B's—Next to The Gage. Old fashioned counter with floats, shakes and sodas. Burgers, hot dogs, salads, and ice cream. Table seating also. Lemonade for $1.75 and burgers from $3.85 show modest pricing. Nice atmosphere. Monday–Sunday 7–10:30, 11:30–3:00. 432-386-4233.

French Company Grocer—206 N. Avenue D. Fresh-made sandwiches and salads to go, cookies and coffee. Open 7:30 A.M.–9:00 P.M. 432-386-4522. www.frenchcogrocer.com.

What To Do/Where To Go

Museum—3rd Street N. and Avenue E. Housed in a one-room adobe schoolhouse (built, 1888), this new volunteer-staffed museum is open Saturday and Sunday. Displays include artifacts of railroading, ranching, and surveying, also period domestic furniture and trappings. To gain access at other times, ask at for a key at Front Street Books.

Walking Tour—Pick up the Chamber's walking tour pamphlet from the Gage or one of the stores and follow your nose to those attractions that appeal to you. Try to find the location of the old windmill that miscreants were handcuffed to before the jail was built. There is not much sign today of the importance of the railroad. The tracks are still in place—three passenger trains pass through weekly in each direction, but none stop. Around 30 freight trains pass through daily. Thirteen points of interest are listed in the pamphlet as well 46 businesses.

What To Do/Where To Go—Health Club

Desert Moon Spa—At the Gage Hotel. "An oasis for the mind, body, and soul." This small spa has two treatment rooms and a much-needed steam room. Desert Moon offers massage therapy, facials, body treatments as well as extensive day packages, all in a beautifully appointed setting. Guests may unwind in the Spa's hydrating Eucalyptus Room. Inquire at Gage reception desk. 432-386-4205.

Gage Fitness—In the Ritchie Building across the tracks from the Gage Hotel. Open free to hotel guests. Open 7–10. Check-in at the Gage reception desk.

What To Do/Where To Go—Desert Gardens

Gage Gardens—Across the tracks, one block east. A quarter-mile trail, orchard, small vineyard, shade trees and seating in 7 artfully landscaped acres, currently being expanded The vegetable garden provides much of the produce for Café Cenizo. Fire pit, and area for receptions/weddings. 432-386-4224.

Pearl Street & Kentucky Avenue Gardens—South 5th Street & Avenue E. A private garden designed with Chihuahuan Desert plants showcasing their beauty, low maintenance, and water use. Stroll the paths, watch the butterflies and birds. Plants for sale. Landscape consultation and design. By appointment, 432-386-4558. Also home to Bodacious Grub, a personal chef service.

What To Do/Where To Go—Galleries/Shopping

Mary Baxter Gallery—Hwy 90 east, 2 blocks from the Gage. A large building with a jackrabbit on the front. Mary Baxter's oil paintings of Big Bend landscapes dominate the space, shared by some whimsical criters sculptured in wire. From her days on a ranch, Baxter captures the subtle beauty of the terrain, producing quiet, soft images on canvas. Hours of opening are irregular since she is often away painting. Call ahead or stop by and follow the instructions in the notebook. 432-386-4041, 432-386-4041. www.baxtergallery.com.

Klepper Gallery—105 N. Avenue D, is owned by writer and artist E. Dan Klepper. He opened this gallery to showcase his large cinematic images of Texas and the natural world. Printed on canvas and paper, and based on photographs, Klepper's artworks profile unusual locations and capture dramatic natural phenomena in full, saturated color. Usually open on the weekends, including Friday afternoons and all day Saturdays and Sundays. www.edanklepper.com. 432-386-4107.

Evans Gallery—4 doors east of the Gage Hotel. The longest established gallery in the Big Bend area, presenting the photographs of James H. Evans. His work is held in major museums and collections nationally. Author of *Big Bend Pictures* (black and white photographs of Big Bend, which represent 14 years of his work here, James has lived and worked in Marathon since 1988, photographing the landscape and people of Big Bend, and is always pushing the creative edge of his work. Featured also are local artists Paul Wiggins (metal work jewelry and belts) and Mimi Litschauer (Marathon painter of 10 years). Open most of the time. If the door is locked, a note on the door will tell you what to do. 432-386-4366. www.jameshevans.com.

The French Company Grocer—206 N. Avenue D. Named after the first general store in Marathon with that "general store" charm. Owner Marci Roberts carries a little bit of everything: staple foods natural foods, fresh fruits/vegetables, fresh-made sandwiches and salads, breakfast burritos, meats and fish, camping stuff, picnic supplies, toiletries, hardware and toys. Sit on the porch with a sandwich, and your computer (Wi-Fi)–the only place to grab a bite in the afternoon. Open 'til 9 P.M. Turn north at the bank. 432-386-4522. www.frenchcogrocer.com.

Pitaya Verde—Three doors east of the Gage Hotel. Fine western wear and boots for men and women. Also handcrafted accessories including belts, buckles and earrings. www.pitayaverde.com 303-408-3122.

Front Street Books—Adjacent to the Gage Hotel. Attractive, well-stocked store, with all the local books you could want, as well as some you might be surprised to find in a village of 458 people. Newspapers, cards, free pamphlets from the Chamber of Commerce, and tourism information are willingly given. Professional, knowledgeable, and friendly. 432-386-4249. www.fsbooks.com.

Purple Sage—Hwy 90 East. Small antique items, glassware, and collectibles incorporating flower arrangements. 40 years of collecting by Jacquelin and Don Boyd, now the items are for sale. Tea pot and oil lamp collection. And a live Pomeranian dog called Miss Charlie. 432-386-4008.

Shaman Springs Gallery—103 E. Hwy 90. Latin American home decor as sell as sculpture and design work. 432-386-4557. www.shamanspringsgallery.com.

What To Do—Excursions

The Post—Cross the tracks downtown, with the new divider barrier, and continue straight for five miles south of town, passing Evans Gallery on your left, brings you to the setting of Fort Pena Colorado, established in 1879 to deal with the Comanches. The name comes from the colored cliffs that overlook the spring-fed watering hole. Some of the foundation and parts of the original buildings may still be seen just north of the post. The post was abandoned in 1893, the last active fort in the Big Bend country. Today it is used by the locals for events such as the annual July 4th dance, as well as weddings and other celebrations. Have a picnic beneath the towering trees, or take out your binoculars to study the many desert birds that pause for refreshment. Swimming is possible, but at your own risk.

Los Caballos—Ten miles south of town on US 385, a historical marker explains Los Caballos, a rare spectacle of scalloped ridges crowning mountains that represent vastly diverse eras of geologic history. The Ouachita Uplift, 300 million years ago, created these and other US ranges–the Ouachitas, Smokies and Appalachians. Forty to 60 million years ago, the geologic movement that formed the Rocky Mountains also 'folded' the Marathon-area mountain ridges crosswise, resulting in wavy layers reminiscent of bucking horses, or *caballos*. Geologists point to these as a fusion of young and old mountains, the Appalachians bumping into the Rockies, seen nowhere else in North America.

Marathon Calendar Of Selected Events

May—Quilt Show. Exhibit of handcrafted quilts, held on the second Saturday of the month.

July—Dance and Cook Off at The Post. On the Saturday closest to July 4th there is a annual outdoor dance at The Post, 5 miles south of town. Local musician-turned-Nashville star Craig Carter and his band traditionally play on this date. This is the place to celebrate with the locals.

September—West Fest. Last Saturday of the month. Cabrito cook-off judged on taste and showmanship. Teams come from all over the region.

October—Marathon to Marathon. The 26.2 mile course starts just outside Alpine and follows US 90 east to Marathon.

November—Cowboy Social and Silent Auction.

December—Fiesta de Noche Buena. First Saturday of the month. Much smaller than Alpine's Gallery Night, but making up for the crowds with more charm and space to move. Every place in town is open and the high desert setting is ideal for browsing, chatting, snacking and buying some excellent art and craft work at non-Houston prices.

Marfa

Elevation: 4,688 feet   Population 1,862

Milton Faver
(1822–1899)

Milton Faver (*Don Melitón*), the first cattle baron of Presidio County, fled the USA as a young man following a duel in St. Louis that he left believing he had killed his opponent. He settled in Chihuahua, married a Mexican woman, and became established in the freighting business along the Chihuahua Trail. After opening a general store in Ojinaga in 1857, he moved north and settled near the Chinati Mountains, buying small tracts of land around three springs, Cibolo, Cienega, and La Morita.

From this modest start Faver developed a herd of 20,000 head of cattle, meanwhile fighting off Indian attacks with a small private army of Mexicans. He later secured a contract to supply the military at Fort Davis with beef and homemade peach brandy, made from the fruit in his orchards. He owned only 2,800 acres of land, mixed cattle with sheep, and ran his herd of original Mexican longhorn stock on the free range.

Unconventional even in those times, Faver was a mystery man to many. He preferred the Spanish language and was guarded by Mexicans in uniform. He was short and of slight build with a beard that in his old age fell to his waist. Formally dressed, speaking three or four languages, a cattleman turned brandy distiller, Faver accepted only gold or silver as payment. Autocratic and individualistic, he paid his ranch hands 12 cents a day and meted out his own justice.

Faver made Cibolo his headquarters and built a 100-foot square adobe block compound with circular defense towers at the north and south corners to protect the inhabitants from Indian attacks and walls 3–4 feet thick. El Fortin del Cibolo, meticulously restored, is open to the public today as a guest ranch.

Faver died in 1889 and is buried on the hill above Big Springs Cibolo, the day and hour of his death are marked in Spanish on the headstone. In a region and at a time when characters abounded, there was no one quite the equal of Don Melitón.

History

The town of Marfa came into existence with the arrival of the railroad in 1883. Within a few years Marfa became the county seat of Presidio County, at that time the largest organized county in the USA with 12,000 square miles. A look at the courthouse, built on a grand scale and visible for miles around, gives some idea of the unbounded confidence of those early days before the turn of the 20th century.

With the arrival of the railroad, Marfa became the loading point for the cattle herds grazing on the lush grasses of the Marfa plateau. Those were the glory days when cattle was king. The earliest pioneer and cattle baron on a grand scale was Milton Faver (see above), the bulk of whose herd ran unbranded and wild on the free range. With the fencing of ranch boundaries more order prevailed, although the region as a whole and the life of the cowboy in particular, was unsettled and turbulent.

The Mexican Revolution and the resulting turbulence along Presidio County's southern border marked a new phase in Marfa's history: the arrival of the military. The military garrison of the 1st Cavalry based in Marfa altered the social balance in the county. With the end of the upheavals in Mexico, life became more settled although the garrison remained. By 1930, relations between Mexico and the USA had improved and an International Polo Competition was staged in Marfa between the Mexican Army and a team from the Marfa garrison (which lost). As a social event, with a 67-piece band playing in the background and a grand ball, taking place in the evening, the event was judged "one of the most brilliant social occasions ever to occur in Marfa."

World War II emptied the town of many local men who were called to the army, but an even larger number of newcomers arrived for pilot instruction at the newly established Marfa Air Field. At the same time that the presence of the military was changing the character of the town, other events were changing the structure of society. The 1950s hit movie, *Giant*, filmed near Marfa, touched on racial attitudes in the area. Unrecognized by many at that time, the county was undergoing a change of racial balance. During World War I the fatalities were all Anglos. By the time of the Vietnam War, they were all Hispanics.

The post war period was marked by the drought of the 1950s, which broke the back of the ranching business, leaving only a few of the largest and strongest of the traditional ranches operating. By this time, the mining industry, which had thrived in the southern part of the county, closed down. This happened most noticeably in Shafter, where silver had been mined in quantity for 59 years. The population of Presidio County went into a thirty-year decline from the fifties through the seventies, not stabilizing until the eighties. It numbered around 5,500, of whom 77% were Hispanic.

Towards the end of the 1900s, the first period of transition took place. This was the arrival in 1976 of Donald Judd, an artist from New York who sought the wide-open spaces of West Texas to display his minimalist art. He purchased the old Fort Russell and converted it to a gallery; other artists with unusual artwork were also invited to exhibit. Judd became a major property owner in Marfa and a regular stream of visitors came from all over to view the installation, as the collection is called. In 1998, a symposium at the Chinati Foundation, the entity that continued following Judd's death, drew visitors from across the nation and from overseas. At the same time, the Marfa Lights phenomenon continued to draw attention to Marfa and the region as a whole experienced a steady growth in tourist visitors.

Of the four main population centers in the Big Bend region, Marfa has been the least active until very recently. Its retail economy was moribund and the housing market was depressed. The Border Patrol complex of offices and housing was a major presence, but remained largely self-contained at the edge of town. The main tourist attraction, the Marfa Lights, whose viewing area is eight miles east of town, remained largely unexploited. By 1999 however, a second transition started. New arrivals, mainly from Texas cities to the east and often connected with the art world, began moving in. They bought property and opened retail businesses, many of them art-related. The social composition of the community and the feel of the town began to change. In the first half of the first decade of the 21st century, this trend accelerated. Property prices went through the roof, art galleries multiplied in number, restaurants proliferated, and articles were even being written: where is the next undiscovered spot? Four years later, 2009, things have quietened down and old-time residents and newer arrivals are taking stock on the changes in their town. Certainly, it has changed radically.

Access/Orientation/Information

US 90 runs east and west linking Alpine 26 miles to the east, Van Horn 74 miles to the west, and intersects with US 67 in Marfa. US 67 connects with Presidio 61 miles to the south, while Texas Hwy 17 connects to Fort Davis, 21 miles to the north.

The main street, Highland Avenue, is also the widest and leads to the majestic courthouse. Chinati Foundation art collection is southwest of town beyond the Border Patrol complex. Follow the signs on U.S. 67.

For more information contact the Marfa Chamber of Commerce, which is located at 207 N. Highland Avenue at the entrance to El Paisano Hotel. Hours: Monday–Friday 8–4.

The Marfa Chamber of Commerce	
Marfa Chamber of Commerce 207 N. Highland Ave. P. O. Box 635 Marfa, TX 79843	Phone: 800-650-9696 or 432-729-4942 www.marfacc.com

Mileage to: Van Horn 74 miles, El Paso 196 miles, Midland Airport 181 miles, Dallas via Fort Davis 473 miles, San Antonio via Del Rio 384 miles.

Public Transportation

Air—The nearest commercial airport is in Midland, 181 miles away. El Paso airport is 193 miles away. Marfa has its own airport, capable to taking small jets. The closest train station is in Alpine, 26 miles away. Call Amtrak 800-USA-RAIL for details of the thrice-weekly service.

Bus—All American Travel provides a twice-daily bus service between Midland and Presidio, which stops in Marfa, going northbound at 10:15 A.M. and 4:50 P.M. and southbound at 1:35 P.M. and 10:35 P.M. 432-229-3001.

Local Publications

The Big Bend Sentinel, coupled with *The International* bilingual newspaper in Presidio, are the county's weekly newspapers. The award-winning *Sentinel* is always alert to border matters and ready to comment on sensitive issues, such as the narcotics business. Check the public library in Marfa for the issue covering the arrest of the local Sheriff who was jailed for life for drug smuggling (1991).

Where To Stay

There are two motels, one historic hotel, one bed & breakfast, an RV Park, a cosmic campground and many guest houses, cottages and apartments to rent.

Where To Stay—Motels

Riata Inn—E. U.S. 90, just outside of town. Unpretentious and friendly 20-room motel, facing the Marfa Lights viewing area. King and queen beds, muted western decor. Rates (two persons, plus tax): king bed $65, two queen beds $65. Pet fee $10. The shady (east) side rooms are more popular. 432-729-3800.

Thunderbird Hotel—600 W. San Antonio Street. Minimalist conversion from a 1959 motel, very new Marfa, very cool. "A fusion of light, wood and concrete textures awaits the visitor" (from the webpage). 24 uniform rooms, with queen bed, some with an additional day bed. Rates vary from $120 to $200 (plus tax) for holiday weekends, with 3-night minimum. Dogs $50 extra. Various packages and specials: Romance, Art Package, Mystery Lights and Mid-Week. A good Continental breakfast is included Friday–Sunday. This is served in the lounge where guests can access Wi-Fi and also play selections from the vinyl library. Courtyard, arbor-covered patio plus small heated pool. Vintage typewriter to borrow. Bikes for rent ($10 for half day), gift shop.

Thunderbird Hotel	
Thunderbird Hotel 600 W. San Antonio Street Marfa, TX 79843	Phone: 432-729-1984 www.thunderbirdmarfa.com

Where To Stay—Hotel

The Hotel Paisano—The renowned architectural firm, Trost & Trost, designed this historic building that dates from 1930. The high-ceilinged, tiled lobby, courtyard, arches and tile roof give this storied old property a touch of elegance. The stars of *Giant*—Elizabeth Taylor, James Dean, and Rock Hudson—all stayed in the hotel, as the exhibits in the lobby show.

A protracted history of disputed ownership, indifferent management, and physical dilapidation came to an end in 2001 with the purchase of the hotel by the Duncan family, owners of Hotel Limpia in Fort Davis. Amenities include a small, heated indoor pool, ballroom, courtyard with an impressive fountain, Greasewood Gallery shops by the entrance, "Giant" Room and Jett's Grill restaurant—open for dinner only. A new Fitness Center has been opened, below the shops, enter from the courtyard.

There are 41 rooms and suites, modernized but faithful to the hotel's history. Bath fittings are old but clean, the radio and the wall pictures are old-fashioned, and the soft furnishings are bright and cheerful. No room phones, and all rooms are non-smoking. Standard rooms (queen bed) rent for $99, deluxe historic rooms (one king or two queen beds) $139–149, patio rooms (queen bed and fireplace in private patio area) $139, and suites (king or two queen beds, plus kitchen, living area and patio) $159-$210. The James Dean room, the Rock Hudson and Liz Taylor suites are predictably popular.

The Hotel Paisano	
The Hotel Paisano 207 North Highland Ave. P. O. Box Z Marfa, TX 79843	Phone: 866-729-3669 or 432-729-3669 www.hotelpaisano.com

The Hotel Paisano

Where To Stay—Bed & Breakfast

Arcon Bed & Breakfast—215 North Austin Street. Turn of the century, two-story Victorian adobe residence in a quiet setting close to the Courthouse. Arcon is an archaic Spanish name for treasure chest and, when you enter, you can see why. The living room is well filled with international antiques and colonial art reflecting the well-traveled life of the Garcia family, your hosts. The bedrooms (the cozy Paris room, the handsome Madrid room and the beautiful London room) offer respectively double, queen and two twin beds with a choice of two bathrooms just across the hall. In the back garden of the inn is the Arcon Casita, a restored territorial-style adobe, with two bedrooms, two bathrooms, sitting room, kitchen and private patio. Prices from $99 to $250 for one room to the whole casita. A full gourmet breakfast with two signature dishes plus menus for vegetarians and diabetics is a feature of the inn. Your hostess Mona Garcia gives tours of the restored WW II barracks with German prisoner of war art on the walls at Fort D. A. Russell in Marfa. Guided ranch tours to a nearby 8,000-acre property are also available.

Arcon Bed & Breakfast	
Arcon Bed & Breakfast 215 North Austin St. P. O. Box 448 Marfa, TX 79843	Phone: 432-729-4826 www.christophers.net/arcon/arcon.htm

Where To Stay—Houses/Cottages/Apartments

El Sueño Marfa—Main House and Casita. 110 West Texas. Victorian adobe home with an upstairs suite (King bed); downstairs bedroom has King bed. TV. Wi-Fi. Fans. The library doubles as a bedroom (two day beds). Huge dining room, excellent kitchen. $350. The Casita offers a queen size bed, TV and full bath. $150. 281-333-5512. www.elsuenomarfa.com.

Grande Dame Marfa—400 S. Dean. Majestic, spacious adobe home. 3 bedrooms plus den, 2 baths. Sleeps 6–10. Vintage furniture. Kitchen. W-Fi. Hammock. $350-$500 night. 512-695-3168. www.vrbo.com/239389.

Kokopelli Cottages—409 East 1st Street. Modern, with one bedroom (Queen bed) and bathroom. A/c. W-Fi. TV. Pets allowed. 432-729-4057/432-386-2585.

La Casita—Detached guest house, 1 bedroom (Queen bed), 1 bath. Own entrance and patio. Kitchen. Artfully decorated in the Marfa spirit. Pet friendly. A/C. WIFI. In a quiet NW corner of Marfa. From $99/night. www.vrbo.com/92118. 432-386-7120.

Marfa Casita Retreat—1107 W. San Antonio, and on W. Dallas, (round the corner). Two houses, sleeps four persons. Weekend, weekly and monthly rates. From $450 per weekend, plus cleaning fee. Full kitchen. www.marfacasitaretreat.com. 831-234-0375.

Marfa 608—"The Art of the Getaway." A 4-bedroom/2-bath ultra chic residence. Full kitchen, hardwood floors, outdoor patio with firepit. Rates begin at $215/night, plus $50/night for each two persons extra. A/C. Wi-Fi. Pets. 713-961-5363. www.marfa608.com.

Marfa Guest Quarters—109 W. San Antonio (office) which is also a wine bar. 432-729-4542. www.themarfaquarters.com

> **The Quarters Guest House at Marfa**—214 E. Lincoln Street. Two-room suite, queen bed, parlor, courtyard.
>
> **Casa Tejas**, (queen bed, fully equipped kitchen, patio),
>
> **Casita Tejas** (one room, double bed),
>
> **Casa Agave** (2-bedrooms, 1-bath, with parlor) and
>
> **The Loft** (2nd story room with queen bed) and
>
> **Casa Gonzales**. Seasonal rates from $69 for two.

Marfa House on the Hill—207 S. Arapejo. Turn of the century adobe home, on the east side of town. 2 bedrooms, one with queen bed, the other with two twin beds. Maximum four persons. Two bathrooms and one outdoor shower. Kiva fireplace. No pets. $260/night including tax, two-night minimum, during peak periods 3-nights minimum. www.marfahillhouse.com. 214-826-4612.

Marfa Vacation Apartments—703 W. Fourth / 203 S.Dean. A variety of accommodations (house, apartments, studio) each with its own designation e.g., "Yellow Studio" which is the smallest (for two), one bed, one bathroom—$75/night. Prices for the one- or two-bedroom apartments $99-$139. All queen beds, A/C, TV, central location. The "White Door" sleeps 4–5; $179/night. 432-386-7120. www.vrbo.com137455/214625.

Simply West—1110 N Ordenar.. 2-bedroom furnished apartment with complete kitchen, in northeast part of Marfa. $185/night. 432-729-4878/432-386-2291.

Windmill Retreat—605 E. Lincoln. Good views. 100-year old adobe home. One bedroom (Queen bed) and sofa bed in living room.

Sleeps 2–4. Kitchen. From $175, with $60 cleaning fee. www.wind-millretreat.com. 212-203-1932. 432-729-4878/432-386-2291.

Where To Stay—Workspace

Casita—Studio space for established creative individuals who want to work in Marfa. Private studio with great energy, skylights and floating stone desk; efficiency living space with a queen bed, good linens, large walk-in shower, Wi-Fi and French press. See images at www.huntsculpture.com or call 432-386-2210.

Where To Stay—Alternative

El Cosmico—El Cosmico, 802 S. Highland Avenue. This new venture is a campground hotel offering accommodation in renovated vintage trailers ($75), eco shack yurts, teepee and tent campsites ($20). Bath facilities available. Visitors are encouraged to use the communal hammock grove, outdoor kitchen and lounge with Wi-Fi access. Music festivals take place periodically, and art shacks are planned. 432-729-1950. www.elcosmico.com.

Where To Stay—RV Parks

Apache Pines RV Park—On US 90 West. At the the western edge of town, with good views to the south. Shade trees. 15 sites. Sign yourself in at the on-site cabin.

Where To Stay—Cibolo Creek Ranch

El Fortín del Cíbolo (Fort of the Buffalo) was the fortress head-quarters of Milton Faver, the first and greatest cattle baron in Presidio County. Today's Cibolo Creek Ranch comprises three different forts, all part of Faver's original empire. Houston businessman John Poindexter has restored each to its nineteenth century glory.

The careful historical research that went into the restoration, in addition to the meticulous work undertaken to achieve authenticity, has led some people to call it the "jewel of west Texas." The first sight of El Fortin del Cibolo is a stunning visual treat where every artifact, piece of furniture, and color combination seems exactly right. The main entrance to the ranch is 33 miles south of Marfa on U.S. 67. El Fortin del Cibolo has 21 finely appointed rooms, a heated pool, Jacuzzi, recreation room, and museum, as well as dining and seating areas. Several miles away El

Fortin del Cienega has five guest rooms within the fort itself, and five in an adjoining hacienda. La Morita, the smallest fort, has a single cottage, the most intimate setting in all three forts.

When Poindexter bought the property in 1990 he set out to achieve maximum accuracy in the historical restoration. Ceilings were built with traditional vigas, or exposed beams. Talavera tiles for the bathrooms were imported from Mexico. Records were searched and old-timers interviewed and a researcher was hired to get every detail right. From the light fittings to the dining room chairs, everything blended. Thick adobe walls with watchtowers and a massive entry gate surround El Fortin. Inside, the bedrooms look out onto a green lawn divided by a stream of flowing water.

The comfort of the accommodations is matched by the gourmet food that comes out of the state-of-the-art kitchen. Depending on the number of guests, dinner may be taken in the dining room, or on the screened veranda. Much of the produce comes from the fort's own garden. A full range of daytime activities are available to guests: bird watching, tours on horseback or by jeep, hiking the canyons, or exploring nearby caves.

Not surprisingly, the luxury and uniqueness of Cibolo Creek Ranch attracts a fair share of celebrities. However, according to the management, the majesty of the setting and the immensity of the west Texas sky at night reduce them to ordinary folk. Other ordinary folk can visit El Fortin del Cibolo once a year in September without payment, when it is open to the public. Otherwise, daily rates for the 21 rooms and suites including three gourmet meals range from $295 (summer, mid-week, queen bed) to $455 (summer, weekend, king bed); higher rates in the high season. There is also accomodation at two nearby sister forts, La Ciénega and La Morita.

Cibolo Creek Ranch	
Cibolo Creek Ranch P. O. Box 44 Shafter, TX 79850	Phone: 866-496-9460 432-229-3737 www.cibolocreekranch.com

Where To Drink

Full Bar at Jett's Grill at the Paisano Hotel and at Padre's at 209 W. El Paso (Wednesday–Sunday). Maiya's on N. Highland Avenue. Wine Bar at Guest Quarters, 109 W. San Antonio which features an Appetizer Menu, open 1–9. Beer and wine at Mando's 1506 W. San Antonio and Borunda's (Wednesday–Saturday). Otherwise, fix yourself up at El Cheapo Liquors on US 90 W.

Where To Eat

Alice's Café—906 W. San Antonio. Popular place. Breakfast burritos, Ranchero plate at breakfast. Tacos, enchiladas and burgers at lunch. Monday–Saturday. 6–2, 5–8 P.M. Sunday 9–11 A.M. 432-729-4188.

Austin Street Café—405 N. Austin. A light, airy eating space in a restored adobe building, art work even in the rest rooms. Discriminating, healthy menu with always fresh ingredients. Try blueberry waffles, hard cooked eggs done right, salads, soups (e.g. tomato basil) and sandwiches all maintain a high, consistent standard. Sunday only, 8–2 P.M. Groups by arrangements. Cakes to go a specialty. 432-729-4653. www.austinstreetcafe.com

Blue Javelina—1300 W. San Antonio. "A roadhouse type menu with some Spanish overtones" was how an employee described the re-opening of this restaurant after a short closure. Set in a 1940s service station and updated in new Marfa style. Thursday–Sunday, 5:30–10 P.M. 432-729-1919.

Borunda's Bar & Grill—113 S. Russell. Beer and wine, limited food. Wednesday–Saturday only 5–10 P.M. 432-729-8163.

Carmen's—317 E. San Antonio. Long a local favorite, has reopened. Carmen felt compelled to come back. The sign outside still reads: "Tie up your horse and come inside." Cinnamon rolls and donuts are again available each morning, in addition to breakfast and lunch fare, like the gorditas and enclilada plate. Monday–Saturday, 6–3. 432-729-3429.

Cochineal—107 W. San Antonio. Two years in preparation, this newcomer extends Marfa's food horizon. Partner Tom Rapp calls the menu Global Home Cooking, and uses produce from his own garden. Partner Toshi specializes in desserts such as date pudding. Twice risen soufflé ($9 is a popular starter, among five), and light fluffy meatloaf ($22) as an entree. Minimal décor. Open every day, 7–10 P.M., also for breakfast from 8 A.M. Friday–Tuesday (huevos rancheros $7.50). 432-729-3300 to reserve.

Food Shark—Mobile kitchen under the shade pavilion by the railroad tracks. Eat outside or in the adjacent dining car. Mainly middle eastern menu like hummus, Lebanese salad, kebabs and baklava and the trademark Marfalafel. Tuesday–Friday 11:30–3:00. 432.729.6540. www.foodsharkmarefa.com.

Frama—120 N. Austin, next to Tumbleweed Laundry. All sorts of coffees, from Big Bend Coffee Roasters, and teas, smoothies and shakes. Blue Bell ice cream. Open every day, 8 A.M.–9 P.M. Seating inside and outside. 432-729-4033.

Jett's Grill—207 N. Highland, in the Hotel Paisano. High ceilinged room with full bar, looking out into the courtyard where there also are tables. Try spinach and strawberry salad, or pistachio-crusted chicken fry. Ten entrees in the $14–$16 range. Burger $10, trout $18, 1lb ribeye $32. Breakfast: 7–10:30 A.M.; Lunch: Friday–Monday, 11:30 –2:00 P.M. Dinner: 7 days a week, 5:30–9 P.M. (10 P.M on weekends. 432-729-3838.

Maiya's—103 N. Highland in the restored Brite Building. Five years of good work. Crisp white tablecloths. Full bar. The menu reflects in its grilled and roasted meats, and homemade pastas, a North Italian bias. Dishes change seasonally. The salads (Grass Salad),Vodka Pasta (a family recipe) and Spinach lasagna are consistently popular. Strong flavored Italian sausage, chicken and seafood dishes add variety. Entrees $17–$30. Extensive wine list. Cool décor with restful Japanese influence. The proprietor as chef. Open Wednesday–Saturday, 5–10 P.M. Wise to reserve. 432-729-4410.

Mando's—1506 W. San Antonio. Formerly a drive-in, now a family-type pool hall, bar and restaurant. Long menu, burgers, steaks and Mexican food. Closed Monday. Open 11–2 P.M., 5–10 P.M. 432-729-3291.

Marfa Table—109 S. Highland New breakfast and lunch spot, between the bookstore and the radio station. Short but tasty menu with emphasis on seasonal, local and sustainable produce. Try migas or florentine muffins $4, organic coffee $2, and for lunch, market salad, a

BLT or spinach lasagna $8. Wi-Fi. Catering. Open Friday–Monday 11–3. Thursday 5–8 P.M. www.marfatable.com. 432-729-3663.

Padre's—205 W El Paso. An eatery, with full bar, and a music joint with extensive game room—all inside a former funeral home. Very new Marfa, and great fun. Burgers, bratwurst, chili and gumbo on the menu. Strong wine and beer selection. Weekly live music, otherwise 45 rpm recordings. An instant hit with the whole community, Padre's is energetically overseen by partner/cook David Beebe. Large patio out back. Open Wednesday–Saturday for lunch and in the evening Bar open til 1 A.M. on weeends. www.padresmarfa.com. 432-7294425.

Pizza Foundation—Highland at Hwy 90. No decor, basic seating (including outside) and great pizzas cheerfully served up. Slice $2.00, whole pizza $14, enough for four people. Salads. Good soft drinks, like Jamaican lemonade. Now serving wine and beer (good choice). 11–9 P.M. Weekends 12–9 P.M. Closed Tuesday and Wednesday. 432-729-3377.

Squeeze Marfa—215 N. Highland. Tucked away on courthouse square. A leafy entrance leads to a small, efficient dining room. In addition to the grilled panini-style sandwiches (6), specialty teas and strong coffee, there are smoothies and Italian sodas. Try Birchermuesli for breakfast and a squeezadilla special for lunch And of course in winter a hot Swiss chocolate drink. www.squeezemarfa.com. Tuesday –Saturday, 9–4 P.M. 800-655-0327, 432-729-4500.

Tacos del Norte—1500 W. San Antonio. New and popular. Tacos, flour or corn, with ground beef from $2, plus gorditas, tostados, burritos and quesadillos. Lemonade and horchata (rice water). Open 7 A.M.–8 P.M., closed Sunday.

Where To Eat—Fast Food

Dairy Queen—704 W. San Antonio. Open every day 10:30–9 P.M. 432-729-4471.

Where To Go/What To Do—Theatre

Goode-Crowley Theatre—Downtown. Check locally to see if there is a performance. Converted from a feed store, this theatre puts on many interesting local and visiting acts.

Where To Go/What To Do—Museums

The Marfa & Presidio County Museum—110 W. San Antonio. The museum comprises nine small rooms in a white one-story building located at the downtown light opposite City Hall. Well-filled, reeking of history, staffed by local volunteers who are part of the story themselves, this homemade museum is a delight. Room One is the history room, showing artifacts dating back to when an ocean covered the region. Then the three periods of exploration and settlement are covered: Spanish, Mexican, and American. Room Two reflects the cattleman's heritage. Room Three, the settler's kitchen with articles from the railroad and the silver mine at Shafter. Don't forget the post office room, across from Room Three. Room Four displays household items, gowns and a baby buggy, for example. Room Five has a special exhibit of photographs by Frank Duncan who arrived in Presidio County in 1916. Room Six displays souvenirs of the military presence in Marfa since 1911 when troops arrived as a result of the Mexican Revolution. In World War II the Marfa Army Air Field was a training ground for pilots. This last room also details the later recreational uses of the Air Field. Open Thursday–Saturday, 1–5.

The Marfa & Presidio County Museum	
The Marfa and Presidio County Museum 110 West San Antonio Marfa, TX 79843	Phone: 432-729-4140

Where To Go/What To Do—Vineyard Visit

Luz de Estrella Winery—Three miles east of Marfa on Hwy 90. Open daily 10–6, Sunday 2–6. Tasting and tours daily. 432-729-3434. www.luzdeestrella.com.

Where To Go/What To Do—Chinati Foundation

In the mid-seventies, New York artist Donald Judd arrived in Marfa, just about as great a geographical contrast as possible. Judd believed that the confines of museums and galleries were not suitable for his artwork, nor the artwork of many of his contemporaries. He had decided that a vast amount of open space was where he needed to be to display his art.

For him, the space in which his art was displayed was as important as
the art itself and the space in Marfa was intended to be a museum for
the permanent installation of a limited number of artists' work. The
Foundation's brochure quotes Judd, who died in 1994, as saying: "It
takes a great deal of time and thought to install work carefully. This
should not always be thrown away. Most art is fragile and some should
be placed and never moved again. Somewhere a portion of contemporary art has to exist as an example of what art and its context were meant
to be."

Judd's work is referred to as "minimalist" and "architectural." His
best-known work is 100 untitled works in mill aluminum (1982–1986),
all different in design, lined up in rows inside the two converted artillery
sheds of what was formerly camp D. A. Russell. The desert sun
streams in through the large windows causing the shapes to change in
appearance according to the time of day. Outside, a line of squat concrete structures, another Judd creation, stretches across the dried grass
compound of the old fort.

First time visitors to Judd's permanent exhibition can react in quite
opposite ways to this part of the collection. Some stand in awe, pacing
up and down the two buildings, staring out of the window at the desert,
focusing on one piece or another, reluctant to leave. Others find the
installation sterile, the setting antiseptic or mechanical, and hurry
through to the other exhibits. These include installations by Claes
Oldenburg; Coosje van Bruggen, whose 25-feet high iron horseshoe, a
memorial to the last cavalry horse, is visible beyond the line of barracks;
and John Chamberlain, whose display of crushed automobile parts is in
a separate building in downtown Marfa.

Other artists whose work is displayed in the restored army buildings
and on the Chinati grounds include Roni Horn, Richard Long, Carl
Andre, Ingolfur Arnasson, Ilya Kabakov, John Wesley, David
Rabinovitch, and Dan Flavin. Flavin was a close collaborator of Judd
and a close friend. His untitled Marfa Project, an installation of colored
fluorescent light, occupying six former barracks, was opened to the
public in 2000.

It took some time after the arrival of Donald Judd for the local towns-
people to realize the importance of the newcomer in their midst. His art

was unfamiliar, but apparently in high demand since Judd had the funds to start buying buildings around town. There was some initial negative reaction born of ignorance of the work and of the man, which only partially changed after Judd's death. TV documentaries, obituaries in national papers, and an increasing number of visitors to Marfa underscored Judd's importance in the field of modern minimalist art.

In 1998, a Chinati Foundation symposium entitled "Art and Architecture" drew an audience from across the nation and overseas. Famous architects spoke in front of an audience of academics, artists, and art lovers. The New York Times sent a reporter. This, plus the opening up of Judd's residence in downtown Marfa by the family foundation created after his death, produced an additional momentum to the Foundation's work, of which the Flavin installation is the most recent example. Along with the "Art and Architecture" symposium there have been symposia in 1995, 2001, and 2006. Around 10,000 visitors a year visit Marfa to see the exhibits.

Visiting days/hours: the collection is accessible by guided tour only, Wednesday–Sunday, in two sections. Tours of Section One begin at 10:00 A.M. and include permanent installations by Donald Judd, Richard Long, Ilya Kabakov, and John Chamberlain. The Chamberlain exhibit is downtown, leaving visitors to have lunch there before resuming. Tours of Section Two begin at 2:00 P.M. and include works by Dan Flavin, Claes Oldenburg, Coosje van Bruggen ("Last Horse"), Roni Horn, Carl Andre, Ingolfur Arnarsson and John Wesley. Admission for the entire collection is $10 per person, $5 for students and seniors. A shorter tour, for those wishing to see only Judd's best known work 100 Untitled Works starts at 3:45 P.M. and costs $5.00. Tour groups can also be scheduled by booking at least two weeks in advance. Visitors are advised to wear protective footwear and hats and to carry a water bottle as temperatures in summer can be high.

To make a reservation, call 432-729-4362 at least three days ahead or check www@chinati.org.

Chinati Foundation	
Chinati Foundation P .O. Box 1135 Marfa, TX 79843	Phone: 432-729-4362 www.chinati.org

Where To Go/What To Do—Judd Tours

There are also tours of Judd's living and working space in downtown Marfa. Tours to La Mansana de Chinati/The Block, where Judd resided operate from Wednesday–Sunday, starting at 4:30 P.M., and last 60–90 minutes. Groups of up to 8 persons, cost $20 each. There are also Studio Tours. Check www.juddfoundation.org. For all tours, you must book at least 5 days in advance by emailing marfatours@juddfoundation.org. The starting point is at 104 S. Highland Avenue, opposite Marfa Book Company. 432-729-4406.

A second tour to other studio space used by Judd leaves at 2 P.M. on Friday and Saturday. $30.

Where To Go/What To Do—Officers Club Historic Tour, Building 98

During WW II, officers from Rommel's Afrika Korps were among the German prisoners of war at Fort D. A. Russell. In what is called Building 98 a lasting testimonial by two of their comrades still exists: murals from floor to ceiling in two large rooms, showing western landscapes. The U-shaped building, now a national historic site. also accommodates a handsome bar in what was the Officers Club which also served as Bachelor Officers Quarters. Today it is the headquarters of the International Women's Foundation. The director of the Foundation escorts visitors on guided tours on Building 98, lasting 1–2 hours and costing $5. Call 432-729-4826 for a reservation.

Where To Go/What To Do—Courthouse/Library

Presidio County Courthouse—This noble, four-story building was built in 1886 and reflects the optimism of the times. It stands at the end of broad Highland Avenue and dominates the town. Built out of brick, it was stuccoed in the thirties, and painted a pinkish color with pale yellow edging on the upper part. Recently the entire building underwent a restoration. A dome surmounts the grand edifice. Inside, the style is equally impressive. Steep wooden staircases lead to the upper floors and thick carved banister railings surround the wells on the landings. Look inside one of the dignified courtrooms. Then proceed ever higher (80 steps total) to the cupola for an outstanding view. Restoration costing $2.2 million was completed 2001, giving the grand old building a new lease on life.

Library—If you are at a loose end, or want to do a quick study of recent history, a visit to the Marfa Library will be productive. This well-run establishment offers a video of Giant to rent and back issues of the award-winning local paper, Big Bend Sentinel, for perusal. Check out May 1997 for reports of the Davis Mountains standoff between Republic of Texas separatist Rick McLaren and a small army of law enforcement officers. In the same month was the shooting death in Redford by a U.S. Marines patrol of a local youth who was tending his goats. The December 1991–January 1992 issues recall the high profile case of discredited Sheriff Thompson, arrested and later jailed for life for drug smuggling. Over one ton of cocaine was found in his horse trailer, parked in the town's rodeo grounds.

Where To Go/What To Do—Golf Course

Marfa Municipal Golf Course—The highest golf course in Texas. This is a good golf course for those who enjoy playing a short game. The greens are on the whole small and elevated and angled towards the fairway, making them hard to hit in regulation and difficult to stay on when pitching. Most greens are protected by a semicircle of trees. This is a nine-hole course with separate tee boxes to make a full round. There is also a practice range. Electric carts must be kept on the cart paths. For green fees call 432-729-4043.

Where To Go/What To Do—Gliding

Rides and Lessons at Marfa Airport—Around Marfa, there are some of the best "soaring" conditions in the world. This family adventure sport is fun and uplifting (no pun intended). Two-seat gliders are used for lessons and rides, which last around 20 minutes. Have a wholly new look at the Marfa Plateau, the Davis Mountains, and the town of Marfa itself. The rides cost $119 with a $20 off coupon found at local Chamber offices. Weather conditions are of critical importance so advance booking is vital. For more information call 800-667-9464 or visit www.flygliders.com.

Where To Go/What To Do—Galleries/Shopping

Arber & Son Editions—128 E. El Paso. A fine art printing and publishing studio and gallery featuring limited edition lithographs of Judd, Nauman, Prince and many others. 432-729-3981.

AYN Foundation (Das Maximum)—Brite Building. 107–109 N. Highland Avenue. Two semi-permanent exhibitions, "Last Supper" by Andy Warhol and "September Eleven" by Maria Zeres. Hours of opening change seasonally so please call 432-729-3315. Or, call Gretchen Coles at 432-729-1970.

Ballroom Marfa—108 E. San Antonio. Previously a Hispanic dance hall which opened in 1927, now a cultural space presenting exhibitions and performances by known and emerging artists in the visual arts, film, performance and music. A leader in the area for encouraging artistic activity. Thursday–Sunday, 12–6. www.ballroommarfa.org. 432-729-3600.

Chinati Foundation—1 Cavalry Row. Internationally known contemporary art museum founded by minimalist artist Donald Judd. Tours 10–12 A.M. and 2–4 P.M. See previous section. 432-729-4362.

Eugene Bender—218 N. Highland Avenue. Shows by con-temporary Texas and New York artists. By appointment. 432-729-3900.

Exhibitions 2d—400 S. Highland Avenue. Rotating ex-hibitions of work by 10 artists, from across the country with an emphasis on reductive and minimal drawing and sculpture, installed in a quiet contemplative environment. Wednesday–Sunday, 11–6. 432-729-1910.

Galleri Urbane—212 E. San Antonio Street. The gallery features the work of emerging artists from throughout the U.S. in 7 shows annually: photography, installation, painting and sculpture. Open Monday–Thursday, 9–6, Friday and Saturday, 9–8, Sunday, 11–4. 432-729-4200. www.galleriurbane.com.

Gallery 111—111 West San Antonio. Art color photography by Leana Clifton. Each picture tells a visual short story. Local scenes. 512-695-3168. www.leanaclifton.com.

Greasewood Gallery—In the Hotel Paisano. Paintings, prints, works in glass and wood by local artists. Open 9–6, Thursday–Saturday, 9–9. 432-729-4134.

The Great Circle Press — By appointment. The working studio of Gretchen Lee Coles, sculptor and cartographer. Contact by email: mapit4u@hotmail.com.

Hunt Sculpture—By appointment only. Conceptually-based, reductively designed, beautifully made steel sculpture and functional pieces.

Featured in collections in USA and Europe. Cranbrook Academy of Art alumni. www.huntsculpture.com. 432-386-2210.

Inde/Jacobs—201 E. San Antonio. Focuses on works on paper by post WW II artists. Also photography from 19th century to present. Wednesday–Sunday. 11:30–5:30. 432-386-0488.

Judd—104 S. Highland Avenue. Guided tours of The Block, former residence of Donald Judd. See section above.

Marfa Book Company—105 S. Highland. A gallery with exhibitions changing frequently with work by local and regional artists. The gallery also periodically hosts literary and music events, and has a large collection of impressive art and architecture books. 10–7 Wednesday–Sunday. 432-729-3906. www.marfabooks.com.

The Marfa Book Company	
The Marfa Book Company 105 South Highland Marfa, TX 79843	Phone: 432-729-3906

Malinda Beaman—Watercolor paintings of local scenes. By appointment. 432-729-3987

Samuel Owen Gallery—106 E. San Antonio. Collection on rare vintage posters from 19th and 20th century. 432-729-4844. 432-729-4844.

Where To Go/What To Do — Shopping

Farmstand Marfa—Every Saturday, under the roof by the railroad tracks. Mainly locally grown produce, but visitors may find a t-shirt, book, pottery or a painting which catches their eye. From 10 A.M. A timely venture by Sandra Harper.

Fancy Pony Land— 203 E. San Antonio. Original handmade clothing by Lorna Leedy, featuring hand-cut vinyl and leather appliqués on colorful, whimsical garments. Also, train-squashed penny jewelry, drawings, books and art pieces. Friday–Saturday, 2–6 P.M. Or by appointment 432-729-7658.

JM Dry Goods—102 S. Dean Street (opposite Ballroom Marfa). Ranch wear, vintage items, and home supplies. Serapes, hammocks,

Mexican dresses, boots. Open Wednesday–Sunday, 2–7. 917-548-7606.

Marfa Interiors/Marfa Bedroom—203 E. San Antonio. The artist/designer owners offer quilts, bedspreads, clothing and furniture, including a line of interior décor pieces, cushions, throws and adornments. Original and unusual. Open Wednesday–Saturday 12—6 P.M. Or by appointment, 917-250-2593.

Marfa Book Company—105 S. Highland Avenue. An extraordinary collection of art books well picked to match Marfa, and a strong selection of other genres. Well managed, modern space with an art gallery adjacent. Regular readings by Lannan Foundation writers take place here on Saturdays at 6:00 P.M. Open 10–7 Wednesday–Sunday. 432-729-3906. www.marfabooks.com.

Moonlight Gemstones—1001 W. San Antonio Street. Quality work by an established craftsman. Paul Graybeal has been working his magic since 1989, custom designing silver jewelry (pendants, bracelets, bolo ties, belt buckles etc.) using remarkable local colored agate as well as rare gemstones from around the world. Monday–Saturday, 10–6. Sundays by appointment.

Moonlight Gemstones	
Moonlight Gemstones 1001 W. San Antonio Street Marfa, TX 79843	Phone: 432-729-4526 www.moonlightgemstones.com

Native Marfa—114 E. El Paso. Unique handmade jewelry highlighting the style, history and landscape of Marfa and the Big Bend. Art work using local stones from the area's principal sights. Inside Christopher's Home Furnishings, www.nativemarfa.com. 432-729-4571.

Paisano Shops—In the lobby of the hotel. Selection of clothing, books, lotions, kitchenware and furniture. Open daily, 9–6, weekends to 9 P.M.

Tienda M—101 S. Highland Avenue. Next to Marfa Book Store. Selected handmade items from the Southwest Mexico including pottery, naturally dyed textiles in cotton, silk and wool, jewelry, baskets, clothing and more. Espresso coffee. Open Wednesday–Sunday.

Wool & Hoop—203 E. San Antonio Street. One of several new artisanal boutiques, Wool & Hoop offers a line of crewel embroidery kits
for the modern crafter designed by artist/author Katherine Shaughnessy.
Also embroidery and sewing supplies including English embroidery
wool, colorful Belgian linen, crafting felts etc. supplies. Open Friday
/Saturday 12–6 or by appointment. 432-386-0386.

Where To Go/What To Do—Pinto Canyon

FM 2810 runs southwest from U.S. 90 W. in Marfa and travels 32
miles on pavement across high, rolling range lands, with superb views of
the Chinati Mountain to the south especially in the morning. Five miles
after the pavement ends, the road drops sharply into Pinto Canyon, and
follows the floor of the canyon for 8 miles before rising again to exit the
canyon above the hamlet of Ruidosa, which is reached after 54 miles.
Any vehicle can usually take this route, although motorcycles may have
a problem. See page 118 for a more detailed description of Pinto Canyon and Chinati Hot Springs, "the magical oasis in Texas' Chihuahuan
Desert."

At Ruidosa where the paved highway restarts you have the choice of
turning left and following FM 1270 for 36 miles to Presidio or turning
right and following FM 170 12 miles to Candelaria. This village has
lost its only store and also its school. A few years ago, the footbridge
across the Rio Grande to the village of San Antonio del Bravo was
removed by the Border Patrol.

The River Road continues north/northwest as an unpaved county
road and crosses one or two creeks, including Cold Water Creek, which
is usually running. Rancho Viejo is near here, under the rim rock at
4,200 feet, and now open to visitors (432-229-4232) It then bears right
through a gap in the Sierra Vieja range. Close to this road are sites
famous in border history, particularly during the turbulent years of the
Mexican Revolution: Brite Ranch, Nevill Ranch, Porvenir, and Pilares
are all known for raids and massacres during the period of hit-and-run
raids and retaliatory pursuits. After 40 slow miles, FM 2017 is reached
which one-mile later joins US 90, 17 miles west of Valentine.

This dirt road passes through some very remote country and all desert
travel precautions should be taken. This journey is not for the casual
driver. A high clearance, all-wheel drive vehicle is a must, also a lot of

water. Check weather conditions before leaving, and check with local Border Patrol or Texas Dept. of Transportation about road conditions. There is also one very steep hill, three miles from Candelaria, impossible to scale from the west without 4-wheel drive.

Where To Go/What To Do—Chinati Hot Springs

Six miles north of FM 170 just west of Ruidosa, and 7 miles west of FM 2810 when it exits Pinto Canyon (both routes are signposted), the Chinati Hot Springs are located in a canyon on the southern flank of the Chinati range within sight of Mexico. This hideaway, little known except by those who have learned of its existence by word of mouth, can be reached in two hours drive from Marfa via Presidio and one hour and 45 minutes via Pinto Canyon. See page 28 for more information.

Where To Go/What To Do—Davis Mountains Scenic Loop

16 miles north of Marfa on U.S. 17, going towards Fort Davis, drivers join the 74-mile Scenic Loop of the Davis Mountains. At this junction with Hwy 166 drivers can either turn left and do the loop clockwise, or continue on through Fort Davis to follow the route in a counterclockwise fashion. See page 128.

Where To Go/What To Do—Prada Marfa

Situated on US 90 just west of Valentine (26 miles from Marfa) is an isolated and currently empty mini boutique. Built of adobe and opened in 2005, the venture is a cooperation between Ballroom Marfa and Art Production Fund. Valentine artist Boyd Elder is the local person appointed to supervise the structure.

The interior previously held a selection of single Prada shoes. The sign on the front says Prada Marfa. Bullet holes in the structure indicate hostility to the venture.

Store as sculpture? An offensive intrusion by elitist newcomers, or a whimsical addition to our changing landscape? At the very least it gives the driver coming from Van Horn a reason for a brief stop.

Where To Go/What To Do—Marfa Lights

Lights and Marfa seem to go together and for most people this unexplained phenomenon is the most common identification with the town. Scientists have done studies and books and papers have been written about the subject. But no one has come up with a satisfactory explanation of the cause of those few, small lights on the horizon. The ghost lights of Marfa are as mysterious today as they were when the early settlers, driving their cattle to Marfa, first saw them. Who can explain their source? Where exactly are they located?

Judith Brueske's booklet *The Marfa Lights* (Ocotillo Enterprises, 1989) sets the scene: "The Marfa Lights of west Texas have been called by many names over the years, such as ghost lights, weird lights, mystery lights, or Chinati lights. They are reported from various places in the Big Bend region in Brewster and Presidio Counties and sometimes from adjacent Jeff Davis County. The phenomenon referred to is the fairly regularly reported appearance of moving, unidentified lights and they are reported most frequently from the area between Marfa, Texas and the place known as Paisano Pass to the east. They appear to travelers along Highway 90, usually to the south of it, on or across Mitchell Flat. The lights are most often reported as rather distant bright lights distinguishable from ranch lights and automobile lights on US 67 (between Marfa and Presidio to the south) primarily by their aberrant movements."

Brueske's 51-page booklet gives a variety of first hand accounts of sightings, accidental and planned, sightings elsewhere, and airborne sightings. There are even cases where tourists swore they had been chased by the lights. Under "Discussion," she covers most of the theories: minerals, static electricity, mirages, and ends the booklet on a tantalizing note.

Descriptions abound concerning the size, shape, color and movement of the lights. In 1988 one account described the phenomena this way: "Poof—there's the first one, a tiny round ball of white light, not exactly still. Then, poof, it splits and becomes two slightly wavering, shimmery spheres. In a minute, poof, another light appears to the right of the other two. And so on. Sometimes only two lights are present, sometimes six."

Another account, from 1963, claimed: "as if on cue, a light appeared far off on the southern horizon. It was a pinprick of light. When I looked at it through a small telescope I had brought for the occasion, I found it was still a small point of light; yet it looked different. It wasn't a star or a planet and it didn't look like light bulbs do at a distance. Soon the first light was joined by a second; then a third; then a fourth; until, finally, we were treated to eleven lights bobbing and bouncing just above the horizon."

The earliest accounts of the lights from Anglo ranchers go back to 1883. Rancher J. E. Ellison reported seeing a strange light as he drove cattle through Paisano Pass on the way to Marfa. He thought they were Apache campfires. Legends grew around that time concerning the cause of the lights, one of which was of the humanist and non-scientific sort. The legend came from Mexican sources and concerned the Indian chief Alsate, who had been captured and executed by the Mexican federales. The lights were said to be the ghosts of Alsate who still roamed the Chinati Mountains.

Through the years various serious and professional attempts have been made from the air and on the ground to explain the mystery. The existence of the Marfa Air Field, a training site for pilots during World War II, provided an opportunity for aerial observations. A recent mayor of Marfa, Fritz Kahl, was a pilot trainer in those days and flew on innumerable occasions at night, when there were no other distracting lights from ranches or automobiles.

He saw the lights frequently and described an early sighting: "We saw these small objects off in the distance. They moved laterally more than vertically. They moved towards us and away from us. They were soft in nature, not a harsh light, pale greens, pale blues, pale yellows, soft reds, but no harsh color. Often oblong, with no rough edges, they moved vertically, but not much. At no time did we ever find the lights hostile or threatening. They didn't run at us, their movement was more slow than fast, very simple, very small, the size of a light bulb."

How do you look for the lights? According to the mayor: "With a great deal of patience. Or, if you are young, with your girlfriend and a six-pack of beer." How often are they out? "They are not out every night in my opinion. They may be down in the grass, but I don't think they're there every night. Probably two nights out of three is a good guess." What do the local people think of the lights? "They're little old fellas out there. They're here. It's just a different sort of thing. They lived with it. The lights are like neighbors."

The mayor had no definitive theory about the cause of the lights and resented those trying to capitalize on the lights to make a name for themselves. The Marfa people certainly can't be accused of that. Only in recent years has the Highway Department provided a parking space on the highway after a rancher donated the land. This is the official viewing area, with a few picnic tables, eight miles east of Marfa on U.S. 90.

Various organized attempts have occurred over the years. Not surprisingly, with a university only 18 miles away in Alpine, students have tried to track down the lights. Using a dragnet effort, with jeeps on the ground and a plane in the air, the lights refused to be captured. Others tried to use triangulation, but the lights kept moving. Others tried to drop markers on the lights, but that effort failed, too. A well-equipped Japanese expedition camped out for several nights, but the lights refused to appear—to the amusement of the Marfa residents.

I have personally seen the lights on several occasions and the descriptions above seem accurate. I had always discounted the theories of people being chased by lights, until one of the guests in my Bed & Breakfast described his own experience. This man, traveling along US 90 around 3:00 A.M. was aware of a bright light behind his car. He slowed down, thinking it might be a police car. But the light did not revolve, nor was it a spotlight. It persisted, so he stopped and got out. The light vanished. The sincerity of the man and his obvious concern for ridicule and the dispassionate, detailed telling of his story, persuaded me that he had certainly seen some light. The mystery continues. So, drop by and check it out for yourself. Even if the lights don't appear when you visit, there are worse things to do than watch the night sky in west Texas while shooting the breeze with other curious visitors.

To view the lights, drive east 8 miles on US 90 to the Marfa Light Viewing Center. This long-needed structure, from a plan devised by Marfa school kids, provides a circular viewing deck equipped with binocular stations, picnic tables, and rest rooms. Read the account (above), or see the video (below) to make the viewing more useful and enjoyable. Look towards the southwest (the highway runs east/west) and use the red light in the middle distance, this is a microwave signal on top of a mast, as your guideline. The lights usually appear on the horizon behind the red light.

Marfa Lights Video—A good introduction to the Mystery Lights is to watch the free video which is played at the Apache Trading Post on US 90 just west of Alpine. This 8-minute film comes from the TV series: *Unsolved Mysteries*. The Apache Trading Post is open Monday–Saturday, 9–5, Sunday, 1–5.

<u>Marfa Calendar Of Selected Events</u>

There are various events involving Gliders during the year. Check www.marfacc.com for current soaring happenings.

April	Marfa Film Festival. 432-729-1948.
May	Memorial Day Weekend. Big Bend Cowboy Hall of Fame and annual Team Roping at Presidio County Roping Arena.
September	Labor Day Weekend. Marfa Lights Festival, Arts and crafts sale, food vendors around the Courthouse, three nights of street dances.
December	First Saturday, evening. Christmas in Marfa.

Monahans
Elevation: 2,799 feet   Population: 6,821

History

Stuck between I-20 and an oil field, Monahans manages to present itself both as an oil service town and as a state park destination. While the price of oil determines the level of prosperity in town and is something the inhabitants can do little about, the continued existence of nearby Monahans Sandhills State Park is something they can influence. In 1998, faced with a threatened closure of their park by the Texas Parks & Wildlife Department, the Monahans community raised $200,000 with the result being that the park remained open and was substantially improved.

In 1881, Pat Monahan, a surveyor for the Texas & Pacific Railroad, dug the first water well between the Pecos River and Big Spring. The community that assembled there was first known as Monahan's Well. In 1883 a post office was established and in 1900 James R. Holman built a hotel to accommodate passengers getting off the train.

Not a great deal happened in the new township of Monahans in the early days of the century. Nearby Barstow, the county seat of Ward County, made a name for itself by winning the gold medal at the World's Fair in St. Louis (1904) for its grape crop. Barstow and surrounding areas had five times as many inhabitants as Monahans, whose population was only 222.

In the late twenties, the discovery of oil in the area led to a twenty-five year period of prosperity during which time forty-two oil fields opened in Ward County. Monahans' population soared. In the 1930s a movie theater opened, a newspaper was started, a hospital was built, and the county seat was moved to Monahans.

Oil was the making of Monahans and it is fitting that the most extravagant feature of the town today is a symbol of oil-producing ingenuity even though it didn't work. The Million Barrel Museum, a near-useless concrete-lined hole in the ground, was built in 1928 by Shell Oil to store excess crude oil before refinement. Unfortunately the seams in the concrete lining leaked and much of the oil seeped away. The idea was abandoned, but the hole in the ground, together with the original Holman House, which was moved from downtown, serve today as a monument to the heyday of oil production.

Eugene Holman, whose father was an early pioneer and community leader in Monahans, was more of a success story. After a lifetime of service in the oil industry, learning the business from the ground up (including time spent in the oil fields of Venezuela), Holman became chairman of the board of Standard Oil Company of New Jersey.

Despite the fluctuations of the oil industry, Monahans has succeeded in maintaining its population level. It also derives some benefit from being only five miles from Monahans Sandhills State Park. This 3,840-acre property was acquired by Texas Parks & Wildlife Department in 1956. Its unique feature is the sand dunes up to 70 feet high, clearly visible from I-20, which are part of a 200-mile dune field that stretches into New Mexico. The proximity to the Sandhills State Park and the location on I-20 makes Monahans a functional stop for visitors. An active Chamber of Commerce and some energetic local participation in events like the Butterfield Overland Stagecoach and Wagon Festival are helping to keep the town on the tourist map.

Access/Orientation/Information

TX 18 runs north/south between Fort Stockton and Hobbs, New Mexico and intersects in Monahans with I-20.

For more information contact the Monahans Chamber of Commerce. Office hours are Monday–Friday, 8–4 P.M.

Monahans Chamber of Commerce	
Monahans Chamber of Commerce 401 S. Dwight Monahans, TX 79756	Phone: 432-943-2187 www.monahans.org

Mileage to: Fort Stockton 51 miles, Odessa 36 miles, Pecos 41 miles, and the New Mexico state line 32 miles.

Public Transportation

Air—The nearest airport is at Midland, 46 miles away.

Local Publications

The Chamber has a map of town and pamphlets including one of the Sandhills State Park. *The Monahans News* is published twice weekly. There is also the *Muddvillenews*, an online newspaper.

Where To Stay—Hotels/Motels

Best Western Inn & Suites—2101 S. Betty Street. 800-780-7234. 432-943-3360.

America's Best Value—702 W I-20 @ TX 18. 800-528-1234. 432-943-4345.

Texan Inn—806 W. I–20. 432-943-7585.

Silver Spur—400 East Sealy. 432-943-5461.

Where To Stay—RV Parks

Country Club R.V. Resort—Next to Ward County golf course. 90 sites. Full hookups with cable TV. $22/night for hookup. There is a small World War II museum in the resort. This is the work of Rodney Venters who has collected 1,000 items and put them on display. Open 7 days a week, 8–6, no charge for admission.

Country Club R.V. Resort	
Country Club R.V. Resort 2000 N. Main Monahans, TX 79756	Phone: 800-622-4308 432-943-7804

Monahans Sandhill State Park—5 miles east of Monahans on I-20. Hookup $14/night, also for tent camping. See the section on the Park below for more detail and contact information.

Where To Eat

Bar H Steak House—901 S. Stockton. Monday–Saturday, 11–9. Sunday, 11–2. "A good steak at an honest price." Consistent and popular. 432-943-7498.

Big Burger—1016 S. Stockton. Collector's memorabilia of old Coke signs. 432-943-5655.

J's Pizza & Burger Shack—2411 S. Stockton. 432-943-6621.

Spotlight Restaurant—2003 N. Main. Formerly a backstage club. Varied menu includes catfish, Sunday buffet, BBQ on Thursday. 432-943-9986.

Sarina's Donuts—432-943-2644.

Pappy's BBQ—Specialty is apple dumplings. 1901 S. Stockton. Truck parking avilable. 432-943-9300.

Pizza Hut—501 S. Main. 432-943-2701.

The Tulip Tea Room—At The Gift Shop. 100 E. Sealy. Monday–Friday, 10–5 P.M. 432-943-5774.

Mexican—Habanero's (formerly Leal's). Try the Don Pablo special. Fred's. Vicky's.

Fast Food—McDonalds, Dairy Queen, Sonic.

Burgers—Howards, Superburger, Fred's, Huddle House (24-hour).

What To Do/Where To Go—Shopping

Through the Pages—121 1/2 E. Sealey. "A bookstore and more" is how this gem of a place describes itself. In addition to an impressive stock of books, the shop carries homemade fudge, toffees and chocolate, arts and crafts, handmade cards and gifts. A vibrant and active venue, whose activities include children's story time on Wednesdays. Wi-Fi and snacks. www.throughthepages.com. 432--943-2456.

What To Do/Where To Go—Museum

Million Barrel Museum—On Business 20, east of downtown Monahans. A 14.5-acre site of historic potpourri. The million barrel concrete-lined tank, built in 1928 and then abandoned due to leakage, is empty and used only occasionally for concerts. Next to the tank are the original Holman House, the old Monahans jail, a section of railroad track with vintage caboose, an eclipse windmill, and a display of antique farm equipment. Weekdays, 10–6, Saturday–Sunday, 10–2, closed Monday. Admission is free.

Million Barrel Museum	
Million Barrel Museum 400 4th Street Monahans, TX 79756	Phone: 432-943-8401

What To Do/Where To Go—Monahans Sandhills State Park

Exit 86 off I-20. The wind-sculpted white sand dunes of this state park stand in sharp contrast to the numerous pump jacks and other industrial paraphernalia that dot the landscape. The extensive sand hills area, covering 3,840 acres, was a substantial obstacle to the wagon trains of the early pioneers as well as to the later railroad builders. Indians knew it better and frequently camped here because pure, fresh water could be found.

Not apparent to the eye is a forest of dwarf oaks (shin oaks, or Havard oaks), which at full maturity reach only 3–4 feet. Underground however, the roots extend as far as ninety feet in order to maintain the miniature above-ground growth. Where these oaks grow, the dunes are stabilized; other dunes, bare of vegetation, shift with the wind.

The newly refurbished Dunagan Visitor Center has a hands-on exhibition that explains the history of the region. The large glass window in the museum serves as a useful vantage point to observe birds as they come to the feeding and watering station outside. A self-guided trail behind the center offers twelve points of interest including a pack rat midden, cactus, sagebrush, and a Havard oak.

For those on a day visit, the Shin Oak picnic area offers shade shelter, tables, and grills. The higher dunes, up to 70 feet high, are located a little further on near the Section House that acts as a snack bar. Discs can be rented at the Visitor Center for $1/hour for sliding down the dunes. There is a second picnic area next to a Pump Jack at the end of 2-mile road from the Visitor Center. There are also 600 acres available for horseback riding.

Entrance to the park is $3.00 per person over 13 years old. Texas State Park Pass holders get in free. Overnight RV camping with electrical hookup costs $14, also tent camping. Check out time is 2:00 P.M. Guests must leave the park by 10:00 P.M. No ground fires; animals to be kept on a leash; quiet in the campground after 10 P.M.

Monahans Sandhills State Park	
Monahans Sandhills State Park P. O. Box 1738 Monahans, TX 79756	Phone: 432-943-2092 Reservations: 512-389-8900 www.tpwd.state.tx.us

What To Do/Where To Go—Pyote Bomber Museum

Pyote, 15 miles west of Monahans, like other communities of the region during the late twenties onwards, enjoyed a dramatic surge of prosperity. By 1929 there were three refineries, five hotels, and two newspapers. The population soared. All of this was due to the Winkler oilfield to the north.

During the Second World War there was a surge of airfield building in west Texas to train aircrews. The Rattlesnake Bomber Base at Pyote gained its nickname from the large number of rattlesnakes found in the area. The base gained some additional fame when the Enola Gay was stationed there after the war. In 1963 the base was closed down. Today it is a prison, another feature of west Texas towns, housing teenagers. The community of Pyote is virtually lifeless, but there is a small museum that houses memorabilia of the World War II era. Open by appointment (432-389-5660), it offers a nostalgic and close up look at the past, down to a pair of officer's dress trousers. The Museum is in a county park that has a swimming pool, picnic area, overnight camping, and a three-hole golf course.

Monahans Calendar Of Selected Events

February	Ward County Livestock Show & Parade.
April	Star Gazing Party, Sandhills State Park.
July	Freedom Fest; Miss Monahans Pageant;
August	Butterfield Overland Stagecoach & Wagon Festival.
October	Wickett Bluegrass Festival.
November	Annual Pecan Show; Monahans Chamber of Commerce Style Show
December	Lighted Christmas Parade; Holiday Open House; Tour of Homes; Christmas and Chili Market.

Presidio

Elevation: 2,594 feet   Population: 7,107

History

In 1760, the Spanish named this place La Junta de los Ríos (the Junction of the Rivers), since this is where the Rio Conchos joins the Rio Grande. The area was home to the Jumano and Patarabueye tribes who lived in villages along the riverbank and tilled the rich soil. It was these settled tribes that the first visitors from the Old World stumbled across two centuries earlier in 1535.

This was Cabeza de Vaca and his three companions who, shipwrecked on the Gulf Coast in 1528, marched across Texas in an effort to reach Spanish settlements. After near starvation and other physical hardships on their lengthy trip, they were amazed to come across Indians growing crops and pursuing sedentary lives.

One hundred years later came the Spanish priests spreading the word of Catholicism. Around 1683, Juan Domínguez de Mendoza, along with Friar Nícolas López, established six missions in the area of Presidio. This is considered Presidio's founding date.

In the following century, the Spanish military moved into the area to protect their northern boundary against increasing attacks by Apache Indians. They established a string of presidios (forts) along the river. The scattering of Indian villages now had a garrison and a penal colony, which occupied both sides of the Rio Grande and became known as Presidio del Norte (1760).

Ninety years later (1848), following the end of the Mexican–American War, the Rio Grande became the international border. On the Mexican side the larger of the two townships was named Ojinaga, after a Mexican general. The town on the U.S. side took the shortened name of Presidio.

During the Mexican Revolution, the whole border region became militarized. In the Presidio/Ojinaga region, Pancho Villa's campaign achieved a quick, dramatic success. Following a siege of the town in December 1913, Villa attacked the federal troops the following month causing their wholesale retreat across the Rio Grande into Texas.

Today the towns are interrelated in economy and family ties, despite the international border. The bridge crossing is open 24 hours and the advent of the North American Free Trade Association (NAFTA) has seen a steady increase in cross-border traffic and a significant increase in Presidio's population. Nevertheless, this is still a quick and easy border crossing compared to major transit points like El Paso and Laredo.

Access/Orientation/Information

U.S. 67 connects Presidio with Marfa 60 miles to the north, then Fort Davis via Texas Hwy 17 to I-10 at Balmorhea. The scenic River Road runs southeast for 50 miles from Presidio along the north bank of the Rio Grande to Lajitas. Crossing the International Bridge to Ojinaga brings the traveler directly to Mexico's Hwy 16 that leads to Chihuahua City (150 miles).

For more information contact the Presidio Chamber of Commerce, located near the "Y" at 202 W. O'Reilly Street. Open 9–5, Monday– Friday.

Presidio Chamber of Commerce	
Presidio Chamber of Commerce P. O. Box 2497 Presidio, TX 79845	Phone: 432-229-3199 www.presidiotx.com

Chihuahua Giant Trail Wagon

Public Transportation

Bus—There is twice daily bus service northbound at 9:00 A.M. and 3:30 P.M. to Alpine, Fort Stockton, Odessa, and Midland. Arrives at 2:30 P.M. and 11:30 P.M. Journey time to Midland Airport is 6 hours. For fares call Presidio bus station at 432-229-3001, Odessa 432-332-5711, Midland 432-682-2761.

Taxi—Presidio Taxi: 432-229-2959. American Taxi: 432-229-2641.

Where To Stay—Motels

Three Palms Inn—Old U.S. 67 North. 51 rooms. Pool. Oasis Restaurant is next door. Ask for one of the newer rooms next to the pool. Rates, including tax from $59 (one person), $65 (two); in rooms near the pool, the rate for two is $69. 432-229-3211.

Big Bend Inn—Next to Thriftway store. Walking distance from bus station. Older property, brightly painted. Small pool. Six compact rooms with two double beds in each. $45/room, plus tax. Lorena will fix a burger. 432-229-3611.

Riata Inn Motel—Newest motel, on Hwy 67 outside of town. $59.89 (one person), $71.90 (two persons), including tax. Computer access. Pool. 432-229-2528.

Where To Stay—RV Park

Loma Paloma RV Park—On FM 170, 4 miles east of downtown, next to golf course. 84 wide, pull-thru sites. Showers. Full hookup $18 including tax. 432-229-2992.

Presidio RV Park—Next to Border Patrol. 40 spaces. 432-229-4286.

Where To Eat

El Patio—Downtown, next to the bus station. Popular. Open 6–9 daily. Also serves beer and ice cream.

El Patio	
El Patio 513 O'Reilly Street Presidio, TX 79845	Phone: 432-229-4409

The Enlightened Bean—Coffee Shop at the "Y." Good coffee, soups, smoothies, steaks and sandwiches, including the 1lb "Juicy Lucy" –$9.25, enough for two. 7 A.M.–6 P.M. daily. Closed Sunday. An enterprising new venture. 432-295-2690.

La Pasadita Taco Shop—On Hwy 67. 8–9 daily. Fast food, Mexican cuisine and buffet. 432-229-4146.

La Escondida Bar & Grill—Like being in the country. Off of Hwy 67 down Utopia road, close to US 67/FM 170 junction. 12–11 P.M. daily, closed Monday. Daily specials. Bar (beer and wine) with pool table, clean restrooms; the juke box can be wheeled outside. Shade trees, outdoor and inside (air conditioned) dining, and dance floor. Green chicken enchiladas ($9) are popular. 432-229-2906.

Oasis Restaurant—Next to Three Palms Inn. Open 6–10 daily. Good desserts. 432-229-3998.

San Jose Panadería—Near the "Y." Family-run bakery, known for its crescent rolls, and for tamales and menudo on Sunday.

Shopping

Nieto's (432-229-3220), **Montana Western Wear** (432-229-3224) and **Spencer's Department Store** (432-229-3324) all on O'Reilly Street offer a full selection of cowboy jeans, belts and hats, as well as a ladies section.

UETA Duty Free Store—Large building close to International Bridge. Some items may be bought on the spot, others like liquor and cigarettes (up to 40% off retail) can only be exported to Mexico at the International bridge. Limit for bringing back liquor: Texans 1 liter, others 4 liters. Tax per liter $1.10. 432-229-3766.

Radio Shack—On N. Business 67 behind Alco. 432-229-3620.

Porter's Thriftway—N. Business 67 in front of First Presidio Bank. Groceries, Western Union. 432-229-3776.

What To Do/Where To Go—Scenery/History

St. Francis Plaza opposite El Patio is an oasis of shade, fountains, and greenery. Santa Teresa de Jesus Church, est. 1683, on O'Reilly Street, was rededicated in October 1983 in its tri-centennial year.

What To Do/Where To Go—Golf

18-hole golf course 5 miles east of town on FM 170 was devastated by the September 2008 floods and, at the time of writing, its future is uncertain.. 432-229-2992.

What To Do/Where To Go—Outfitter

Angell Expeditions—Provides trips or bike to remote places in the Big Bend. In safety and with professional staff, this outfitter offers mountain biking, jeep tours, rock climbing and hiking in the area. www.angellexpeditions.com. 432-229-3713.

What To Do/Where To Go—Excursions

Shafter, 20 miles north on U.S. 67. Two thousand feet higher than Presidio, thus providing some relief from the heat in Presidio. For the few teachers and border officials who choose to live here, it is the ghost town of Shafter. In 1856, Colonel Shafter discovered a surface vein of silver in the foothills of the Chinati Mountains about two miles from present-day Shafter and a mine was started.

The town swelled to more than 2,000 residents and a church, school, stores, and cafes were established. During World War II, lead was extracted to aid the war effort. But problems of water and extraction were increasing in the deepest workings, and in 1942 the company closed down the mine and sent the miners away. Shafter became a ghost town.

Across the creek, next to the cemetery, is a simple and effective pictorial record of the town's mining and social past. Plans have been presented again recently to re-open the mine and to reinvigorate Shafter as a tourist attraction. This time there seems more likelihood of this happening, but time will tell.

Ojinaga—Sister city of 30,500, straight across the Rio Grande. No immigration formalities. Toll bridge. See page 77 for details of restaurants and sights in "O. J."

Chinati Hot Springs—A magical Oasis. 36 miles northwest on River Road FM 170 to Ruidosa, then a further 4 miles on a dirt road (clearly marked on FM 170). Containing lithium, arsenic and a variety of other natural healing minerals, the springs (110° F constant temperature) were used by indigenous people for centuries. In the 1930s the Kingston family opened the Springs to the public, and in recent years substantial improvements have been made.

Today, visitors can drop in for a day ($12.50 per person for day use), but an overnight stay, or longer, is recommended for the waters, the ambience and interraction with other guests to have effect. Overnight camping, including use of the mineral baths, costs $15 per person. Seven cabins, ranging from El Corazon ($75) to the El Presidente Suite ($125), are dotted around the property. There is a group hot tub for those whose cabins do not have a private bath. There is also, above the property, a welcome cold pool. No food is included in the rates but a modern kitchen enables visitors to fix their own food. Rates do not include tax. Located in a remote canyon on the flanks of the Chinati range, overlooking the Rio Grande with views across to Mexico, there are few better places to rejuvenate yourself, while taking an occasional hike along local trails. Getting there is half the adventure, and the webpage or the helpful hosts will tell you how to arrive via Pinto Canyon. 432-229-4165. www.chinatihotsprings.com.

Fort Leaton State Historical Site—On August 8, 1848, just after the end of the U.S.–Mexican War, four Americans drifted into Presidio del Norte from the Mexican interior and crossed the Rio Grande into Texas. The leader of the group was Benjamin Leaton, who had been employed by the governments of Sonora and Chihuahua as a "scalp hunter"—a collector of Indian scalps for bounty.

Leaton settled down quickly in Presidio, farming the rich alluvial soil, opened a trading post, and developed a lucrative trade in weapons with wandering bands of Apache and Comanche Indians. Before he died in 1851, Leaton also built the fort, which officially bears his name. Local residents, however, believing Leaton also collected Mexican scalps, refuse to dignify his memory and refer to the historic site by the Old Spanish village name, *El Fortín*.

The Burgess family, who owned a successful freighting enterprise on the San Antonio/Chihuahua Trail, took possession of the fort and lived there until 1926. Following their departure, the adobe structure fell into ruins and was finally donated in 1968 to the state of Texas by then owner Frank Skidmore of El Paso. What the visitor sees today is a great adobe fortress perched on the edge of a terrace overlooking the Rio Grande.

Approaching the entrance to the fort along a walkway, take a look at the signs describing the fort's history, which were erected in the 1960s. Make use of the several picnic sites with shade shelters, a useful spot for a snack before entering the fort. The small cemetery lies off to one side. The six graves are all of the Burgess family.

The total area of the site (buildings and surroundings) is just over 23 acres. Exhibits inside the fort include information on the agricultural Indians who farmed the floodplains in the 15th century, Spanish colonization, and the emergence of the Mexican Republic and the arrival of Anglo-Americans in the mid-19th century. Artwork, models, artifacts, and original photographs describe the importance of the Chihuahua Trail that passed by the fort.

Wandering through the 25 rooms open to the public, visitors can get an impression of the history of the region through the ages and also of the sinister history of the Leaton family. Following Leaton's death, his widow married Edward Hall who was later murdered for failing to repay a debt. In 1875, Hall's stepson (Leaton's son) murdered his stepfather's killer who had meanwhile moved into the fort.

Guided tours are now available thanks to a program that attracts local students as docents to the park. These interpretive tours cost $3 Two self-guided nature trails have recently been laid out next to the Fort.

Located three miles southeast of Presidio on FM 170. Fort Leaton State Historical Site is open from 8–4:30 daily. The entrance fee is $3 for adults, $2 seniors, children under 12, free. Entrance is free with a Texas Parks Pass.

Fort Leaton State Historical Site	
Fort Leaton State Historical Site P. O. Box 2439 Presidio, TX 79845	Phone: 432-229-3613

Presidio Calendar Of Selected Events

February—Annual Asado Cook-off sponsored by the Chamber of Commerce. Great cook-off of pork meat and red chili sauce, with prizes. Games for the kids, folkloric dancers, mariachi bands, vendor booths. For information call 432-229-3199, or 877-229-3199.

March—Art Festival, sponsored by the Chamber of Commerce.

October — Santa Teresa Fiestas. Santa Teresa de Jesus Church. 432-229-3235.

October–April — Living history tours at the fort.

December — La Posada del Fortin. Borderland Christmas is celebrated with song and dance, including a solemn devotional procession and a lighthearted *piñata* contest. For information about other events, call 432-229-3613.

Sanderson
(Top of The Big Bend)
Elevation: 2,900 feet   Population: 843

Most visitors to Big Bend use I-10 as their access route, usually turning off at Fort Stockton and heading south. An alternative route for those coming from San Antonio is US 90. This route is slightly shorter and more scenic. It leads to Del Rio, the Judge Roy Bean Visitor Center at Langtry, and to Sanderson before reaching Marathon. West of Del Rio, US 90 also provides access to Lake Amistad National Recreation Area and Seminole Canyon State Historical Park.

Sanderson, 120 miles west of Del Rio, is tucked into Sanderson Canyon amongst rolling hills and stark desert. Once a booming town due to the sheep and goat ranches nd major railroad hub (Terrell County is the scene of the last horse-mounted, train robbery in Texas), Sanderson suffered a severe economic downturn when the railroad closed its hub in 1995. However, due to escalating energy prices, oil and gas activities in the area are currently booming. However, due to escalating energy prices, oil and gas are booming in the county, along with sustainable energy enterprises and expansion of the U. S. Border Patrol facility. A private citizens group has undertaken efforts to save and restore Sanderson's historic 1882 railroad depot.

Designated by the Texas Legislature in 1998 as the "Cactus Capital of Texas," the community has been making a concerted effort to develop its nature tourism draw. With assistance from Texas Parks & Wildlife, a nature hiking trail winds around the town on its steepridges. The annual Prickly Pear Pachanga festival, held each Columbus Day weekend, celebrate all things cacti with seminars on native plants, conservation and sustainable living. Cactus-themed contests, food, arts and crafts booths attract visitors from the Big Bend region and across Texas. Sanderson's largely-unchanged look has increasingly attracted "big city folks" who like the picturesque vintage adobe architecure, remoteness of the town and the low prices of property. Recently, new gift, art, antique and collectible shops have opened along its main street (Hwy 90).

The Visitor Center, Hwy 90 and 3rd St., provides information about the Trans-Pecos region and Big Bend National Park. Includes an interesting cactus garden walk with stone pictographs showing the history of Terrell County, and a walking tour brochure with points of interest and local history.

Terrell County Visitor Center	
Terrell County Visitor Center P. O. Box 4869 Sanderson, TX 79848	Phone: 432-345-2324 www.sandersontx.info

How To Get There

By car on US 90 from Del Rio (120 miles east) or from Marathon (53 miles west); on US 285 from Fort Stockton (65 miles north).

By train with Amtrak. (three times weekly). www.amtrak.com. A request stop only, must be arranged in advance.

Where To Stay

Sandersons' accommodations include four motels, one Guest House, and one RV park.

Where to Stay—Motels ($40–$65 for two people)

When booking a motel, ask if they cater to construction crews since this may affect the peacefulness of your stay.

Outback Oasis Motel—14 rooms, 888-466-8822, 432-345-2850.

Budget Inn—26 rooms, 432-345-2541.

Desert Air Motel—16 rooms, 432-345-2572.

Sunset Siesta Motel—13 rooms, 877-674-3782, 432-345-2200.

Where to Stay—Guest House

Granny's Guest House—On 4th Street. Built in 1927, Granny's Guest House offers three rooms, one big bath, a kitchen, and stone patio. Lovingly restored and filled with furniture and collectibles. Price is $95 for up to 6 persons in three bedrooms with the run of the whole house. Helpful, amiable hostess Mrs. Hinkle lives adjacent. Coffee and tea provided. 432-345-2949.

Where to Stay—RV Parks

Canyons RV Park—28 hookups. 432-345-2916.

Where to Eat

Dairy King—Mexican food, chicken fried steak. Open 11–2, 5–8. 432-345-2254.

The Brown Bag—125 Oak Street (Hwy 90). Monday–Saturday 10:30 A.M.–2:00 P.M. Sandwiches, soups and salads To-Go. 432-345-3086.

Round House Café—309 W. Oak Open 10–2, 5–8. Closed Monday. Mexican, sandwiches, steaks. Salad bar. Sample plates: Rueben sandwich ($6.75), 5 oz. burger ($6.00), Fajitas plate ($10.50) and rib eye steak ($17.95). John Gonzalez who was Executive Chef at College Station for 20 years, has come back home. He intends to use only the freshest materials in his cooking, including locally grown produce and home-made sauces. Discount for seniors. 432-345-2481.

Eagle's Nest Café—109 E. Oak. Burgers, chicken fried steaks Barbeque on Saturdays. 432-345-3065.

What To Do—Museum

Terrell County Memorial Museum houses early Anglo settler artifacts, as well as genealogical records. Located at the corner of 2nd Street and Mansfield, across from the courthouse and lawn. 432-345-2936.

What To Do—Visits

The Snake House—Adjacent to the Outback Oasis Motel. Live snakes on display. A display of local reptiles and education center. Call Roy Engeldorf for admission. 432-345-2850

Terrell County Memorial Park—Dedicated to the lives of those lost in the June 1965 flood. Picnic tables and playground equipment.

Scenic Overlook—A trail up the hill behind Sanderson leading to the Water Tower, with great views of the town and surrounding area. The Cactus Capital Hiking Trail begins near Centennial Park and winds through Homing and Javelina Hills, around the Sanderson High School football and track fields, and ends at a spot near Hwy 90 and Wilson Street. Check with Visitor Center for more details.

East Gate Park—A unique art gallery painted on monoliths of local limestone. The art work celebrates the history and icons of Terrell County, from the time predating Native American culture to the cowboys and railroad culture of today. A must-see activity.

Sanderson Calendar Of Events

January	Terrell County Fair.
April	Buzzard Rally for motorcycle enthusiasts; Big Bend Open Road Race, 100 entries traveling at up to 200 mph, between Fort Stockton and Sanderson; Sheriff's Easter Egg Hunt; Historic Dryden Church Easter Sunrise Service.
May	Cinco de Mayo.
June	St. James Summer Festival.
July	Fourth of July parade, old-timer reunion, car show, and street dance.
October	Prickly Pear *Pachanga* (party), celebration of the cactus.
November	Turkey Shoot, start of mule deer hunting season.
December	Christmas lights and pageant, Hunter Feast banquet.

Study Butte
Elevation: 2,167 feet   Population: 160 (est.)

Named after a miner, Will Study, and pronounced "Stewdy Beaut," this scattered township is the last stop for services before entering the Big Bend National Park, 3 miles further south on Highway 118. The locals call it the "Study Butte–Terlingua microplex" and there is some truth in the linkage since it is hard to see where one ends and the other begins. At present, there is a local dispute. Some say the community at the intersection of Hwys 118 and 170 is Terlingua, because that is where the Terlingua post office is, and that Study Butte starts further south on Hwy 118. In Terlingua Ghostown and areas adjacent, the people say that the Study Butte/Terlingua demarcation is at Terlingua Creek (and that is the dividing line used here).

Like Terlingua, Study Butte's early history was mining, and the mounds of ore refuse from the Study Butte mine are visible to the left of the highway. The ore was cinnabar (mercury), the same as was being mined in Terlingua, but the closing down of the mine, which was owned by Diamond Shamrock, occurred about 30 years later than the Terlingua mine, in 1973. Study Butte sits at the intersection of Hwy 118 and FM 170 and offers two motels, a bank, post office, several eating places, a stables, a laudromat and some stores.

Information

Big Bend Chamber of Commerce representing Big Bend National Park, Terlingua, Study Butte, Lajitas, and Terlingua Ranch. 432-371-2427. www.bigbendchamberofcommerce.com.

"Visit Big Bend" (Brewster County Tourism Council) promotes Study Butte, Terlingua, and Brewster County outside of Alpine. There is no on-site office, but the organization has an efficient brochure and webpage. 877-244-2363. www.visitbigbend.com.

Services

Post Office—Monday–Friday, 8–1, 2:30–4:30.

Bank—Monday–Friday, 8:30–11:00, 2:00–4:30, open to 6 P.M. on Thursdays. ATM machine.

Towing — Terlingua Auto Service, 432-371-2223/2384.

Car Rental — Terlingua Auto Service (jeep and car rental) 432-371-2223.

Beauty Shop—Hats Off Hair Care, Wednesday–Friday, 432-371-2815.

Cycle Tek—For all motorcycle needs. 432-371-2560.

Hardware Store—Bee Mountain Hardware, Monday–Friday, 8:30–5; Saturday 10–2. 432-371-3113.

Laudromat—In the arcade at the "Y".

Desert Lotus Healing Arts—Massage therapy, bodywork, yoga. 432-371-2160.

Jeep Rental—Terlingua Auto Service. $125/day for up to 150 miles. 432-371-2223.

Where To Stay—Motels

Big Bend Resort and Mission Lodge—These two motels face each other across Hwy 118 at the intersection with FM 170. The Resort has 51 non-smoking rooms from motel units to a small house. Rates from Double Queen bedroom $99 to small/large duplex $149 / $169 to VIP House (sleeps four) $199. The Mission Lodge offers a Single Queen bedroom for two persons and apartments $99. Additional adults $10; rollway $10; pet fee $20. Also RV Park, Gift Shop, Golf Course, Café, Convenience Store with Gas Station. No check in after 10 P.M.

Big Bend Resort / Mission Lodge	
Big Bend Resort / Mission Lodge P. O. Box 336 Terlingua, TX 79852	Phone: 877-386-4383 or 432-371-2218 www.bigbendresortadventures.com

Chisos Mining Company Motel—At Easter Egg Valley. An older property with some character including Burr Rabbit curios shop. Single ('cozy') one-bed rooms from $57.23, double two-bed rooms with TV from $75.76. Cabins (small, large, really large with kitchenette sleeping up to 6 persons from $98-$153. Condos ("Santa Fe" and "Cliff Dwelling") from $141.70. www.cmcm.cc. 432-371-2254.

Chisos Mining Company Motel	
Chisos Mining Company Motel P. O. Box 228 Terlingua, TX 79852	Phone: 432-371-2254 www.cmcm.cc

Where To Stay—Bed and Breakfast

Ten Bits Ranch—("Somewhere...Out There"). 15 miles north of Study Butte on Hwy 118, then 2.3 miles west on North County Road. Four guest rooms with queen or double beds, with continental breakfast. Two-night minimum. Rates $159–$199 per room/night for two persons depending on the season. $25/night per extra person. Total capacity 10 guests. An off-the-grid facility. Breakfast is taken in the Cantina. Your host is an archeologist/paleontologist and conducts Dinosaur Excavations twice a year on the ranch. 866-371-3110. www.tenbitsranch.com.

Where To Stay—Cabins

Wildhorse Station—6 miles north of Study Butte on Hwy 118. A little different, and popular. Seven cabins/trailers, with one to three beds. Fully furnished with complete kitchens. Four of the cabins are on the side of Wildhorse Mountain facing west. Rates, typically, for Cabin No. 1, which hangs off the mountain side, are $80 for two, to $100 for up to 4 persons in the three-bed cabins. Snacks, ice, and cokes available at the store. 432-371-2526.

Where To Stay—RV Parks

Big Bend Resort—126 sites. Full hookups from $26–$29. Tent camping $15/night, double occupancy, discounts for longer stays. Extra person $3/night. Showers/Laundry. 432-371-2218.

Study Butte RV Park—Next to Study Butte store. 15 sites, $18/night. Owner Larry Harris also carves sotol walking sticks for a low, low price and does unusual silverware art work. 432-371-2468.

Where To Eat

Chili Pepper Café—Next to the Post Office. Open daily 8 A.M.– 9:00 P.M. Mexican food, burgers, daily specials. Beef and shrimp combo fajitas are popular. 432-371-2233.

Che!—A new café on Hwy 170 at Terlingua Springs Market, next to the creek. Salad bar and soups, with emphasis on organically grown food. Build your own sandwich. Pay by weight. Quick and affordable says Chad the owner. Monday–Friday, 11–3. 432-371-2662.

Rio Bravo Café—FM 170 just west of the intersection with Hwy 118. Only six tables, and one is reserved for the family. Family-run, with a colorful décor. A recent visitor reported: "The enchiladas are served casserole-style, not rolled, and the chili rellenos kicked my butt!" Open Monday–Saturday 11–3, 6–9. 432-371-2101.

Big Bend Resort Restaurant—At the "Y". Open daily for breakfast 6–10, lunch 11–3. Tex Mex fare including Picadillo plate. Convenience Store. Beer and wine. 432-371-2483/2291

Kathy's Kosmic Kowgirl Kafe—aka The Pink Place. One mile west of the Y on Hwy 170. Unmistakable, unconventional, outdoor eatery, popular with river guides. Good in winter in front of an open fire, ok in summer under the shade tent. Big 3-egg breakfast burritos ($5), lunch might be a burger, sandwich or BBQ. Kathy dispenses food and wit through the serving window. Open Thursday–Monday, 6:30 A.M.–3:30 P.M. www.kosmickowgirl.com. 423-371-2164.

Terlingua Springs Market—Half mile west of Hwy 118 intersection. Natural foods, good coffee, fresh veggies. Monday–Saturday, 9–noon, 3–6. 432-371-2332.

Shops/Galleries

Alice Knight's Art Studio—Opposite Terlingua Springs Market, set back from the highway. Pottery, Paintings, Prints and other local work, especially CDs . Open "at my leisure" says manager Ron. 432-371-2328.

Quilts etc. by Marguerite—Handmade quilts, made by herself and by other quilters, and handicrafts. Next to the Hardware store below Bee Mountain. Marguerite Chanslor. 432-371-2292.

Many Stones Gifts—On Hwy 118. Fine jewelry hand crafted by the proprietor, stained glass, precious and semi-precious stones, mineral specimens, and eclectic surprises. Many native and exotic cacti, also air plants (*tillansia*) Open most of the time. 432-371-2994.

Burr Rabbit Curios—Classic souvenir shop in the Chisos Mining

Company motel. Rocks, fossils, and kitschy memorabilia. Good prices. 432-371-2254.

Maverick Mountain Rock Shop—Hwy 118 just south off Rough Run Creek. The oldest mineral marketplace in Brewster County. Proprietors live on site. Drop in at any reasonable hour.

Study Butte Store—Open 7–10 daily. "At the traffic light." Colorful South Brewster County emporium. Crowded with chatting locals, and tourists buying beer or peering at posters by the entrance. Ice, gas, liquor, and video rentals. 432-371-2231.

Cottonwood Store — New and efficient Across the street. Groceries, beer and wine, other necessities. Open daily 7–9, Sunday 9–7

What To Do—Ultralight Flights

$30 for 40 minutes. Hwy 170 4 miles west of junction with Hwy 118. Inquire at Chisos Mining Co. Motel 432-371-2254. During peak season only.

What To Do—Golf

Big Bend Resort Golf Course—Adjacent to the motel. A true desert course where accuracy is rewarded. A par 72 with nine holes that use 18 tee boxes. Carts available. 432-371-2218.

What To Do—Horseback Riding

Big Bend Stables—On Hwy 118 near the Y. Long-established, competent outfit with fully-trained personnel. Guided trail rides from $40/hour. Other short rides to the Old Mine, to Indian Head and Ocotillo Mesa (with lunch), as well as sunset rides. In addition, an imaginative choice of longer multi day trips includes: Combo Trips (ride and raft); 2- to 3-day trips into Big Bend Ranch State Park to the back-country, or focusing on geology or archeology. Four- and five-day riding trips into Chihuahua State, Mexico are for the adventurous (passports needed). www.lajitasstables.com. 800-887-4331, 432-371-2212.

What To Do—River Rafting, Jeep Tours, Hiking

Desert Sports—Mountain Biking a specialty, also other trips. See description on p. 999. www.desertsportstx.com. 888-989-6900, 432-371-2727.

Far Flung Outdoor Center—Full-service outfitter offering raft trips, jeep tours, ATV trips, shuttles, and rentals. With 30 years experience, Far Flung offers a complete slate of river trips from a half-day to 10 days on the Lower Canyons. Most popular is the Santa Elena Canyon overnight. Mariscal and Boquillas Canyons are the two other medium length trips. Prices from $66 for the half-day trip to $1,800 for the 72 mile, 10-day Lower Canyons. There is an emphasis on nature instruction from the river guides. Similarly, the Jeep Tours will take you to places you could not get to on your own, and your driver will show you things you would have missed by yourself. The most popular tour is the 3-hour Camp 360 tour ($64) which involves a steep climb up a dirt track to a mountain-top viewe across the whole area. Another in-demand tour is Round the Bend where the driver takes you into Big Bend national Park and explain the geologic formations along the Maxwell Scenic Drive. This all-day tour ($129) visits Santa Elena Canyon and returns via the Old Maverick Road. FFOC also organizes two seasonal hiking tours within the national park for Elderhostel. Check www.eldershostel.org. For full details of FFOC jeep tours, river trips, ATV tours, rentals and shuttles, go to www.farflungoutdoorcenter.com. 800-839-7238, 432-371-2489.

Big Bend River Tours—At Hwy 118 and FM 170. The oldest, full-service outfitter in Big Bend country. A full slate of river, jeep and hiking trips throughout the area, from half-day to multi-day, including combo trips (e.g. saddle and paddle). At one end of the selection is the half-day float trip for those short on time but keen for the river ex-perience. Three miles is a good distance to get a sense of adventure, yet not too long to exhaust families. Trips depart at 8 and 2. $67/$72 per person. There is the overnight trip through Santa Elena Canyon, Big Bend's most popular canyon, which gives participants time fully to appreciate the appeal of the Rio Grande, soaring limestone walls, a sense of remoteness and the silence of an early evening before a tasty meal is set before you. $310 per person. Other services include hiking only, canoe ($50/day) and raft rentals, shuttle service from Midland, El Paso and Alpine (airport or train), and a low water trip (smart idea) into Santa Elena Canyon called the "Boomerang" Adventure. Promotional Trips (Dad goes free on Father's Day) are also on offer from time to time. www.bigbendrivertours.com. 800-545-4240, 432-371-3033.

Terlingua & Ghostown

Elevation: 2,835 feet
Population: 78 (est. year round)

History

"Close to nature, far from civilization, Terlingua was a quicksilver mining town. In 1902 Howard E. Perry established the Chisos Mining Company. Terlingua was Perry's town. By the end of World War I, Terlingua quicksilver dominated the industry in the U.S., but by 1942 Perry declared bankruptcy and Terlingua became a ghost town."[*]

After World War II came a shift in land use. Previously mining and ranching prevailed. In the 1940s mining went bust and ranching has been struggling ever since. The establishment in 1944 of the Big Bend National Park to the east of Terlingua saw 800,000 acres become public property for recreational use. A little over fifty years later, a large chunk of land to the west of Terlingua became a state park: the 270,000-acre Big Bend Ranch State Park.

Terlingua Ghostown comes as a stark contrast. Mine shafts covered with gratings, pieces of rusting machinery, low standing walls without any roofs—all randomly scattered across the side of a mountain—indicate that there was previous life here. In the early years of the Twentieth Century 2,000 workers worked and lived in the area.

To the first-time visitor Terlingua still looks like the remains of something from the past, part industrial, part residential. But in the past twenty-five years significant changes have taken place, some subtle, others more obvious. A new community has developed, part of it catering to tourists, the other part acting as home to a growing number of artists and others escaping city life.

Two sorts of newcomers arrived. First the river guides who steer the canoes and rafts through the Rio Grande canyons. These fit, mainly

[*] *The Terlingua Area* by Dimitri Gerasimou (DeGe Verlag, 1964).

young, outdoor types are seasonal employees of the local rafting companies in the area. Despite a continuing shortage of water in the Rio Grande, river trips are still one of the main tourism attractions.

"What attracts people to Terlingua today is the austere landscape, the big sky and a connection between these physical features and where they are in their own life," says David Lanman, a musician from Ohio who came to Terlingua. Lanman played music, opened a Bed & Breakfast, changed his mind, and then left to live in Marfa. But his summary of what attracts artists and others to this corner of the desert rings true. Artists, musicians and sundry other escapees from elsewhere make up the second, larger number of Terlingua newcomers.

Talented musicians, famous as well as unrecognized, are attracted to this area and impressive live music can be heard year-round in such local restaurants as the Starlight Theatre in the Ghostown. Artists painting hubcaps, doing watercolors, producing silver jewelry or throwing pots emerge from time to time from their simple, sometimes primitive homes

Terlingua Graveyard

to put on shows of their work. Having no water or electricity is no stigma. "You must take a vow of poverty to live here," said one old river guide, only half jokingly.

Quicksilver

Mercury, from which the popular name quicksilver comes, has been in use for over 2,500 years. In the Seventeenth Century it was used to determine atmospheric pressure. In the Eighteenth Century, Fahrenheit invented the mercury thermometer. At the end of that century, Edward Charles Howard discovered that mercury could be used as a primer to detonate gunpowder in cartridges and shells. The discovery and extraction of mercury in Terlingua came at a timely moment, just prior to World War I.

Howard E. Perry, founder and president of the Chisos Mining Company, was a Chicago industrialist who won the Terlingua property in a poker game. He was an autocratic, single-minded industrialist whose sole aim was to reduce expenses and maximize profits. Extremely secretive, wary of everyone, and responsible to none but himself, he was totally incapable to changing his policies or adapting new techniques. Personal relationships did not exist for him. Typically, in 1940 he fired without notice his manager of 25 years. In 1942 the company closed down.

Chili Cookoff

"To understand how upwards of ten thousand usually normal people gather in a remote corner of Texas desert to drink beer, taste chili, raucously applaud a wet T-shirt competition and engage in general silliness it is necessary to go back to the late 1960s. This was the era of the Vietnam War, bell-bottoms, hippies and anti-war protests and the 'Summer of Love.' Chili and everything associated with it was definitely out. Tofu, bean sprouts, and brown rice were the choice of the flower children that dominated the popular culture of that time.

"The chili movement started in Dallas about then, the plot hatched by a group of men sitting around talking over a pot of chili and cocktails. One of the men, race-car designer Carroll Shelby, mentioned some property he owned down in the Big Bend including a ghost town named Terlingua. He wanted to sell the property but couldn't find anyone who knew anything about it. What he needed was a publicity stunt.

"A second man, Tom Tierney, suggested that a chili cookoff be held. Dallas Morning News columnist Frank X. Tolbert, also in the group, pounced on the idea and carried it a step further. Having read a recent column by food writer H. Allen Smith in the New York Times entitled "No One Knows More About Chili Than I Do," Tolbert proposed a chili cookoff between Smith and Wick Fowler, their host on the evening of the meal in Dallas.

"The cultural superiority of Texas over New York was at stake when Smith and Fowler turned in their entries in front of a substantial crowd, which had made its way to the middle of the Chihuahuan desert later that year. Aware of the PR value of the moment, the judges declared a tie, meaning that everyone had to come back and do it again next year.

"For some reason, the entire surreal picture of a mass of beer-drinking people crowded around two men stooped over two black pots of chili in the middle of nowhere while a country-western band played, was just what people were looking for during the gloomy year of 1967. The Cookoff was born. From that point it took off, developing into a rivalry between two factions that lasts to this day. Actually two cookoffs take place near Terlingua at the same time."

From the Big Bend Quarterly, Fall 1999.

Chili Cookoff

Terlingua Today

Now, thirty years into the new tourism-led economy, Terlingua/Study Butte is showing distinct signs of change, including concrete and regulations. One of the reasons that led those early escapees from the big city to search out a remote desert location was an absence of laws. Not that they were necessarily escaping from the law—at least not many of them. Like hippies, some of whom were also attracted to Terlingua, they were looking for an alternative lifestyle.

The opening of Big Bend High School and the construction of new roads demanded some agreement on regulations by a population that likes to call itself "a herd of mavericks." As life becomes more regimented, the look of the Ghostown is changing. More affluent newcomers have built homes in southwest adobe style. Tourist-oriented businesses have opened up. To the first-time visitor the external appearance looks decidedly frontier, but the underlying character is changing as the place grows. The old timers are still to be seen, some at the bar of the Boatman's Grill, others outside on the porch of the Terlingua Trading Company drinking a six-pack and watching the tourists.

Note
Terlingua Ghostown is clearly marked and roughly occupies the old mine town. The beginning and end of Terlingua and Study Butte have recently been under dispute locally. For the point of view of identification, this book uses Terlingua Creek as the dividing line between the two communities.

Orientation

Four miles west of Study Butte, twelve miles east of Lajitas, and half-a-mile off FM 170, Terlingua Ghostown is a mix of old mining remains and new commercial and residential buildings scattered across a south-facing hillside within sight of the Chisos Mountains.

The origin of the name is not agreed on, but the most popular explanation is that it comes from *tres lenguas*, or three languages: Indian, Spanish, and English.

Information

The Brewster County Tourism Council is responsible for promoting the region. They do not have an on-site office. The Big Bend Chamber of Commerce provides business and tourist services and sponsors Big Bend Community Recycling and Green Scene. A handy calendar of events is available at www.bigbendchamberofcommerce.com. 432-371-2427.

The Brewster County Tourism Council	
The Brewster County Tourism Council P. O. Box 335 Terlingua, TX 79852	www.visitbigbend.com

Last Minute Low Budget Productions produces plays several times a year at the Behind the Store chili cookoff venue on Hwy. 170. This group also sponsors the annual Home Tour of Terlingua (in late January) which features homes with alternative building styles, and a new Garden Tour, scheduled for late August, providing a rare insight into residents' lives. For specific dates and further information, contact Martha Stafford 432-371-2399.

Events

Chili Cookoff—The annual chili cook offs take place on the first weekend of November. These events are mainly for outsiders—up to 10,000 invade the area temporarily. Local participation is confined to one or two local chili cooks.

Word Off—By contrast, the "Word Off," which takes place in the Terlingua Springs Coffee Shop in February, is very much for locals—writers, poets and anyone else who chooses to read something, written by them or by someone else. The diversity, creativity and humor of the residents of South Brewster County is nowhere more evident than during the "Word Off."

For information on local events look for the *Terlingua Moon*,
a weekly broadsheet posted in the area.

Services

Wi-Fi—at Espresso Y Poco Mas coffee shop in the Ghostown, and the Starlight Theater.

Massage—Desert Lotus Healing Arts. Massage, facials and foot treatments. In the ghostown. Call 432-371-2160 or 432-386-0305.

Where To Stay—Hotels, Rooms

Holiday Hotel—Behind the Terlingua Trading Post (which acts as booking agent), this former tourist court now offers 6 rooms, artistically restored with antiques and local art by Ghostown owner Bill Ivey. Two 2-rooms suites, two rooms with bath, and two with shared bath. Queen-size beds. $100-$150. www.bigbendholidayhotel.com. 432-371-2234.

Upstairs at the Mansion—Located in one restored section of the ruined Perry Mansion, the home of mine owner Howard E. Perry, this one-room hotel is a short stroll from the Ghostown center. Your room has its own entry, up some stairs with a small library outside. Simple touches of minimalist décor give an idea of history. Views over the Ghostown. Fan. Full-size and twin beds. $75/night. Bathroom down below, shared with owner Kaci Fullwood. 360-713-3408.

La Posada Milagro Guesthouse & Casita—"The Miracle Inn" owner, Mimi Webb-Miller, a known figure in these parts, offers rustic ambience in carefully restored former ruins, located high on the Ghostown hill with spectacular views of the Chisos Mountains. Four rooms, refrigerated air; three with queen beds and one with bunk beds, with private (in the Chisos Honeymoon Room) or shared bath. Sun deck. Two courtyards. $145 for one person for the bunk bedroom ($25 per extra person), $185–$210 for two persons. Wi-Fi. La Casita, separate building, king bed, jacuzzi, complete kitchen, private porch $350. 432-371-3044. www.laposadamilagro.net. Or, drop in at the coffee shop Espresso y Poco Más (below the Guest House) to book on the spot.

Terlingua House—Two miles west of the Ghostown, this nicely furnished adobe-style complex comprises four bedrooms and two baths in three separate buildings. Amenities include a complete kitchen, and a telescope for night sky watching. Set in 15 acres of native vegetation, Terlingua House has easy access and complete privacy, located under a sheer limestone escarpment, and enjoys great views of the Chisos Mountains. Two of the bedrooms have queen beds; the Studio, known as the homeymoon suite, has a double bed. Higher rates during Chili Cook Off, special offers during the summer. Can sleep up to 8. Rates are $220/night with a cleaning fee of $75. Two-night minimum. www.terlinguahouse.com. 325-473-4400.

El Dorado Hotel—A recent structure located at the entrance to the Ghostown. 20 modest rooms have been completed, and the bar / restaurant is now open. Rates from $79 (one person, full size bed), $89 (two full-size beds) to $125 (king size bed with jacuzzi). www.eldorado-hotel.com. 800-371-3588, 432-371-2111.

Where To Stay—Camping

Las Ruinas Camping Hostel—2- and 4-person tent camping, adjacent to the Boatman's Bar. Wood floor, bunk beds. Use your own sleeping bag, or rent one. Showers and restrooms shared. Outdoor kitchen. $22 for two, $36 for four persons. 9 sites for own tent camping $12/night. Book at Boatman's Bar. 432-371-2291.

Where To Stay—House Rental

Candelilla House—In the Ghostown. Two bedrooms, sleeps up to 5 persons. Composting toilet. $165 and up, depending on number of guests. 432-294-0441

Rock House—4 miles west of Lajitas. A fishing camp set up in one large room, including 2 queen beds, and two other beds, on the very bank of the Rio Grande. Sleeps 6–8. $200/night. Book through Terlingua Trading Post 432-371-2234.

Study Butte, five miles to the east, has several motels. Lajitas Resort, 12 miles to the west, has a variety of deluxe accommodations.

Where To Stay—RV Parks

BJ's RV Site — Behind the Terlingua Store and the site of one of the annual cookoffs. At other times of the year it is very quiet. $20 for full hookup, two persons. Showers. Laundry. 432-371-2259.

Big Bend RV Park—Located at Terlingua Creek, 35 sites bordering the creek and adjacent to La Kiva restaurant. $12 for full hookup. Tents sites $2.50 per person. Showers. 432-371-2250.

Where To Eat (Ghostown)

Starlight Theatre—Well-known, colorful restaurant/bar installed in the adobe remains of what was formerly the local movie theater (1930). Colorful décor, a full bar, and (often) live music, are complemented by an imaginative menu, such as Wild Boar Sausage as one of the Previews ($3–$13) and Chick Fried Antelope, steaks, Curry Vegetable with Chicken for Feature Presentations ($13–$33). Open daily for dinner, 5:30–9:30. Bar open 5–12 (til 1:00 A.M. on Saturday night). 432-371-2326. www.starlighttheatre.com.

Starlight Theatre Restaurant

Ghost Town Café—On the left while approaching the Ghostown. Open 7 days, 7–3 summer, 6–5 winter, for breakfast and lunch. Cheap and filling. Eat here if you want to talk to everyone in the café and in the kitchen. Smokers inside, non-smokers outside. Breakfasts include the popular chili cheese omelet, also biscuits, gravy and sausage ($3). Specials include tilapia on Friday, and chicken fried steak on most days. 432-371-3000.

High Sierra Bar & Grill—At the El Dorado Hotel. Open noon to 9:45 P.M. Wine and beer at the bar. Occasional art shows. 432-371-2111.

Where To Drink (Ghostown)

Starlight Theatre—Described above.

Boatman's Bar and Grill—A casual hangout, popular with locals. Big garage doors opening onto a patio set the scene and provide a spectacular view of the Chisos Mountains. Large beer selection, also wine. Pool table, large screen TV. A dance floor and stage have recently been added, allowing the many local musicians to perform. Book here for tent camping. Snacks (mini pizza, chili and beans), also served after 10 P.M. Open daily, evenings 4–midnight (till 1 A.M. on Saturday night). 432-371-2219.

High Sierra Bar & Grill—Described above.

Outside The Ghostown

La Kiva Restaurant & Bar—By Terlingua Creek on FM 170, 3 miles west of the "Y" in Study Butte. Long a feature of south Brewster County, this cave bar/restaurant is fun and lively. Their special cocktails like The Mind Eraser (kahlua), and the 30 tequilas (from $1.50 at Happy Hour to $64 a shot for the rarest) match the menu which lists ribeye steaks (from $12–$17), pork ribs ($15), chicken ($8.50) as well as salads and sandwiches. There's karaoke on Tuesday and Open Mike on Wednesday, and usually live music on Friday/Saturday. Open evenings from 5–midnight (till 1:00 A.M. on Saturday) every day of the year. 432-371-2250. www.lakiva.net.

Long Draw Pizza—Hwy 170 two miles west of Terlingua Ghostown. Nancy, the owner, serves pizzas described as "wonderful" by a food critic. The "Grumpy Ed" (blue cheese, Canadian bacon, chicken topping), named after the founder, is particularly popular. Wednesday–Sunday from 5–10 P.M. 432-371-2608.

Kathy's Kosmic Kowgirl Kafe—One mile west of the Y at Study Butte is The Pink Place. Unmistakable, unconventional, fun. You're likely see to river guides in the early morning polishing off a 3-egg-breakfast burrito with cheese and beans. Mainly outdoor seating; fire in winter, shade in summer. Lunch is a sandwich, burger or BBQ. Kathy dispenses food and chat through the kitchen window. Drive-in movies are screened, May–September. Open Thursday–Monday 6:30 A.M.–3:30 P.M. Closed Tuesday–Wednesday. 432-371-2164. www.kosmickowgirl.com.

Shops/Galleries

Terlingua Trading Company—In the Ghostown. No one along the border knows retailing better than owner Bill Ivey, who previously owned the Lajitas Trading Post. Excellent on books, strong on jewelry, also Mexican imports, Indian crafts, and a whole lot more, not forgetting the 6-pack of beer that you can take outside and drink on the porch. Open daily. 432-371-2234. www.GhostTownTexas.com.

Leapin' Lizard Studio & Gallery—Just north of the Starlight Theater, the Leapin' Lizard offers locally created fine and folk art, jewelry, hand crafted light fixtures, photographs, and is also the showroom for owner Bryn Mawr's original watercolor desert landscapes. Locally made treasures from $30, fine art from $300 to $3,000. The porch is an inviting place to rest, cool down, and enjoy the views of the distant Chisos Mountains. www.leapinlizardterlingua.com. 432-371-2775.

Terlingua Store—On Hwy 170, close to Ghostown entrance. Well stocked with foodstuff, drinks. Adjacent, is the Frank X Tolbert Chili Cook Off site. Also BJ's RV Park.

What To Do

Buy a pamphlet at Terlingua Trading Company ($1 goes towards the church fund) and follow the instructions, in particular:

Visit the cemetery. Check out the 400 graves of old residents, Mexican and Anglo, buried side by side. Also, on the south side, a newer grave (2007) of the Burro Lady, Judy Magers, who wandered the area's highways for many years with her burro. The Day of the Dead (November 2) is a major celebration here.

Visit the Church, behind the Starlight Theater. Non denominational, used for weddings snd funerals, also for yoga classes and reunions. New floor, and new stained glass windows—a work in progress.

Menagerie Press. Lauren Stedman does quality printing on antique presses.

What To Do/Where To Go—Horseback Riding

Big Bend Stables—See listing under Study Butte. 800-887-4331, 432-371-2212.

What To Do/Where To Go — Rafting/Biking/Hiking

Desert Sports (Terlingua) — On FM 170 just before Ghostown turnoff. A wide selection of trips including Guided Trips (Mountain biking; canoeing and rafting; Multi Sport Trips (Hike, Bike, Boat) and Rentals, also shuttles. Bike and Canoe rentals and bike repairs. Organizers of the Mas o Menos 100k Marathon, this small and dedicated outfit specializes in bikes: from a 4–6 hour ride around Lajitas, to 2- and 3-day trips along the Old Ore Road in the National Park or into the Solitario (the Hermit), the main geologic feature of Big Bend Ranch State Park.

Desert Sports (Terlingua)	
Desert Sports P. O. Box 448 Terlingua, TX 79852	Phone: 888-989-6900 or 432-371-2727 www.desertsportsx.com

Additional Reading

Quicksilver — Terlingua and the Chisos Mining Company by K.B. Ragsdale. 1976.

Chronicles of the Big Bend by W. D. Smithers. 1999 reprint. A must for anyone wanting to know how the Big Bend country was shaped in the first half of the 20th century. 1999 reprint.

Tales from the Porch by Blair Pittman. The real stuff from old timers. 2008.

Terlingua Teacher by Trent Jones. Teaching in the one-room schoolhouse and being a Terlingua resident in the early 70s. 2010 reprint

Why Terlingua? by Carl Leatherwood. A recent arrival describes the local people. 2009.

Federico Villalba's Texas by Juan Casas. Story of a successful Mexican pioneer in Big Bend. 2008.

Big Bend and Texas Mountains Travel Guide. Free bi-annual travel guide to the whole region. Available locally at Chambers of Commerce and motels. See www.bigbendtexasmountains.com.

Terlingua Moon. Monthly broadsheet with local news and events.

Valentine

Elevation: 4,300 feet est.   Population: 160 est.

History

"Valentine, the smaller of Jeff Davis County's two towns, is on U.S. Highway 90 and the Southern Pacific Railroad in the southwestern part of the county, thirty-six miles west of Fort Davis. It was founded and named when the Southern Pacific Railroad crew, building east, reached the site on February 14, 1882. Trains began running the next year, and a post office was established in 1886. In 1890 Valentine had a population estimated at 100, two saloons, a general store, a hotel, and a meat market. Two years later only one saloon was left, but the population had risen to an estimated 140. Valentine became a shipping point for local cattle ranchers, and by 1914 the town had an estimated population of 500, five cattle breeders, a news company, a real estate office, a grocery store, a restaurant, and the Valentine Business Club. A decade later the population had fallen to an estimated 250, but it rose again to 500 by the late 1920s and to 629 by the early 1930s. In the late 1970s the town had an estimated population of 226, a high school, an elementary school, and two churches. The estimated population rose to 328 in the early 1980s and in 1990 it was 217."

— Martin Donell Kohout

Reprinted with permission from the Handbook of Texas Online, copyright Texas State Historical Association, 1999–2001.

Valentine Today

No grocery store, no café, no gasoline, not even a pay phone. Two churches and around 160 inhabitants among whom are artist Boyd Elder and mountain lion tracker Henry McIntyre. The big event of the year takes place in the post office around Valentine's Day when 15–18,000 pieces of mail arrive to be redispatched with the Valentine stamp. If you wish to add to that number, send the card to U.S. Post Office, Valentine, Texas 79854.

However, recently a dentist has opened, also a library on the north side of the highway as you drive through town.

Van Horn

Elevation: 4,010 feet   Population: 2,435

Situated 119 miles east of El Paso and 47 miles west of where I-20 separates from I-10, Van Horn lies in the extreme west of the Central Time zone. It advertises itself as the crossroads of The Texas Mountain Trail and is surrounded by distant mountains on all sides, in some of which mining (for marble and talc) still takes place. There is a flourishing pecan orchard to the south of town, but apart from that not much is happening on the land as ranching has slowly wound down. The town's main purpose is serving travelers on I-10.

The name comes from Lt. James Judson Van Horn, who was in command of the U.S. Army garrison at the nearby Van Horn Wells when he was taken prisoner and held captive for two years by Confederate forces. Twenty years later in 1881 when the town was founded, it was named after the lieutenant. It might have been more appropriately named Van Horne, since Major Jefferson Van Horne, commander of Fort Bliss in El Paso in 1849, reportedly discovered the wells that are located twelve miles south of town.

The wells were used by the Mescalero Apaches for years and were well known to travelers on the San Antonio to El Paso coach route in the 1850s. A sign on U.S. 90 commemorates the wells' discovery and refers to a battle fought nearby between soldiers and Indians in 1879, as the so-called "Buffalo" soldiers of the U.S. Army gradually cleared the way for safe passage of the stagecoaches.

As the Crossroad of the Texas Mountain Trail, Van Horn promotes itself as a great place at which to base travels to many of the regional attractions. The drive north of Van Horn on State Hwy. 54, along the eastern edge of the Sierra Diablo range, is one of the most beautiful drives in Texas. El Capitan, the prominent feature of the Guadalupe Mountains National Park, grows increasingly majestic, and the traveler has an opportunity to appreciate its full magnificence at the road side picnic area at its base.

As a Texas Main Street City, Van Horn is making significant progress toward community development and beautification, assuring its role as an oasis in the vast Chihuahuan desert and as a base for regional travel opportunities.

284

Access/Orientation/Information

Interstate 10 runs east/west and is intersected by Texas 54, which goes north 55 miles to Guadalupe Mountains National Park, and U.S. 90, which runs southeast 74 miles to Marfa.

For more information contact the Convention Center and Visitors Bureau, which is open daily and handles all tourism inquiries.

Van Horn Convention Center and Visitors Bureau	
Convention Center & Visitors Bureau P. O. Box 448 Van Horn, TX 79855	Phone: 866-424-6939 or 432-283-2682 www.vanhorntexas.org

Mileage to: El Paso is 119 miles, San Antonio 450 miles, Houston 610 miles, and Dallas via I-20 is 508 miles.

Public Transportation

The nearest commercial airport and train station are in El Paso, 119 miles away. Buses travel round the clock east and westbound on I-10. Greyhound buses stop at Pilot Truck Stop.

Local Publications

Van Horn Advocate—A weekly–Thursday.

Services

Hospital and Rural Health Clinic—800 Eisenhower. 432-283-2760 (hospital), 432-283-9194 (clinic).

Towing Service—Juan's Auto Repair. 915-345-4217.

A & A Repairs, 805 E. Broadway. 432-283-9048

Where To Stay—Motels

Eighteen motels and one new hotel provide over 700 rooms. Many of the motels, in fact most of the town's business is on Broadway, are parallel to the interstate. Comfort Suites, yet to be finished at the time of writing, will be the newest motel. Hampton Inn is the most recently completed motel. The historic Hotel, 100 E. Broadway is now open. This famous building, designed by architects Trost & Trost, first opened in 1930. Today its 38 well restored rooms rent from $69-$129. A restaurant and bar will open soon. www.hotelelcapitan.net. 877-283-1220. 432-283-1220.

Desert Inn—401 E. Broadway. 432-283-9030.

America's Best Value Inn—1705 W. Broadway. 432-283-2410.

Budget Inn—1303 W. Broadway. 432-283-2019

Days Inn at Van Horn—600 E. Broadway. 432-283-1007.

Economy Inn—1500 W. Broadway. 432-283-2754.

EconoLodge—1601 W. Broadway. 432-283-2211.

Hampton Inn—1921 S.W. Frontage Road. 432-283-0088.

Holiday Inn Express—1905 Frontage Drive. 432-283-7444.

King's Inn—1403 W. Broadway. 432-283-2617.

Knight's Inn & Suites—1309 W. Broadway. 432-283-2030.

Motel 6—1805 W. Broadway. 432-283-2992.

Ramada Ltd.—200 Golf Course Drive. 432-283-2780.

Royal Motel—300 E. Broadway. 432-283-2087.

Sands Motel—805 E. Broadway. 432-283-9247.

Value Inn—901 W. Broadway. 432-283-2259.

Super 8—1807 Frontage Road. 432-283-2282.

Taylor Motel—900 W. Broadway. 432-283-2266.

Village Inn—403 W. Broadway. 432-283-2286.

Where To Stay—RV Parks

There are 254 spaces available at 4 RV Parks on East and West Broadway and at the KOA on US 90 at Hamper Lane.

Where To Drink

Don & Ruby's Lounge—711 Laurel Street.

Gilbert's Lounge—313 E. Broadway.

El Capitan Bar—102 E. Broadway (coming soon).

Where To Eat

Papa Chuy's Spanish Inn—1200 W. Broadway. 432-283-2066. Papa Chuy's billboards greet you from the highway: "Praise be the

Lord," or, if you have passed it, they tell you so. Patio dining is offered along with smoking and no-smoking sections inside. Outside, a large sign reads "John Madden Haul of Fame" recognizing the support and publicity given by the hefty ex-football coach to Chuy's. Tacos, gorditas, fajita plates, chili verde plates, and machaca (chopped beef cooked with fried vegetables and cheese sauce, with beans and rice) are some of the many items available in this popular restaurant. Open 9 A.M.–10 P.M.

Cattle Company Restaurant—1703 W. Broadway. 5–10 P.M. only. Best for steaks. 432-283-1163.

Sands Restaurant—805 E. Broadway. Charbroiled steaks and burgers. Buffet changes daily. Part of Tommy Lee Jones 2005 movie "The three burials of Melquiades Estrada" was shot here.

Mija's Restaurant—400 E. Broadway. New. Great Mexican food. 432-283-1334.

Lizzy's—400 E. Broadway. American and Mexican food. 432-283-1521.

Country Grill—I-10, Golf Course Drive. American and Mexican food, daily specials, salad bar and buffet. 432-283-2343.

Papa's Pantry—Next to the enormous Pilot Travel Center at I-10 and US 90. This all-purpose restaurant gets high marks for their attention to small details, like their Mickey Mouse pancakes for kids. 432-283-2302.

McDonalds, Wendy's, Subway, Charlie Bigg's Fried Chicken, Pizza Pro's, and Dairy Queen are all easily visible.

What To Do/Where To Go

Van Horn is a useful pit stop catering to the bulk of travelers who are simply stopping to fuel, to eat, or stay the night. But, if you need to take a stroll along Broadway before or after your meal, drop by Los Nopales (Fancy Junk Yard), next to Chuy's, for antiques, books, native plants, and a whole lot of other stuff that has appeared from somewhere and fills the cluttered rooms. Joy or Gerald Scott know the area and can advise you where to go or what to eat.

Museum—If you have free time in the afternoon check to see if the Clark Hotel Historical Museum, 112 W. Broadway, is open. Normally it is open 9:00–5:00P.M., Tuesday–Saturday. The old hotel bar lines one wall and a mining exhibit describes mine workings of the area, some of which are still functioning. Slogan for Van Horn from the museum: "This town is so healthy we had to shoot a man to start a cemetery." Attributed to A. S. Goynes who was shot a year later in 1892. 432-283-8028.

Museum Thrift Shop—"Once Over Lightly" is a non-profit thrift shop that helps support the Clark Hotel Museum. It is housed in the east wing of the museum and filled with irresistible goodies: books, knickknacks, clothing, household items and jewelry.

Our Lady of Fatima Catholic Church—Has a grotto in the churchyard in honor of "Our Lady," the statue was brought over from Portugal in 2001.

Okey D. Lucas Park—across the street from the Convention Center/Visitor's Bureau at 1801 W. Broadway.

City/County Park—Located at 206 Austin, has a playground, picnic area, basketball courts, sand volleyball and swimming pool.

What To Do/Where To Go—Ranch Tours

Only 15 minutes from downtown Van Horn, Red Rock Ranch (known locally as the McVay Ranch) is open to the public for daytime driving tours. The ranch contains one of only four natural Precambrian rock exposures in the Northern Hemisphere.

In addition to this geologic feature, the ranch terrain reveals wind carved rocks, canyons, and hidden desert life. The two-hour tour also includes a visit to a movie set, one of the filming locations for Lonesome Dove, and to a working talc mine. For information, call 800-735-6911. www.redrockranchtours.com.

What To Do/Where To Go—Golf

Mountain View Golf Course—Closed Mondays. Green fees: $10 weekdays, $12 weekends. 432-283-2628.

Shopping

Los Nopales—Also known as Fancy Junk Shop. Antiques, books, native plants, and sculptures by Gerald Scott. A must see. 432-283-7125.

Trading Post—501 W. Broadway. Jewelry and souhwestern gifts. 432-283-2299.

El Capitan gift shop—102 E. Broadway. Coming soon.

Red Rock Ranch Tours—5305 W. Broadway. Art Gallery and fine jewelry.

"Once over Lightly" Thrift Store—in the Clark Hotel Museum. 112 W. Broadway. 432-283-8028.

Van Horn Calendar Of Events

January	County Stock Show.
February	Texas Crossroads Cowboy Gathering.
April	Building Bridges Art Show.
May	Cinco de Mayo.
June	Third weekend. Frontier Days and Rodeo Celebration.
July	Fourth of July Celebration.
August	Mountain View Golf Tournament.
September	The Dollar J Classic.
October	Halloween Costume Ball, Howloween Dog Costume Contest.
November/ December	Trans Pecos Big Buck Tournament.
December	Annual Lighted Christmas Parade & Show and Sell.

Part VI
Big Bend Background

Top Ten Books on the Big Bend
(In-print books only)
(Alphabetical by title—compiled by Front Street Books)

1. ***Below the Escondido Rim*** by David Keller. (Center for Big Bend Studies, 2005). Gripping history of the O2 Ranch.

2. ***Beneath the Window: Early Ranch Life in the big Bend Country*** by Patricia Wilson Clothier. (Iron Mountain Press, 2003). The author's memoir of growing up on the Wilson ranch which became the heart of Big Bend National Park.

3. ***Big Bend: A History of the Last Frontier:*** by Ron Tyler. (Texas A&M University Press, 1996). Comprehensive, readable treatment of the area.

4. ***Big Bend: A Homesteader's Story*** by J. O. Langford with Fred Gipson. (University of Texas Press, 1995). Long-time favorite story of an early pioneer.

5. ***Big Bend Vistas*** by William McLeod. (Texas Geological Press, 2003). A geological exploration of the Big Bend.

6. ***I'll Gather My Geese*** by Hallie Stillwell. (Texas A & M University Press, 1991). A warm and humorous autobiography set in early Big Bend and written by a legendary ranchwoman of great heart and grit.

7. ***A Naturalist's Big Bend*** by Roland Wauer. (Texas A & M University Press, 1973). The all-encompassing account of one of the nation's outstanding natural systems.

8. ***Federico Villalba's Texas*** by Juan Casas. (Iron Mountain Press, 2008). A family memoir, the first published account from the Mexican perspective.

9. ***Quicksilver*** by Kenneth B. Ragsdale. (Texas A & M University Press, 1984). The story of the tough and colorful history of Terlingua's mining district.

10. *Up To My Armpits: Adventures of a West Texas Veterinarian* by Dr. Charlie Edwards. (Iron Mountain Press, 2002). A charming memoir of 50 years of a ranching practice centered around Marfa.

Other popular titles, specific to Big Bend (1998-2006):

The River Has Never Divided Us by Jefferson Morganthaler. A history of the La Junta area. (2004).

Big Bend Pictures by James Evans. A mighty book of Evans' best known photos. (2003).

Tales from the Terlingua Porch by Blair Pittman. Good tales. (2005).

Texas Outback by June Redford van Cleef. Picures and text about ranching on the Last Frontier. (2005).

Drug Lord by Terence E. Poppa. Life and death of a Mexican kingpin. (1998).

One Ranger by Joaquin Jackson. Stories (1966-1993) from a Texas Ranger's point of view. (2005).

My Goose is Cooked by Hallie Stillwell. More tales from Hallie who died at age 99, just a few months shy of her 100th birthday. (2004)

Indian Tribes Of The Big Bend From 1535

Human beings have lived in the Big Bend area for ten to twelve thousand years. Evidence of Paleo-Indian culture in the region dates to around 9,000 BC. The first identifiable group to leave their mark was the Archaic people, around 6,000 BC, who occupied water sites, which exist today, and hunted with the atlatl, a throwing spear. The start of the history of modern day Big Bend began in 1535 when Cabeza de Vaca, the first Spanish explorer to visit the area, stumbled across a farming community near present-day Presidio.

On his five-year odyssey across Texas from Galveston Bay, where he had been shipwrecked, Cabeza de Vaca and three companions moved from group to group of Indians, sometimes held captive, sometimes welcomed as a healer. These were bow-and-arrow carrying descendants of the Neo-American Indians.

De Vaca must have been astonished, after the hardships his group had suffered, to come across such advanced living. Here were people living in houses and growing crops along the fertile banks of a large river. These village-dwelling Indians were the Jumanos and this was probably the most remote of their pueblo settlements, far from the majority of their tribe who lived in New Mexico, Arizona, and Utah. Their civilization was declining in prosperity when de Vaca arrived.

The Spanish had little interest in the barren area of Big Bend; their sights were on the riches of present-day New Mexico. Starting in 1581, a few missionary expeditions entered the area, but for the most part the predominant Chisos Indians, based in Mexico, but using the Big Bend during summer months, were largely undisturbed.

The arrival of the Spanish in northern Mexico attracted the attention of a different, more aggressive and mobile Indian tribe, the Apaches. In the late 1600s, the Apaches, who had drifted down from northwest Canada and had settled in New Mexico, came under attack from the Comanches. Named Mescalero Apaches, because they ate the heart of the "mescal" or century plant, they moved further south into the rugged, uninhabited land of the Big Bend.

But to exist in this unyielding land, the Apaches had to resort to mounted raids into Mexico for livestock and slaves. So fierce and skilled in battle were they that by 1740 they dominated Big Bend and became known as Chisos Apaches, "the most successful mountain folk, desert dwellers and guerrilla fighters this country has ever known." This in turn caused the Spanish authorities to establish, in 1772, a line of forts to protect the northern frontier, but these were slow in being built, ineffectual, and soon abandoned.

Meanwhile, another element entered the scene: the Comanches—superb horsemen. These nomadic buffalo hunters extended their domination across the southern Plains, west Texas, and southeastern New Mexico, and were soon looking south across the Rio Grande at the ranches and settlements of Mexico. Raiding with impunity, they waited until September of each year. Then, "the painted warriors crossed the Pecos and swept down past the flat-topped hills and on up the long, empty, gently sloping desert floor towards the blue mountains, threading the Santiago at Persimmon Gap, and fording the Rio Grande at Lajitas."

Thrusting deep into Mexico as far as Durango, they picked the area clean. Driving livestock, horses, and captives northward, they recrossed the Rio Grande and headed for Comanche Spring at present-day Fort Stockton. So frequent and productive were these raids over a hundred-year period that a trail as much as a mile wide, scuffed bare by a thousand hoof marks and littered with the bleached bones of cattle and horses that had died on the way, remained as evidence years later.

The Spanish were unable to contain these raids from the north, but the situation changed rapidly following the Mexican War of 1848 and the establishment of the international border along the Rio Grande. On the U.S. side, a line of forts was established—including Fort Davis (1854) and Fort Stockton (1867)—to protect the westbound travelers on the Butterfield Stage route as well as the pioneer ranchers who were beginning to arrive in the region. The arrival of the U.S. Army in the region coincided with the linking of the railroad and was the beginning of the end of Indian attacks. Colonel Grierson's careful campaign to keep the Indian chief Victorio on the run was successful. In 1889, Victorio was trapped by Mexican forces south of the Rio Grande and killed. With the end of the Indian threat, the day of the cattle empire arrived.

Rocks Of The Big Bend

"A heap of stones thrown down by the Great Spirits after they finished creating the Earth." This was the explanation given by the Apache Indians for the formation of the Chisos Mountains, their home for many years. Today's geologists give a different reason. The Big Bend national park is first and foremost a geological park. Its unique features, which are the main reasons for its establishment in 1944, are primarily related to rocks. The Geologic Society did the first surveys of the region and the first superintendent of the National Park, Ross Maxwell, was a geologist.

The same can be said for the wider Big Bend region: the scenic qualities are the result of its geologic history. Low rainfall and desert conditions produce erosion, which strips away surface vegetation and leaves the rock exposed. But, initially we need to look at what was going on underground over the past millions of years to see how we are left with today's aboveground features.

Two major rock types are found in the Big Bend, sedimentary and volcanic. The oldest exposed rocks in the area are found at Persimmon Gap, the northern entrance to the National Park, and further north at Los Caballos marker on US 385 south of Marathon. This older rock, dating back 300 million years, contains fossils from the time when the whole area was lush and moist. Present-day North America was at that time connected to Europe and Asia and straddling the equator. The rock at Los Caballos is of the same age as the Appalachians and the Ouachitas in Arkansas.

Later (200 million years ago) the continents split and moved apart: a warm, shallow sea covered what is now Big Bend. Today's park began to form its geologic shape 75–100 million years ago as faulting lifted up bedrock to form mountains, and erosion set in, producing sediments in the valleys. The shallow sea began a gradual retreat to its present location, the Gulf of Mexico. It left behind layers of limestone, which form the walls of the Santa Elena, Mariscal, and Boquillas canyons as well as the towering cliffs of Sierra del Carmen across from the Rio Grande Village.

About this time the second mountain-building process began. The Rocky Mountains, formed of uplifted sediments by the compression of the earth's crust, started to rise. The Del Norte/Santiago range to the north of the park is a spur of the Rockies and Mariscal Mountain is the southernmost feature of the range within the USA. Thus, the newer Rockies and the older northeast pointing Ouachitas came together. Nowhere else in the USA can traces of the two major mountain ranges be seen within eyesight at one place.

While a look at the topographical map will confirm the coming together of the two mountain ranges, within the Big Bend park itself the scene is more confusing. Thirty-eight to thirty-two million years ago there was a long, interrupted period of volcanic activity in Big Bend. This activity is responsible for the brightly colored volcanic ash and lava layers in the park, and for most of the mass of the Chisos Mountains. In other areas, the rising magma of the volcanic eruptions spread sideways and, upon cooling, formed intrusive igneous rock, later revealed through erosion and visible today in many areas such as Maverick Mountain and Grapevine Hills.

The final major feature in the region is faulting: fractures appearing in the earth's crust. When subterranean stresses caused the earth's crust to stretch and then fracture, the result was the land surface to one side of the fault slipped down. The Terlingua Fault, seen at the mouth of Santa Elena Canyon, is the result of such a split; the canyons reach up to 1,500 feet and the same layer of rock is found 1,500 feet below the lower ground surface, i.e. a total drop of 3,000 feet.

Erosion continues today, mainly as a result of water. Rare as it is, when it arrives, the results are dramatic. While not visible to the eye, we can be sure the changes are ever-so-slowly occurring and will continue to alter the shape of the land indefinitely.

What Time Is It?

If we represented the 4.6 billion year span of geologic time on earth as a single calendar year, the oldest rocks in Big Bend would have been deposited on the 21st of November! No record of the preceding 324 days is to be found in the park area.

The building of the Ouachita Mountains in Big Bend would have taken place on December 17th. The remains of these mountains are seen only near Persimmon Gap in Big Bend National Park and near Marathon.

Uplift and folding in Big Bend, associated with the building of the Rocky Mountains, occurred on the morning of the 27th of December. Volcanoes dotted the Big Bend landscape from early morning on December 28th to midday on the 29th.

Basin and range faulting began at midnight the same day and continues today. The Rio Grande established the flowing drainage to the Gulf of Mexico at 7:00 A.M. on December 31st and began carving the canyons of Big Bend!

The Time Is Now! Come & Visit The Big Bend.

Jim Glendinning

Photo Credits

James Evans—*Chisos Mountains from Old Ore Road* (page 3), *South Rim With Agave* (page 26), *Rancher Ike Roberts* (page 96), and *Big Bend National Park* (page 111). James moved to Marathon in 1988. He has been photographing the people and landscapes of Big Bend ever since. His work has appeared in many national and regional magazines and is in personal and museum collections. James owns and operates Evans Gallery in Marathon. He can be reached on the web at www.jevansgallery.com or 432-386-4366.

Jim Glendinning—*Inside Santa Elena Canyon* (page 11), *Entrance To Santa Elena Canyon* (page 31), *Alpine & Twin Peaks* (page 143), and *Chihuahua Giant Trail Wagon* (page 254). Author and guide to the Big Bend. Runs tours to Copper Canyon, Mexico. Email: jimglen2@hotmail.com.

Jean Hardy—*Balancing Rock* (page 25), *Century Plant* (page 61), *The Gage Hotel* (page 206), and *Marathon Motel* (page 210). Jean moved to Marathon in 1993 from Houston. She was gardening editor and managing editor of Houston Home & Garden and later worked as a freelance editor and writer, with her work appearing in numerous regional magazines. She owns and operates Front Street Books in Alpine and Marathon. 432-837-3360 or 432-386-4249.

Holland Hotel—The photographs *Terlingua Welcome Sign* (page 271), and *Starlight Theatre Restaurant* (page 279) are courtesy of The Holland Hotel, Alpine. www.hollandhotel.net.

Carolyn A. Hoyt—Photo of *Clayton's Overlook* (page 57) courtesy of Carolyn Hoyt, Executive Director, Chihuahuan Desert Nature Center.

Martha King—Curator of the Annie Riggs Museum, (*Annie Riggs Museum*, page 188) from her private collection.

Victoria Lowe—*Hotel Paisano* (page 225). Fort Davis photo-illustrator and graphic designer who keeps her dues paid in the Cinematographers Guild "just in case." She does other jobs as necessary to keep food on and under the table for a large family of pets. 432-426-2506.

Luc Novovitch—*Cerro Castellan* (page 19), *The Rio Grande* (page 35), and *Terlingua Graveyard* (page 272). In 1998, after traveling widely in Europe, Africa, and Asia, photographer Luc Novovitch came to the Big Bend area. Immediately enthralled with the desert and mountain landscape, he moved to Marathon six months later and established the Sotol Gallery. He now works as a freelance photographer in Tennessee. www.offiwent.com.

Blair Pittman—All cover photos. Photojournalist and Nature photographer Blair Pittman, has had a love for Big Bend since his childhood. He now lives near Terlingua in the heart of Big Bend writing the stories he has heard on the Terlingua Porch. Blair was a photographer for *National Geographic* and the *Houston Chronicle*.

Sam Richardson—*Chili Cookoff* (page 274). Long-time resident, guide and editor in South Brewster County. He now lives in Taos, New Mexico.

Marsha J. Seyffert—*Lucifer Hummingbird* (page 94).

Alice Stevens—*Chinati Peak* (page 121) and *Double Windmills* (page 131). Alice lives near Alpine. She is a photographer, jeweler, potter, cook, location scout, and now the owner of One-Way Plant Nursery in Alpine where she also sells her scenic postcards. 432-837-1117.

Linda Walker—*Riding to San Carlos* (page 83). Owner of Lajitas Stables in Lajitas and Study Butte, and Big Bend Stables in Fort Davis. For horse trails in Big Bend, to San Carlos, Mexico and in Copper Canyon, Mexico call 888-508-7667.

Big Bend River Tours—*On the Rio Grande* (page 87). Established 1980, the only rafting company in Lajitas, BBRT invites readers to "Come and share the magic of the Rio Grande." Operates year-round. 800-545-4240.

Texas Jeep Expeditions—*Jeep Country* (page 91). Far Flung Outdoor Center can be reached by phone at 800-359-4138, local 432-371-2634 or via their website: www.farflungoutdoortravelcenter.com.

Also, thanks are due to the following for permission to use their photographs: Big Bend Ranch State Park for *Closed Canyon* (page 36), *Longhorn Roundup* (page 40), and *Abandoned In The Big Bend* (page 135); Fort Davis National Historic Site for *Buffalo Soldiers Reenactment* (page 66) and *Officers' Quarters* (page 170); McDonald Observatory for *McDonald Observatory* (page 68); and Lajitas Resort for *Lajitas Resort* (page 198).

General Index

Accommodations Index

(Hotels, Motels, Lodges, Inns, B&B's, Cabins, Cottages,
Guest Ranches, Camping & RV Parks)

Restaurant Index

Bar Index

Galleries Index

ABOUT THE AUTHOR

Jim Glendinning arrived in the USA from Scotland in 1961 after graduating from Oxford University. For the next 30 years he worked on both sides of the Atlantic, mainly in tourism. As a tour guide and travel writer, he visited 118 countries before happening upon Alpine, Texas in 1992. He decided to stay and opened a bed & breakfast called The Corner House. He continues to write travel articles, runs small group tours to Copper Canyon, and offers guide service in the Big Bend area and to Scotland and Ireland. 432-837-2052. Email: jimglen2@hotmail.com. See also: www.smallgroupsmexico.com.

512 364
9301